Web Farming for the
Data Warehouse

The Morgan Kaufmann Series in Data Management Systems

Series Editor, Jim Gray

Web Farming for the Data Warehouse
Richard Hackathorn

Database Modeling and Design, Third Edition
Toby J. Teorey

Management of Heterogeneous and Autonomous Database Systems
Edited by Ahmed K. Elmagarmid, Marek Rusinkiewicz, and Amit P. Sheth

Object-Relational DBMSs: Tracking the Next Great Wave, Second Edition
Michael Stonebraker and Paul Brown with Dorothy Moore

A Complete Guide to DB2 Universal Database
Don Chamberlin

Universal Database Management: A Guide to Object/Relational Technology
Cynthia Maro Saracco

Readings in Database Systems, Third Edition
Edited by Michael Stonebraker and Joseph M. Hellerstein

Understanding SQL's Stored Procedures: A Complete Guide to SQL/PSM
Jim Melton

Principles of Multimedia Database Systems
V. S. Subrahmanian

Principles of Database Query Processing for Advanced Applications
Clement T. Yu and Weiyi Meng

The Object Database Standard: ODMG 2.0
Edited by R. G. G. Cattell and Douglas K. Barry

Introduction to Advanced Database Systems
Carlo Zaniolo, Stefano Ceri, Christos Faloutsos, Richard T. Snodgrass, V. S. Subrahmanian, and Roberto Zicari

Principles of Transaction Processing
Philip A. Bernstein and Eric Newcomer

Distributed Algorithms
Nancy A. Lynch

Active Database Systems: Triggers and Rules For Advanced Database Processing
Edited by Jennifer Widom and Stefano Ceri

Joe Celko's SQL for Smarties: Advanced SQL Programming
Joe Celko

Migrating Legacy Systems: Gateways, Interfaces, and the Incremental Approach
Michael L. Brodie and Michael Stonebraker

Database: Principles, Programming, and Performance
Patrick O'Neil

Atomic Transactions
Nancy Lynch, Michael Merritt, William Weihl, and Alan Fekete

Query Processing for Advanced Database Systems
Edited by Johann Christoph Freytag, David Maier, and Gottfried Vossen

Transaction Processing: Concepts and Techniques
Jim Gray and Andreas Reuter

Understanding the New SQL: A Complete Guide
Jim Melton and Alan R. Simon

Building an Object-Oriented Database System: The Story of O_2
Edited by François Bancilhon, Claude Delobel, and Paris Kanellakis

Database Transaction Models for Advanced Applications
Edited by Ahmed K. Elmagarmid

A Guide to Developing Client/Server SQL Applications
Setrag Khoshafian, Arvola Chan, Anna Wong, and Harry K. T. Wong

The Benchmark Handbook for Database and Transaction Processing Systems, Second Edition
Edited by Jim Gray

Camelot and Avalon: A Distributed Transaction Facility
Edited by Jeffrey L. Eppinger, Lily B. Mummert, and Alfred Z. Spector

Readings in Object-Oriented Database Systems
Edited by Stanley B. Zdonik and David Maier

Web Farming for the Data Warehouse

Richard D. Hackathorn
Bolder Technology, Inc.

Morgan Kaufmann Publishers, Inc.
San Francisco, California

Senior Editor Diane D. Cerra
Director of Production and Manufacturing Yonie Overton
Production Editor Cheri Palmer
Editorial Assistant Belinda Breyer
Cover Design Ross Carron Design
Cover Photograph © 1998 The Image Bank/Ross M. Horowitz
Text Design Rebecca Evans & Associates
Composition Proctor-Willenbacher
Illustrations Lineworks, Inc. and Ken Truhan
Copyeditor Judith Abrahms
Proofreaders Sharilyn Hovind and Christine Sabooni
Indexer Ty Koontz
Printer Edwards Brothers, Inc.

Designations used by companies to distinguish their products are often claimed as trademarks or registered trademarks. In all instances where Morgan Kaufmann Publishers, Inc. is aware of a claim, the product names appear in initial capital or all capital letters. Readers, however, should contact the appropriate companies for more complete information regarding trademarks and registration.

Morgan Kaufmann Publishers, Inc.
Editorial and Sales Office
340 Pine Street, Sixth Floor
San Francisco, CA 94104-3205
USA
Telephone   415 / 392-2665
Facsimile   415 / 982-2665
Email   *mkp@mkp.com*
WWW   *http://www.mkp.com*
Order toll free 800 / 745-7323

03   02   01   00   99   5   4   3   2   1

Library of Congress Cataloging-in-Publication Data
Hackathorn, Richard D., (date)
   Web farming for the data warehouse / Richard Hackathorn.
       p.   cm.
   Includes bibliographical references (p.   ) and index.
   ISBN 1-55860-503-7
   1. Data warehousing.   2. World Wide Web (Information retrieval system)   I. Title.
   QA76.9.D37H32   1998
   658.4'038'0285574––dc21   98-46063
                                                                       CIP

To my family, Linda, Eric, and Robin,
for allowing Dad to sneak off to his cave
for many hours over the past year.
And to Shellie, who faithfully guarded me
during those long hours.

Foreword

The Web revolutionizes the way we gather and process information. The revolution is just beginning. Millions of us have learned that the quickest way to find something is to search the Web. This simple fact is just dawning on corporations.

Hackathorn points out that "the Web is the mother of all data warehouses." Most new information instantly appears on the global Internet. The volume and velocity of this information is completely different from what we traditionally deal with—it is huge, it is instant, and it is inexpensive. That's the good news; the bad news is that Web information quality varies enormously.

Corporations cannot afford to ignore the information-gathering potential of the Web. The Web can help them find the best suppliers and anticipate trends, and it can more quickly inform them about external events. Web farming gathers, analyzes, and abstracts this huge information source into alerts, news reports, and recommendations. It allows organizations to know more about their customers, their suppliers, and their competitors.

This is the first book to make the case for Web farming. Hackathorn describes the opportunity, offers case studies of successful Web farmers, provides a tutorial on the underlying technologies, and then gives you a recipe for setting up a Web farming operation within your company. If Hackathorn is right, and I think he is, most organizations will have Web farms within five years.

The book is written in a concise and accessible style. Hackathorn brings his vision, humor, and 25 years of experience in building database systems and applications.

Jim Gray
Microsoft Research

Contents

Preface

My experience in writing this book was like taking a long journey, in an intellectual sense. I started with great enthusiasm, fascinated by each new sight along the way. My mood soon mellowed as I encountered the magnitude of the task. Each turn and each hill brought continual disappointment that the end was not in sight. After more than a year of effort and over four hundred pages of text, the journey seems as if it is still beginning. There is no end in sight.

The area of Web farming is an emerging technology area whose exploration has just begun. It is a fascinating journey, whose implications will deeply affect the management of enterprises in the future. In fact, this technology merely uncovers more fundamental issues.

The journey of exploring Web farming is one that I would now like you to join. It is much more fun with a few colleagues along for the trip. We will need at least three to five years of additional work before the journey is finished. Even then, there will probably be numerous other avenues to explore.

Your help in completing this task is critical. We should form a community of professionals who are dedicated to evolving the concepts and methodology of Web farming. The Web site http://webfarming.com/ has been established for this purpose. Please visit and interact about this new area.

Inception of the Idea

I remember well the moment when the idea of Web farming came to me. I was at the CIO Conference in March of 1997. I was sitting in a semiboring presentation by a vendor explaining its efforts with data warehousing. My mind wandered toward more interesting matters. On my notepad, I wrote that "the Web is the mother of all data warehouses" and sketched the basic architecture. It is amazing to me that the points in those notes endured as major topics of this book.

Audience

The primary audience for this book consists of the many visionaries within the data warehousing community. This group includes the implementation teams and the end user line-of-business partners. The implementation teams typically include people such as project managers, data analysts, database programmers, data modelers, application designers, end user coordinators, business analysts, and project architects.

A second target audience includes the information technology (IT) managers and IT planning staff members, especially within large organizations. To these people, Web farming is a practical step toward knowledge management—a way to push the curve on exploiting business intelligence by leveraging their investment in data warehousing. This audience should pay particular attention to the skills and patience required to establish the infrastructure for Web farming.

A third target audience is the group of vendors who provide products and services to the data warehousing marketplace. This marketplace is changing rapidly. Technology-oriented products that drew great attention a few years ago have given way to business-oriented products that deliver real value.

A final target group includes the many people involved with commercial information sourcing, providing, and brokering. With a few exceptions, this area has been a diverse cottage industry, rarely generating large revenues. With the global marketplace of the Internet and the leverage point of data warehousing within businesses, there is potential for an explosion of growth within this industry. This book may guide these developments in some small way.

Topic Sequence

This book is organized into four parts that flow in an agricultural sequence—plowing, planting, cultivating, and harvesting.

Part I. Plowing the Soil

 1. Motivation
 2. Perspectives
 3. Foundations

Part II. Planting the Seeds

 4. Methodology
 5. Architecture
 6. Management

Part III. Cultivating the Plants

 7. Standards
 8. Tools
 9. Resources
10. Techniques

Part IV. Harvesting the Crop

11. Society
12. Challenges

The first part provides the motivation for Web farming, along with the proper perspectives and foundations for approaching this new area. The second part gets into the heart of Web farming by suggesting a methodology and an architecture and also deals with the management issues of implementing these activities within an enterprise. The third part describes the technical aspects of Web farming in terms of standards, tools, resources, and techniques. The fourth part concludes with the societal issues of privacy, intellectual property rights, a proposed code of ethics, and a list of challenges that await future Web farmers.

Volatility of the Web

You should be aware that this material was compiled in the early half of 1998. As the book was going into production, many URL references and even company names were changing (and even disappearing). The topic of Web farming certainly reflects the high volatility of the Web itself. You should be sensitive to this inherent volatility and check any references for current validity.

In an effort to deal with the volatility problem, a Web site has been established for you. See http://webfarming.com/ for the latest information (and current links) concerning Web farming.

Embedded Story Line

I have added a story line about a fictitious company involved with Web farming. The story line is shown in shaded boxes and appears in installments throughout the book. Its purpose is to highlight some major issues, making it easier for you to identify similar ones within your company.

Acknowledgments

Writing this book was a humbling experience for me. The complexity of the task seriously drained my energy and intellect. As a writer, what I do not know seems to overwhelm what I do know. If I had written this book alone, the book would not have been completed.

First, I would like to acknowledge the support and encouragement of Diane Cerra, Cheri Palmer, Antonia Richmond, and the other good folks at Morgan Kaufmann Publishing. Publishing a book is so much more than cramming keystrokes into a word processor.

Second, the team of reviewers were excellent in balancing soft nudges with harsh criticism—both of which were required to steer me in the proper direction. In particular, I would like to thank Karen Watterson, Prem Mehra, Alan Meyer, Christopher

Ryan, Dave Brumbaugh, Paul Brian, Colin White, Jim Gray, Gayle Niss, Kyle Geiger, Ken North, Jim Warner, and Claudia Imhoff.

Third, the visual contribution of Ken Truhan, the illustrator par excellence, is significant. Over coffee and bagels, Ken took my muddled ideas, painted with verbal handwaving, and quickly converted them into visual reality with a few pencil strokes. With each illustration, our hope is that you will chuckle a bit and then feel the firm kick in your rear.

Finally, the Center for Innovation of the Eaton Corporation provided the opportunity to transform these ideas into reality. In particular, the insights and encouragement of Ralph Castain, Bill Saylor, and Stephanie Hoffman are greatly appreciated.

## Part One

Plowing the Soil

## Chapter One

Motivation

A large agricultural concern is serious business, involving large capital investment and huge amounts of labor. Likewise, you should approach Web farming as a serious business. The capital investment is of the intellectual kind, but the labor part is still hard work.

This chapter introduces the concept and objectives of Web farming as refining Web content for business intelligence and, in particular, as input to a data warehouse. The chapter conveys the reasons that this content is valuable to an enterprise, along with the difficulties of achieving the objectives of Web farming.

Figure 1-1
The Web as a Haystack

Amid the chaos of the Web is a diversity of ever-changing information, some of which is of great value to your enterprise. The objective is to cultivate these information resources systematically. That is the theme of this book.

This book explores the nature and limitations of such cultivation by defining a new area called *Web farming*. Our goal is to move from an information-gathering activity that is often haphazard and individualized to one that is structured and systematic. Specifically, our goal is to move Web content into the managed context of the data warehousing system. By validating and transforming Web content, you can establish linkages with other business factors (such as sales patterns and inventory levels), thus greatly enhancing the information impact for the enterprise.

1.1 Nature of the Global Web

The Web is one of the most intriguing social phenomenon of our age. Like radio and television, the Web is a new medium for communication. Like automatic teller machines and telephone catalog ordering, the Web is a new marketplace for commerce. Like newspapers and magazines, the Web is a new channel for societal awareness. Like libraries and universities, the Web is a new stimulus for knowledge creation and dissemination. If the histories of earlier technologies are indicative of Web technology, we have not yet imagined its true impact on society.

Gathering Web content that is valuable to an enterprise seems like a simple task. You should merely tap into the vast information resources of the Web and store the relevant content in the data warehouse for use throughout the enterprise. However, achieving this objective is difficult because of the nature of the Web's paradigm, its dynamics, and its diversity.

1.1.1 The Paradigm

The paradigm of the Web is radically different from that of the data warehouse. A typical page from the Web is a free-form mixture of text, images, unusual objects (audio, video, 3D worlds, etc.), and many context-dependent links to other Web

Figure 1-2
...and the Haystack Is
Constantly Changing

pages. A typical table from a data warehouse is structured into a format adhering to the conventions of the relational database model.

Adapting the old programming term *spaghetti code,* we might say that Web content is spaghetti data (i.e., it has links to everywhere but little discipline). As we dip into the mass of Web pages, we retrieve an unruly mess of things! Jim Gray of Microsoft Research gives a succinct description of this situation:

> The Internet and the Web are the database designer's worst night-mare. The Web is all pointers, circles, and arrows with no structure whatsoever. Every node that you come to, every entity, has its own private structure. . . . about 30 percent of the pointers are busted.[1]

1.1.2 The Dynamics

Web content is extremely dynamic, constantly changing. Consider the Web as a hay-stack. Finding something useful on the Web is like finding a needle in a haystack, as illustrated in Figure 1-1. The situation is more complex because of the dynamics of the Web. The analogy is more accurate if people are adding and taking away hay while you look for that needle. The difficult task of finding the needle becomes even more so, as in Figure 1-2.

Interesting Event

After 40 years of hard-copy news on the IT industry, *Datamation* magazine stopped publishing its printed version in February 1998. Since then, it has been a Web-only publication, at http://www.datamation.com/. Given the volatility of our industry and the cost of printed media, is this the future for IT trade publications?

---

1.   J. Gray, interview, *DBP&D,* May 1996, 32.

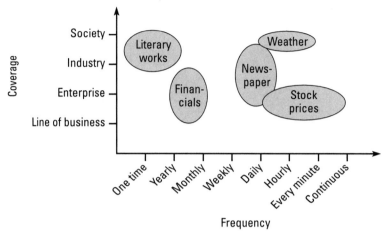

Figure 1-3 Dynamics of the Web

In database management terms, the dynamics of Web pages are similar to those of a busy database without concurrency controls. There is no isolation level of repeatable-read on the Web! Further, Web content is increasingly retrieved through procedural execution, rather than through static retrieval from directory files. In other words, a simple request for a Web page often invokes an SQL retrieval that invokes a complex stored procedure against a database.

Question *Can we depend on the stability of Web content?*

The stability (or lack thereof) of Web content is both its strength and its weakness. No one would expect a daily newspaper to have the same content tomorrow as it does today. The whole value of the newspaper lies in its volatile nature. Its content must track current reality. Likewise, the value of Web content lies in its ability to track current reality.

On the other hand, if you need to know about an event that happened last month, today's newspaper is of little value. The value then resides in an archive at a library, where you can retrieve and study the newspapers from last month. Likewise, the value of Web content also lies in the ability to archive and index to track past reality.

The point is that we must be very smart in managing the time attributes of Web content. An intelligent blending of linking to current content and capturing old content is required. Web content without a historical context is of little value.

Consider the frequency with which information is published on the Web versus the coverage of that information, as in Figure 1-3. At the upper left, literary works and historical texts would be ageless and relevant to all of society. Toward the right (more frequent events), there is a range from weather forecasting on a daily basis to weather alerts on a hourly basis. Stock prices are interesting in that there is a wide range of granularity and of time periods to consider. The information content of the Web is rapidly moving toward the right, both in tracking volatile events and in covering the total spectrum of events.

1.1.3 The Diversity

The diversity of the Web challenges our imagination. Every day brings new forms of creative expression on the Internet, some of which bring with them questions as to their social value.

The diversity of the Web is universal and global. Many see the Internet as a ubiquitous utility, weaving together the information society of the future.

> [The Internet] will become invisible, like a utility, like electricity or water. People will stop talking about URLs and downloading, the technologies we are so absorbed with. It will become so central to our lives that it will become invisible.[2]

And others tell of its enormous reach:

> My body may be stuck in this chair, but with the Internet my mind can go to the ends of the universe.[3]

The sheer size of the Web is overwhelming; it is estimated by some to be eight terabytes and doubling every six months. Moreover, these estimates cover only the unrestricted static content of the Web. The restricted Web sites and Web pages driven by Web-enabled databases may easily double these estimates.

The Internet Archive[4] began archiving the entire Web in early 1996 and has at least three snapshots of over half a million active and unique Web sites. As of December 1, 1997, the Internet Archive had captured more than eight terabytes of content, with a new snapshot taken every 30 to 60 days. The total number of Web sites is doubling every six months. Each Web site contains a median of 300 Web pages; typically, 50 sites have more than 30,000 pages.[5] The number of Web pages is estimated at 80 million pages for the entire Web. Each page usually consists of 5 KB of HTML text, 5 images of 15 KB each, and 15 links to other pages. The average age of a typical Web page is only 44 days.

---

2. Interview with Kim Polese, CEO and cofounder of Marimba, Insider Profile, CMP Net, November 1997.
3. Stephen Hawking, *A Brief History of Time.* Hawking is a professor at Cambridge University.
4. See http://www.archive.org/ and Z. Smith, The Truth About the Web, *Web Techniques,* May 1997.
5. These numbers are somewhat misleading, since dynamic pages (pages generated on demand from database contents) have become more widespread.

The implication is that we face two challenges in dealing with this diversity. The first challenge is filtering all this material to find the few seeds of information that contain real business value. The second and greater challenge is cultivating those seeds so that they grow into an entire crop of information for the enterprise.

1.2   Combining the Web with Data Warehousing

Both the Web and data warehousing (DW) are hot technologies receiving considerable attention within the IT industry. The application of Web technology to data warehousing is an intriguing combination. However, does such a combination have practical value?

In several areas, the combination has proven highly successful. Publishing warehouse data via an intranet (i.e., a secured network internal to a company) has become a very productive approach. Web technology (such as the HTML protocol, generic browsers, and Java applets) is being adapted for mechanisms to deliver warehouse data from Web-enabled databases. The generation of dynamic pages from Web-enabled databases and the addition of Java applets (to manipulate data locally) to the browser has made whole new areas of data analysis and data mining possible, primarily within an intranet environment.

On the other hand, no one has yet seriously considered taking content from the World Wide Web and using it as input to the data warehouse.

Typical reactions to using Web content tend to be negative. Web content is too unreliable and unstable. The interaction with Web sites is too messy. Transformation of hypertext into a structured database is often impossible. Images and sound have no machine-discernable content. Besides, data external to the organization have little value to the business.

Question *Why is surfing the Web so unproductive?*

Everyone who has surfed the Web for information has experienced long periods of frustration interspersed with brief moments of elation. It is certainly a black hole for consuming your time. However, we are getting better at creating tools and using techniques for more productive discovery and acquisition of Web content. The intent of Web farming is to change this haphazard personal activity into a systematic group activity.

1.3   External Information for Business Intelligence

This book argues for the usage of Web content. There are significant problems in dealing with Web content; however, the benefits of using external information for business intelligence are far more significant.

Figure 1-4
Studying Your Navel
Can Be Dangerous

As markets become turbulent, the old way of doing business becomes less viable. Doing business as usual is a risky strategy. And data from internal operational systems is becoming less relevant to managing your business.

An enterprise must know more and more about its customers, its suppliers, its competitors, government agencies, and many other external factors. The information from internal systems should be supplemented with information about external factors. The synergism of the combination creates the greatest business benefit for the enterprise.

The majority of data warehousing efforts result in enterprises that focus inward, while instead the enterprise should be keenly alert to the external world. Current warehousing efforts are like studying your navel while a dangerous animal approaches. As shown in Figure 1-4, this is not the best approach.

Professor Peter Drucker, the senior guru of management practice, admonishes IT executives to look outside their enterprises for information. He has predicted that obsession with internal data will lead to their being blindsided by external forces.

> The single biggest challenge you face is to organize outside data, because change occurs from the outside.... Management is swamped with inside data but doesn't have any more real information than it did 40 years ago, and the quality of decisions has not improved.[6]

From the global perspective, the Web is the mother of all data warehouses! Valuable information about external business factors is readily available on the Web and is becoming more so each hour. When the data is volatile, the Web is the only viable delivery medium.

---

6. C. Wilder, Drucker: Look Outside, *InformationWeek,* February 16, 1998.

The Web is the mother of all data warehouses!

While a few web resources (e.g., direct feeds of stock quotes) are used as data sources, the immense resources of the Web are largely untapped. Information derived from the Web has terrific potential if only we can make business sense of it all!

1.4   The Objectives of Web Farming

Web farming is not haphazard surfing of the Web, wandering from one intriguing item to another. Nor is it a one-time thorough search of the Web.

On a continuous and systematic basis, Web farming must deliver, to the right people at the right time, information that is relevant to the enterprise. In effect, the Web farming system should act as the eyes and ears of the enterprise, focusing externally on important changes in the business environment. Web farming is the systematic refining (or cultivating) of information resources on the Web for business intelligence.

Web farming is the systematic refining of information resources on the Web for business intelligence.

Web farming has the following specific objectives:

1. To continuously discover Web content that is highly relevant to the business.
2. To acquire that content so that it is properly validated within a historical context.
3. To structure the content into a usable form that is compatible with the data warehouse.
4. To disseminate the content to the proper persons so that it has direct and positive impacts on specific business processes.
5. To manage these tasks in a systematic manner as part of the production operations of a data center environment.

The challenge is to wade (with big boots) through the Web, discovering and acquiring those items that provide an understanding of external impacts on the enterprise. The benefits of Web farming can be global in scope for the enterprise.

Figure 1-5
The Farmer and God

1.4.1 Why the Term *Web Farming*?

The term *Web farming* is "cute," almost unprofessional in tone. However, there is a serious side to Web farming that draws strength from its analogy to agriculture.

First, farming is hard work. There is an old joke about the effort required in farming. Two city folks (shown in Figure 1-5) survey a beautiful farm. They say to the farmer, "God and you sure did a great job with this place." The farmer pauses in thought and replies, "Yes, but you should have seen it when God had it all to himself."

Of course, we are not belittling the contribution of God, for that is certainly essential. Plants need the sun and rain to grow. However, God also works through the farmer, who applies those resources appropriately. The farmer doesn't blast those little cornstalks with a firehose, but gently moistens them over time and nurtures them in their growth. The value comes from applying resources to a problem with considerable effort and patience. Likewise, Web farming requires considerable effort to apply the "natural" resources of the Web, which in their raw form can be quite ugly and unusable.

Second, it is Web *farming,* not Web *mining.* The joke about the farmer would not work if it featured a miner. Web mining would be like harvesting a fully grown crop in the field, gathering wild berries in the forest, or finding gold nuggets in a mine. The implication would be that valuable information is already present somewhere on the Web, just waiting to be found and used. The emphasis would be on seeking and collecting an existing resource, rather than on the hard work required to make that resource valuable.

Third, Web farming is serious business. To most people, surfing the Web is like planting a small garden in the backyard, as shown in Figure 1-6.

Figure 1-6
The Different
Scales of Farming

To be a reliable and valuable function, Web farming should be treated more like a large agricultural business, involving many people and several thousand acres of farmland. The basic principles have some similarity to those of a backyard garden, but the scaling of a personal garden into an agricultural business does change the methodology, architecture, tools, and techniques.

Fourth, a large-scale farm must also be managed with an eye to financial objectives, while a small garden can be justified as just a hobby. The objective of Web farming is to increase the productivity of providing business-relevant information that is valuable to an enterprise.

Suppose the Web farming system scans 100 units of Web content in an afternoon. To be of value to the business, the content must be structured into a meaningful format, loaded into a database, packaged into documents, and disseminated to the proper people. The end result may be only one or two units of content that are actually of value to the enterprise. How can the system be improved so that the 100 units of content that are scanned will produce 20 to 30 units of useful information?

Question *What types of organizations could benefit the most from Web farming?*

Large multinational firms in rapidly changing markets will be the first ones to exploit the benefits of Web farming. These firms typically have the resources and motivation to mold an emerging technology into a productive system. However, the successful adoption of any technology often depends on just a few critical individuals who have the vision and the leadership skills to realize that vision. Such people can carefully evolve a Web farming system to produce real business benefits.

Finally, Web farming should not be confused with the term *Web farms,* which sounds similar but refers to a different concept. A Web farm is a traditional glass-house approach to configuring and managing multiple Web servers within a centralized

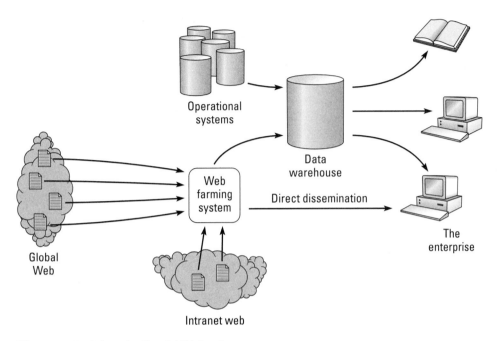

Figure 1-7 Information Flow in Web Farming

facility.[7] The main point about Web farms is the ability of a corporation to manage hundreds of geographically dispersed Web sites as though they were all a single system. Hence, Web farms and Web farming are very different concepts.

1.4.2 Information Flow

As shown in Figure 1-7, the data warehouse occupies a central position in the information flow of a Web farming system. Like operational systems, the Web farming system provides input to the data warehouse. The result is the dissemination of refined information about specific business subjects within the enterprise.

The primary source of content for the Web farming system is the global Web, because it can provide external perspectives on the business of the enterprise. As a content source, the global Web can be supplemented (but not replaced) by the intranet web of the enterprise. This intranet web is typically made up of internal web sites, word processing documents, spreadsheets, and email messages. The content of the intranet is usually limited to internal information about the enterprise; this leaves out an important contribution of Web farming.

Most information acquired by the Web farming system will not be in a form suitable for the data warehouse. It will consist of either unstructured hypertext or

---

7.   D. Eskow, Harvest Profits from Web Farms, *Datamation*, March 1997, 44.

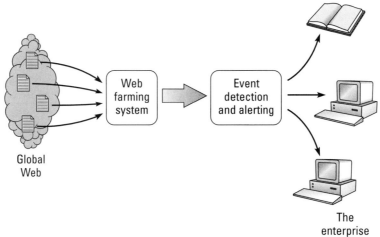

Global
Web

The
enterprise

Figure 1-8   Web Farming for Event Alerting

unverified tabular values. In either case, that information must be refined before it is loaded into the warehouse. Even in its unrefined state, the information could be very valuable to the enterprise. The ability to disseminate this information directly to the proper people may be required in addition to disseminating via the warehouse.

There are two variations on the information flow described above: one to support event alerting, and another to support strategic analysis.

The first variation, outlined in Figure 1-8, focuses the Web farming system on *event alerting*—detecting relevant events in the business environment and alerting the proper persons within the enterprise. Such events include news flashes on AP wire outlets, stock prices, SEC filings, press releases, weather warnings, and so forth. There is little processing of the content; the emphasis is on quickly disseminating the raw content to the appropriate persons.

The second variation, outlined in Figure 1-9, focuses on *strategic forecasting*—modeling the relevant dynamics of the business environment and forecasting its future patterns.

The source content is usually 100% external data, with a heavy longitudinal time dimension spanning several years. Favored Web providers are governmental sites and commercial databases. The applications of Web farming for strategic analysis are similar to advanced data-mining applications in customer retention, fraud detection, and purchasing patterns. In fact, some of the same techniques can be applied to strategic forecasting.

In these two variations, the data warehouse plays a secondary role. In some enterprises, the warehouse may not exist or may be contained within a distant group. In the strategic forecasting variation, the warehouse may be optionally incorporated into the information flow. Predictions of key parameters in the business environment (e.g., interest and inflation rates, market growth potentials, or supplier availability) could be fed into budgeting and planning applications within the warehouse.

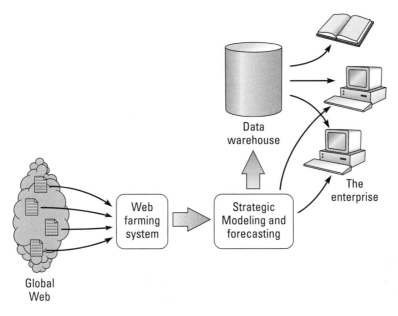

Figure 1-9 Web Farming for Strategic Forecasting

Although the data warehouse may not be essential, it will be easier for an enterprise that has to develop a mature understanding of data warehousing and has experienced several successes. In this way, the business justification and initial directions for establishing a Web farming function will have been established for this enterprise.

1.4.3 Reliability of Web Content

The reliability of Web data is an important concern. Consider the following:

If you hear "Buy IBM stock because it will double in value over the next month," your reaction should depend on who made that statement and in what context. Was it in a random conversation overheard on the subway, a chat with a friend over dinner, or a phone call from a trusted financial advisor? The same is true when you are judging the reliability of Web content.

> Errors using inadequate data are much less than those using no data at all.
> —*Charles Babbage*

Most people have a "flaky-free" image of Web content. In reality, the Web is a global bulletin board where both the wise and the foolish have equal space. The fact that content is acquired from the Web should not reflect positively or negatively on its quality. Think of Web resources in terms of quality and coverage, as shown in

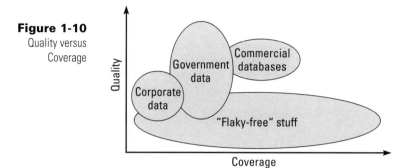

Figure 1-10
Quality versus
Coverage

Figure 1-10. Toward the top are information resources of high quality (i.e., accuracy, currency, and validity); resources toward the right have wide coverage (i.e., scope, variety, and diversity). Note that information resources of the Web appear in all parts of this figure.

The commercial online databases from Dialog Information Services and similar vendors have traditionally supplied businesses with high-quality information about numerous topics. However, the complexity of using these services and their infrequent update cycles have limited their usefulness.

The usefulness of governmental databases has increased tremendously in recent years. Not so long ago, public information could often be acquired only by spending many hours of manual labor at libraries or government offices. The EDGAR database, maintained by the U.S. Securities and Exchange Commission, contains extensive information on every publicly traded company and is updated daily.

Corporate Web sites often contain vast amounts of useful information in white papers, product demos, and press releases, eliminating much of the need to attend trade exhibits to learn about the "latest and greatest" in a marketplace.

The "flaky-free" content occupies the lower half of the figure. Its benefit lies not in the quality of any specific item but in its constantly changing diversity as it tracks the business environment minute by minute. The "flaky-free" content acts as a wide-angle lens to avoid tunnel vision within your marketplace.

1.4.4   A Step Toward Knowledge Management

Web farming is about information refinement—converting data into information and then into knowledge. Web farming provides a means for extending existing data warehousing systems into knowledge management systems. In other words, Web farming is a practical step toward knowledge management for an enterprise.

Web farming is a practical step toward knowledge management for an enterprise.

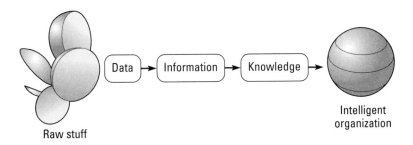

Figure 1-11   Making an Intelligent Organization

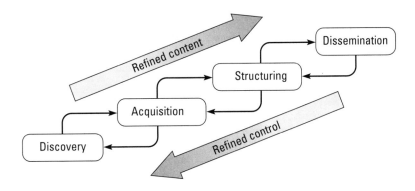

Figure 1-12   Information Refining

As we will see in the next chapter, and as shown in Figure 1-11, information is data that changes individual decisions, and knowledge is information that changes business processes. Information must *make sense* to a person; the data must be transformed so that it fits into a cognitive model of business for that person.

Likewise, knowledge must *make sense* to a group of persons; information must be transformed so that procedures for conducting business are changed. This type of knowledge should not only change our business processes, but also change the way we do business, and may even change the business in which we are situated.

When a data warehouse is first designed and implemented in an enterprise, there is a lot of analysis and reengineering of data from operational systems. The same is true for Web farming. Before Web content can be loaded into a warehouse, there must be a refining of that information.

We have defined four processes for refining information as part of Web farming. As shown in Figure 1-12, the processes are discovery, acquisition, structuring, and dissemination—or DASD for short. These processes have a bidirectional flow. The left-to-right flow refines the content of information, making it more structured and better validated. The right-to-left flow refines the control of the processes, which becomes more selective and discriminating.

The first process is *discovery:* the exploration of available data to find those source items that are related to a specific topic or issue. A business analyst is the primary participant in this activity and requires intelligent search tools.

The second process is *acquisition:* the continuous collection and maintenance of identified source content. This processing requires a stable operations environment and a large storage capacity.

The third process is *structuring:* the analysis, validation, and transformation of data into refined information (i.e., data that changes decision behavior).

The fourth process is *dissemination:* packaging of (decision-changing) information and delivery to the appropriate consumers, either directly or through a data warehouse. A range of dissemination mechanisms is required, from rigid, predetermined schedules to ad hoc queries.

1.4.5   Rendezvous with the Data Warehouse

The most difficult part of Web farming is the rendezvous with the data warehousing system—especially matching the data structure inherent in the Web content with the data schema of the warehouse.

Question *Is data warehousing necessary for Web farming? Would knowledge management be a better focus?*

There is a danger that Web farming will evolve independently of data warehousing. That would be a long-term mistake. The business value of Web farming results ultimately from highly structured data that is precisely targeted to specific points in a critical business process, such as carrying out a request from a customer. All the decision support and knowledge management in the world cannot replace the benefits that come from a few satisfied customers.

Consider a typical data schema for a sales warehouse, as shown in Figure 1-13. In this warehouse, we have sales data by customer, product, and store, aggregated on a weekly basis. Let's assume that we have mostly corporate customers, rather than individuals, as in a large office furniture company.

Web farming would be of value in enhancing the demographics of customers, as in Figure 1-14. If you add information on customer demographics, selective marketing can be performed based on the profitability and the requirements of customers. By knowing what types of customers buy what types of products at which stores, you can promote specific sales and anticipate demand. The demographic information is added to the customer dimension so that analyses of specific customers are improved by the demographics.

As experience with the demographics matures, data mining techniques can cluster customers into segments based on demographics, as shown in Figure 1-15.

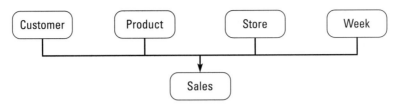

Figure 1-13   A Typical Schema for a Sales Warehouse

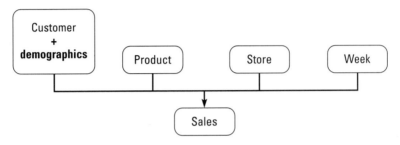

Figure 1-14   Adding Customer Demographics—Part I

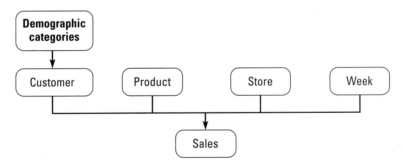

Figure 1-15   Adding Customer Demographics—Part II

Then demographics can be categorized into meaningful categories and become a separate analysis dimension.

Another example of using Web farming to enhance a data warehouse is the addition of demographics on the store. Using zip codes and even the full store address, census data about the communities surrounding the store can be added as another business dimension, as shown in Figure 1-16. This enhancement can lead to more effective management of stores based on their communities and to more effective placement of new stores.

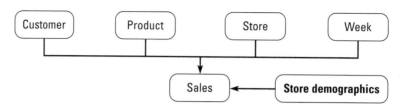

Figure 1-16   Adding Store Demographics

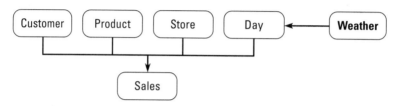

Figure 1-17   Adding Weather Data

Question *Where do Web farming and data warehousing meet?*

Web farming will be an agent of change (even of a disruptive sort) in the controlled and structured world of data warehousing. We believe that this is a necessary change—a maturing of the basic objectives and concepts of data warehousing.

The discipline of data warehousing has finally fulfilled its promise of business benefits. In retrospect, those benefits were "low-lying fruit"—the easy accomplishments (relatively speaking) of cleaning up the sins of monolithic legacy systems.

With Web farming, we must deal with messy Web content by resolving some messy issues. No longer can we rely on simplistic assumptions like this one: "If our operational system collected this data, it must be of value to our business."

A final example involves adding data about weather to the warehouse, as shown in Figure 1-17. Seasonal variations have always been an important part of sales analysis. However, a sudden heavy snowstorm, or an intense hailstorm, can also affect sales of specific products. This example shows that timely flow of Web content into the warehouse can aid in the day-to-day management of the business.

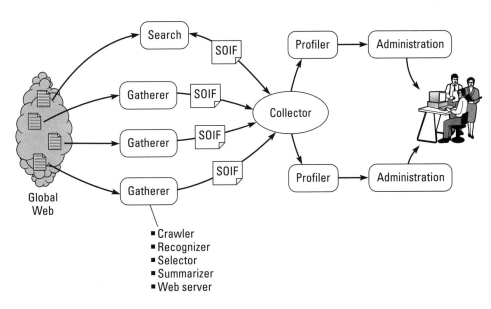

Figure 1-18   Architecture of IBM's Grand Central Station

1.5   Illustrations of Web Farming

Although there is no single illustration that incorporates all the aspects of Web farming, the illustrations in this section do cover most of the spectrum.

1.5.1   IBM's Grand Central Station

Our first illustration of Web farming, diagrammed in Figure 1-18, is a research project at IBM Almaden Research Center called Grand Central Station (GCS).[8] As a busy on-ramp for the Information Highway, its objective is to find and summarize Web content and disseminate the content to various persons based on their interest profiles. The architecture is based on distributed Gatherers and a common interchange format from the Harvest project at the University of Colorado. The Gatherers can be distributed geographically (e.g., one in Europe and another in Australia) and merge their results in a central Collector server. The common format for interchanging results is the Summary Object Interchange Format (SOIF), an important mechanism for conveying metadata and summaries of Web objects.

---

8.   B. Schechter, Information on the Fast Track, *IBM Research*, no. 3, 1997, 18–21.

1.5.2 Junglee Virtual Database

The Junglee Corporation[9] has commercialized research at Stanford University to turn the Web into a single virtual database. Using specific wrappers around Web sources, a uniform metadata drives a database engine to process queries joining multiple sources. This technology has been applied to classified job ads (e.g., *JobCanopy* in the San Jose area) and e-commerce (e.g., ShopCanopy for 40 merchants in eight categories). Because of this technology, Junglee was acquired by Amazon.Com.

1.5.3 Gaining Competitive Information

An article in the *Wall Street Journal* has reported on recent efforts to gain competitive information using Internet newsgroups. Scott Lucado, an analyst for an IT firm specializing in outsourcing, scans the help-wanted or jobs-available ads in newsgroups, looking for inside information about other firms.

> Companies tell "a great deal about their technology in help-wanted ads," Mr. Lucado says. "Sometimes I wonder whether organizations realize how much sensitive information seeps out."[10]

DejaNews[11] offers free services for indexing the vast quantities of material generated by newsgroups.

1.5.4 Supporting the Call Center

Free Market Partners, a national direct-marketing venture division of the Provident Bank, uses Open Text Livelink to disseminate information internally to its call center and externally to its customers directly.

> Free Market Partners is using Livelink to create a database of company knowledge, which can be accessed by call center employees to immediately answer customer questions across a wide range of categories. Livelink's ease of deployment enabled the company to make over 1200 intellectual capital projects accessible online within months. Free Market Partners will also use Livelink to create an extranet, enabling better communication with hundreds of vendors and customers concerning contract negotiations and project updates. [12]

---

9. See http://www.junglee.com/.
10. H. Lanchaster, Web Sites That Help You Do Intelligence the Intelligent Way, *WSJ*, March 31, 1998, B1.
11. See http://www.dejanews.com/.
12. Open Text Further Strengthens Market Penetration in Financial Services Industry, *Business Wire*, February 10, 1998.

Introduction to Company and Its Business

Given in installments, this is a story line about a fictional company to high-light specific issues regarding Web farming.

ABC Manufacturing is a global supplier of pipe and fittings to oil production firms. In recent years, its business has fluctuated wildly, based on external factors such as political unrest, commodity markets, refinery capacities, aggressive competitors, and government incentives. ABC must better anticipate customer demands. A top priority is understanding the various factors affecting their top 10 customers, which account for 73% of their business.

Next installment is on page 34.

1.5.5 International Currency Monitoring

A simple Web farming system was developed from Microsoft VisualBasic components to monitor international currency functions.[13] Operating on a workstation, the system monitors finance Web pages for changes, retrieves a page, and parses the retrieved page to obtain the useful data. The system connects to three specific sites, which are predefined but can be supplemented with more sites. With a time delay of approximately 20 minutes, it retrieves currency exchange rates (such as USD to GBP) along with stock prices and news headlines containing specific keywords. The data, including linking information, source, and a date/time stamp, is currently loaded into several Microsoft Access tables. The user can choose the currency for display and ask for recent headlines.

1.5.6 Strategic Forecasting for a Manufacturing Conglomerate

Staying on top of the diverse markets of Eaton Corporation is not an easy job. Spanning engines, transmissions, and a thousand other components in vehicle and power plants, Eaton is monitoring hundreds of markets for technology shifts, emerging competitors, and governmental regulations. Based on the methodology and architecture presented in this book, WebFarming.Com[14] is developing a Strategic Outreach System to support strategic forecasting of these markets.

---

13. Private conversation with Andy Billington, Focus Online Ltd., London, UK.
14. See http://webfarming.com/.

1.5.7 Monitoring Visa Applications for the U.K.

The U.K. Foreign and Commonwealth Office[15] has equipped over 200 of its embassies, consulates, and high commissions with Excalibur RetrievalWare to manage over 15 million documents. The goal is to support antifraud initiatives for standardization of visa applications by recognizing unique patterns based on concepts, meanings, and logical word associations.

1.5.8 HP Manages Knowledge for Its Professional Services Organization

Hewlett-Packard Company[16] has developed Productivity Researcher for its Professional Services Organization. Using the Infonautics EKMS-Direct product, Productivity Researcher is a central online repository of professional-services documents, including white papers and presentations. Employees will use the Productivity Researcher to store and locate shared documents and information, allowing consultants to address client requirements rapidly and efficiently.

1.5.9 IBM Offers a Window into Patent Information

A special IBM Web site[17] offers a database of patents issued in the U.S. during the last 27 years—over 2 million patents. The display of the results can highlight clusters of similar patents or ranking patents according to areas of interest. An analysis tool called MAPIT, from Manning & Napier Information Services, compares the contents of thousands of patents and automatically produces the visualizations. The need exists to incorporate the analysis of patent information for R&D planning, competitive intelligence, licensing management, and strategic market research. In particular, investment banking firms can determine the intellectual assets of potential acquisition or investment candidates.

1.5.10 Supporting the Deregulation of Electric Power

TIBCO Software offers TIBPower, a real-time trading and risk management system for the emerging deregulated electric power industry, including the independent power providers. TIBPower enables you to buy, sell, and trade power contracts in real time, including power futures and options, like other marketable energy commodities. TIBPower also provides access to live market information by tapping into

---

15. *Business Wire,* March 4, 1998.
16. *PR Newswire,* July 2, 1997.
17. See http://patent.womplex.ibm.com/respage.html.

Dow Jones, Reuters, Platts, Knight-Ridder and other news/data feeds, displays real-time spot prices for natural gas and oil, delivers later power pool energy prices, weather maps and forecasts, tracks political developments that might affect prices, and integrates new adapters for news sources and exchanges like NYNEX, Continental Power Exchanges and others.[18]

This initial chapter has shown the motivation for Web farming by describing the nature of the Web, the relationship of the Web to data warehousing, the need for external information for business intelligence, the objectives of Web farming, and finally some illustrations. The next two chapters expand on these topics by providing further perspectives on the objectives and a foundation for the discipline.

---

18. *Business Wire,* September 30, 1997.

Chapter Two

Perspectives

A core activity of farming is taking many little things and organizing them into useful big things. The seed, fertilizer, water, and sunshine are the basic ingredients. The result is the crop, harvested and ready for market. Likewise, Web farming is the process of taking raw data and transforming it into structured information and then into organizational knowledge.

This chapter paints a perspective for understanding the concepts and benefits of Web farming. Its purpose is to position the potential impacts of Web farming in the mainstream of organizational thought. The value of Web farming comes from the benefits, to the enterprise, of transforming data first into information and then into knowledge.

Be patient with this chapter. Quickly browse through it on your first reading. Pick out one or two points that are important to you. In any case, enjoy the illustrations.

The chapter first discusses the fundamental process for leveraging data into knowledge. The challenges of managing the enterprise are described within today's business environment; this description is followed by a rethinking of the basic way we work within the enterprise. Finally, we discuss the two essential elements of the *data-to-information-to-knowledge* process: first sharing information, and then creating information markets.

Figure 2-1
Managing the
Enterprise: Past
versus Present

Why would an enterprise expend the effort and the funds for Web farming? The answer lies deep within the fabric of the enterprise, and involves much more than using the hottest technology in some exotic manner. The answer should involve a clear understanding of your enterprise and a pragmatic vision for its future.

2.1 A Sense of Urgency

We are facing a major dilemma! Radical changes in the business environment have shifted our focus from incremental improvements for cost reduction to radical innovations for corporate survival.

Incremental improvements for cost reduction $\rightarrow$ radical innovations for corporate survival

We have moved from a business environment that is like steering a ship across a placid ocean to one that is like landing an airplane at a crowded urban airport, as captured in Figure 2-1.

We face many more choices than ever before. From a world with a few dimensions, we are thrust into one with numerous dimensions. Uncertainty has increased. We cannot predict the nature of critical business issues for next year. The wisdom of rules of thumb that served our enterprises well in past decades no longer seems relevant for today's markets.

Moreover, our response time has declined. We no longer have the luxury of examining and researching an issue for one or two years before making major capital expenditures. We must gather all available information quickly and make decisions immediately.

We must recognize that these changes are profoundly affecting the basic nature of work and are affecting the use of information technology within our enterprises.

Business firms today face a set of challenges different from those of past centuries or even past decades. The global economy has pushed competition within marketplaces to new levels of intensity, resulting in major shifts within industries. As Hammer and Champy warn,

> Adequate is no longer good enough. If a company can't stand shoulder to shoulder with the world's best in a competitive category, it soon has no place to stand at all.[1]

Businesses are finding that they are competing in ways that are totally unexpected. The vaguely defined group of indirect competitors often have severe negative impacts on sales revenues. The same company is sometimes viewed as a partner and sometimes as a competitor, often flipping its perceived status on a weekly basis.

The current marketplace has also shifted the balance of power from the producers to the consumers. "Customer is King!" and "Outrageous Customer Service" are themes of popular management books.[2] This shift has driven enterprises to total customer responsiveness, including the customizing of products and services for individual customers. To achieve this responsiveness, reaction to changing market conditions must be fast, even if damage to existing business units occurs.

> [The] chief skill is doing things fast; permitting the market to tell it [the enterprise] whether or not it's on target; and killing off fast what the market rejects. . . . It adds up to "how to destroy your company before a competitor does."[3]

The current business environment is best summarized as "semiorganized chaos." A misunderstood fact about the theory of chaos is that it is not about random behavior. This theory examines what appears to be random behavior but is in fact behavior produced by simple deterministic systems. In practical terms, a chaotic system can be usefully studied and its mechanism discovered. And under certain conditions, its behavior can be controlled.

Tom Peters, in *Thriving on Chaos,* expanded on this theme with a lengthy list of prescriptions for dealing with this chaotic environment.

> The true objective is to take the chaos as given and learn to thrive *on* it. The winners of tomorrow will deal proactively with chaos, will look at chaos per se as the source of *market* advantage, not as a problem to be got around.[4]

To explore these changes, let's define an enterprise and the crises faced by enterprise systems.

---

1. Hammer and Champy, 1993, 21.
2. Peters, 1987.
3. Peters, 1992, 14.
4. Peters, 1987, xiv.

2.1.1 What Is an Enterprise?

In an informal sense, an enterprise is any group of people who have a high degree of common purpose or mission. We typically think of an enterprise in the commercial sense—as a profit-making corporation that manufactures products or offers services to other corporations or individuals. In this case, the purpose is defined as bottom-line numbers on the financial report, which are somehow affected by the commerce in the products and services offered by the enterprise. However, enterprises are of many sizes and shapes throughout the world—from a small one-person store to a large governmental agency.

Several important factors characterize an enterprise. First, the *coherence* of its purpose determines the degree to which its members both understand and support the enterprise's purpose. Second, the *organization* of the enterprise specifies the structure and processes for coordinating activities and allocating resources within the enterprise. Third, the *shared information* within the enterprise provides the basis for this organization. The most important kind of shared information is a common worldview held by its members: a view of the economy, its marketplace, customer motivations, product preferences, and so on. A part of this worldview is formalized in computer databases, as we will discuss later; however, most of it is conveyed person-to-person through the modern equivalent of storytelling around tribal campfires. In all cases, the factors—coherence of purpose, organizational structure, and shared information—are closely interrelated.

2.1.2 The Crisis in Enterprise Systems

An enterprise system is the formal information system constructed by the enterprise to assist in the coordination of business processes and the allocation of resources across internal (and external) organizational boundaries. In small organizations, the enterprise system subsumes all formal information systems; it is the one and only information system for the enterprise. In larger organizations, the enterprise system is contrasted with information systems catering to division, group, or departmental units.

As the nature of enterprises has been changing, the nature of enterprise systems has also been dramatically changing. The supporting technology is radically changing. The underlying infrastructure can become obsolete on a monthly basis. Established methodologies are discarded for quick-and-dirty trial and error. The professional skills become irrelevant, decaying with a three-year half-life. Moreover, the IT function within the enterprise endures intensive scrutiny.

Our decade has brought a profound rethinking of the fundamentals of *enterprise systems*—systems that support end-to-end business processes, cutting across internal organizational boundaries and bridging out into other enterprises. Enterprise systems are the basis for the centralized coordination and resource allocation necessary for a coherent enterprise.

Progress with our enterprise systems, however, is often measured by the shattering of the glass house into fragmented client-server islands or by the erosion of databases by uncontrolled data extractions. Dramatic leaps in applying new information technology seem so close, yet continue to be slow to deliver real business value.

> *Dramatic leaps in applying new information technology seem so close, yet continue to be slow to deliver real business value.*

Enterprises in the new nanosecond millennium will be subjected to a different set of challenges from that of just 10 years ago. With great sacrifices of efficiency, the new requirements will drive enterprise systems to seek

- Total customer responsiveness
- Quick reaction to market conditions
- Continuous product differentiation

The importance and validity of enterprise systems are real, regardless of the radical changes in the business environment or in information technology. There is a continuing and critical need for enterprise systems. Its importance is at the heart of responding to the challenges, as Hammer and Champy write:

> In [business] re-engineering, information technology acts as an essential enabler. Without information technology, the process could not be re-engineered.[5]

2.2 Leveraging Data into Knowledge

Transforming data into information, and then into knowledge, has been a fundamental challenge facing our society for centuries. Over the last 30 years, IT has certainly sharpened our focus on this challenge and has enabled us to be more effective. As we hurtle into the next century, our ability to leverage data into knowledge effectively will be at the core of our society and its commerce.

> *As we hurtle into the next century, our ability to leverage data into knowledge effectively will be at the core of our society and its commerce.*

Dataquest estimates that corporations will be spending $4.5 billion by 1999 to better leverage their knowledge resources.[6] Leading organizations are adopting

---

5. Hammer and Champy, 1993, 44.
6. C.F. Ross, Knowledge Management Focus Report, *Dataquest,* 1996, 31, as reported in *Business Wire,* DataWare Technologies, September 29, 1997.

knowledge management techniques and tools at a quickening pace, blending cultural changes with technology to realize the benefits. Examples of companies investing in knowledge management with impressive returns are reported as follows: [7]

- Dow Chemical has increased annual licensing revenues by $100 million by managing its intellectual assets.

- Silicon Graphics has managed its product-information communications processes and reduced sales training costs from $3 million to $200,000.

- Skandia Insurance has reduced the start-up time for opening a corporate office in Mexico from seven years to six months.

- Steelcase has realized an upswing in patent applications and a threefold increase in productivity after implementing knowledge sharing processes across multidisciplinary customer teams.

- Texas Instruments has avoided the cost of building a $500 million wafer fabrication plant by leveraging internal knowledge and best practices (i.e., selection of the most effective business procedures).

- Chevron has realized $150 million in annual savings on power and fuel expenses through knowledge sharing in energy-use management.

- Booz-Allen & Hamilton has achieved over $7 million in annual savings by reducing the time needed to find and access accurate employee and collaborative information.

2.2.1 Data, Information, and Knowledge

The key to understanding the nature of the data-information-knowledge spectrum lies in the following definitions:

- *Data* is the accumulation of raw observations acquired at various points along a business process. Data in itself has no value to an individual, or to an organization, until effort is expended to transform it into information.

- *Information* is data that changes decisions. To be information, data must make sense to people in terms of their mental models of the business and must make a difference in the decisions that they make.

- *Knowledge* is information that changes business processes from an organizational perspective. In other words, knowledge effects changes in the procedures and techniques that an organization applies in the creation and delivery of its product or service.

---

7. *Business Wire,* DataWare Technologies, September 29, 1997.

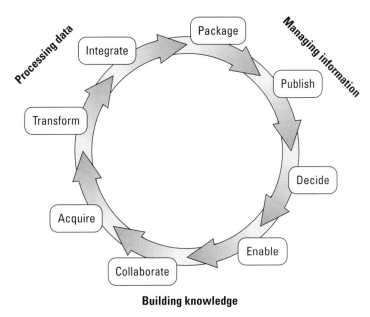

Figure 2-2 The Data-Information-Knowledge Spectrum

Data is a collection of observations.

Information is data that change individual decisions.

Knowledge is information that changes organizational processes.

Increasing value is generated as we move from data to information to knowledge. This flow proceeds as follows:

- *Processing data* means capturing raw observations in a machine-readable (or other useful) format, validating its accuracy, filtering out unrelated data, and assembling the remaining data into consistent structures.
- *Managing information* means transforming data into useful representations that map to our mental models of business activities.
- *Building knowledge* means discovering within the dynamics of information the effective patterns for organizing people to achieve the goals of the enterprise.

An elaboration of this flow is the eight-step circular execution of activities shown in Figure 2-2. Processing data begins in the upper left segment as Acquire, Transform, and Integrate. Managing information continues in the upper right segment as Package,

---

A Simple Experiment at ABC Manufacturing

Steve, director of Data Warehousing, got a call from Susan, CIO of ABC. "I like your proposal for Web farming," remarked Susan. "It certainly is in synch with the Know-Thy-Customer initiative. I would like to commit some resources, but let's ease into this new area slowly so that we understand the benefits to our business."

Steve assigned Alice, one of the better business analysts on the DW staff, to the Web farming experiment. "Spend about half time initially, and get some training on Web search techniques," Steve told Alice. "Treat it as a learning experience for all of us, and keep us posted on a weekly basis."

Next installment is on page 71.

Publish, and Decide. Finally, building knowledge concludes in the lower segment as Enable and Collaborate. The cycle continues as the changed decisions and processes acquire further data about the business.

2.2.2   Knowledge and Power

As our manufacturing economy shifts to an information economy, workers shift from using the firm's capital equipment for manufacturing to using their own knowledge for information production. In other words, the major assets of the firm leave the building after work each day and perhaps return the following day.

The traditional view of knowledge is as a power base to affect organizational politics. In other words, one should "wheel and deal" with knowledge as if it were a durable commodity. The person with knowledge has power over others within the framework of organizational politics. Knowledge should be hoarded and released to others sparingly and only in return for favors.

The contemporary view of knowledge is more open and pragmatic. In this view, you should "use or lose" knowledge as if it were a volatile commodity. Hoarding knowledge only leads to its obsolescence within turbulent markets.

> Therein lies one of the great paradoxes of the knowledge economy. As the possessor of knowledge I can sell it, trade it, or give it away, and yet I still have it. I can turn around a day later and sell, trade it, or give it away again. In order to continue this process I must continually renew, replenish, expand, and create yet more knowledge.[8]

---

8.   Allee, 1997, 10.

For using your knowledge, choose one of the following:
Wheel and Deal   *or*   Use or Lose

The process of renewing knowledge is critical in today's business environment. As in landing that airplane at an urban airport, the readings on the instrument panel an hour ago or even 10 minutes ago are worse than useless. Not only must information be current and accurate, but the knowledge of how to acquire, process, and disseminate information must be equally current and accurate.

Achieving the effective sharing of knowledge is not easy, and it is at the heart of managing the knowledge asset. This is not a technology problem. Ernst & Young used Lotus Notes to gather the collective wisdom for their worldwide consultants. But their effort produced little in the way of results:

> The problem: Many consultants. . . were resisting the program because they had no incentive to use it. On the contrary, sharing knowledge and information via Notes might have harmed an employee's own chance of advancement within the firm by putting valuable information in the hands of a coworker who might then grab the spotlight for a job well done.[9]

This transition in sharing knowledge will continue to be difficult for many, as Jeanne Harris of Andersen Consulting has remarked:

> Some companies are still staffed by people who believe knowledge is power, and they aren't about to give it up to their co-workers. I'd say those are organizations that are in trouble.[10]

The ultimate goal is to gradually change the culture so that everyone is convinced that knowledge sharing is in their best interest, regardless of the incentives. In other words, the benefits from tapping into a common knowledge base exceed any costs from disclosing your secrets to others.

2.2.3 Managing the Knowledge Asset

What is the knowledge asset? Thomas Steward, in *Intellectual Capital*, gives a concise definition: "intellectual material—knowledge, information, intellectual property, expertise—that can be put to use to create wealth; it is collective brainpower."[11]

---

9. M. Halper, Everyone in the Knowledge Pool, *ComputerWorld Global Innovators,* December 8, 1997, 8.
10. D. Bank, Know-It-Alls, *Wall Street Journal,* November 18, 1996, R28.
11. Steward, 1997, x.

A *Wall Street Journal* article by David Bank also captures the motivation for managing the knowledge asset:

> The premise behind the boom [in knowledge management] is simple. Employees hold a wealth of knowledge and expertise about their company—from its products, customers and competitors to its production processes and internal technology. But much of that knowledge is held in bits and pieces by various individuals or sections of a company. If these bits and pieces could be gathered and distributed throughout the entire company, the reasoning goes, the shared knowledge—a sort of collective IQ—would become a powerful force. Workers could use the pool of information create competitive advantage and increase revenue.[12]

The article goes on to state that this collective IQ is becoming more attainable with advances in technology, particularly Web-based intranets. A survey by Dataquest estimated that corporate spending on knowledge management consulting will grow from $410 million in 1992 to $4.5 billion in 1999.

An astute researcher of knowledge management is Yogesh Malhotra, who offers a deeper definition:

> Knowledge Management caters to the critical issues of organizational adaptation, survival and competence in face of increasingly discontinuous environmental change. Essentially, it embodies organizational processes that seek synergistic combination of data and information processing capacity of information technologies, and the creative and innovative capacity of human beings.[13]

His definition acknowledges the turbulence of the business environment and the emphasis on business processes. It also points out that the solution lies in the "synergistic combination" of the hard (i.e., information technology) with the soft (i.e., human capabilities).

Another difficulty of managing knowledge is underestimating the breadth of the knowledge within the typical enterprise. From an excellent discussion by Verna Allee, we can visualize the knowledge asset as an iceberg.[14]

Figure 2-3 illustrates that tangible assets (such as patents, trademarks, and copyrights) are a visible but very small part of knowledge assets within an enterprise. Beneath the surface lies considerably more. Most of the intangible assets are not in structured databases or even in machine-readable form.

---

12. D. Bank, Know-It-Alls, *Wall Street Journal*, November 18, 1996, R28.
13. Y. Malhotra, Virtual Library on Knowledge Management, 1997, http://www.brint.com/km/.
14. Allee, 1997, 35.

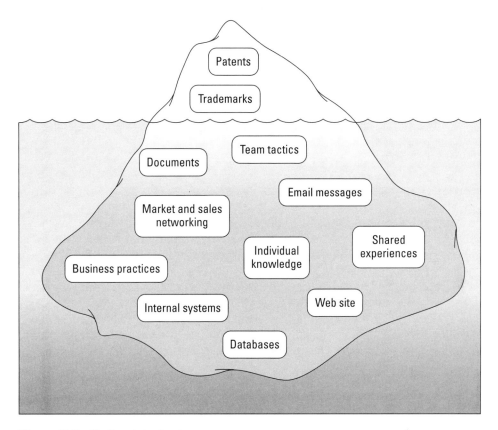

Figure 2-3 The Knowledge Asset

In his book *The New Wealth*, Karl Sveiby gives a vivid account of the rise and fall of Saatchi & Saatchi, an advertising group based in London.[15] This was a firm (specializing in "arty" marketing) whose wealth was entirely dependent on creative skills applied in innovative ways. Through ceaseless acquisitions, an empire arose ... until creative talent fled and stock value waned. Within a few years, the firm was at a fraction of its peak value.

The moral, as Sveiby states, is that the old economics of growth does not apply to creative endeavors. The acquisitions of Saatchi & Saatchi diverted attention from its core competencies. Managing knowledge industries is not like managing manufacturing industries.

One way of measuring the knowledge asset is simply to subtract the net book value of a publicly traded firm from its market value. This measure does assume a

---

15. Sveiby, 1997, 13–18.

degree of rationality in the stock market—a debatable assumption. According to Sveiby, this difference is the invisible part of the balance sheet and consists of

- Employee competence (ability to react properly to uncertain business situations)
- Internal structure (patents, strategies, models, and systems)
- External structure (customer and supplier relations, organizational image)[16]

2.3   Rethinking the Way We Do Work

To cope with our new business environment, we must rethink the way we do work—in a very fundamental sense. Across the global expanse of business processes today, the vast majority of activities are modeled on those of the Industrial Revolution in the early part of this century. Simply put, the model is as follows: Decompose a business process along functional lines, delegate the functional pieces to specific organizational units, and exercise control through hierarchical authority relationships.

This template for doing work has served our society very well! Moreover, it will continue to do so, far into the next century. However, we need to balance this template for doing work against one that has greater flexibility to cope with constant changes in our business environment.

2.3.1   Molded by the Industrial Revolution

Over 200 years ago, Adam Smith suggested, in *The Wealth of Nations,* new ways of organizing work within enterprises through the division of labor.[17] At that time, the usual organization called for one person to perform the entire business process, from raw materials to final product. As the enterprise became successful, the process was scaled up by adding apprentices to assist the craftspeople in noncritical aspects of the process. This scenario describes the craft-based industries before the industrial revolution.

At Smith's suggestion, a business process was divided into a sequence of simpler tasks (i.e., functional decomposition). Each task was assigned to one person, who would perform it repetitively. Over time, the person would become more proficient at that task, increasing both the quality and the quantity. Later, special tools and machinery would be developed to assist with that task. This was the birth of the Industrial Revolution.

In later years, Henry Ford and others adapted these simple suggestions into the massive manufacturing assembly lines of today. As history clearly shows, this

16. Sveiby, 1997, 18.
17. Smith, 1910.

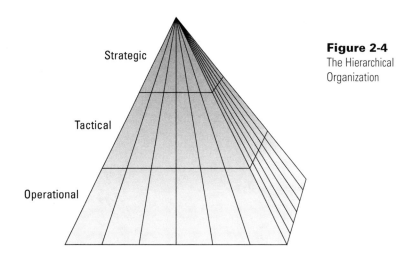

Figure 2-4
The Hierarchical
Organization

seemingly minor shift in organization resulted in enormous increases in industrial production.

An important by-product of decomposing the business process into simpler tasks was specialization into functional units. As people became more specialized, each performing a particular task, they were increasingly identified with the task, rather than with the overall business process. Thus, workers started to be grouped into functional units. With the functional units emerged an organization based on a hierarchical (or pyramidal) control structure, which was called a *bureaucracy*. Figure 2-4 illustrates the hierarchical structure.

It is important to realize that during the Industrial Revolution, bureaucracies became very successful. Every person in the enterprise was accountable to clear measures of the enterprise's purpose. The enterprise was capable of being scaled to very large sizes. Massive economies of scale were realized. Therefore, many benefits of our society today are directly attributable to bureaucracies.

Times have changed! In our *small-is-better* era, bureaucracies are getting bad press. Is the bureaucratic organization a relic of the past? Is it no longer applicable to modern enterprises? In particular, the following changes in enterprises are occurring:

1. Organizations are shifting from hierarchical to flattened (horizontal) structures.

2. Business processes are being redesigned for better responsiveness to customers.

3. Individuals as members of teams are given greater responsibility and authority.

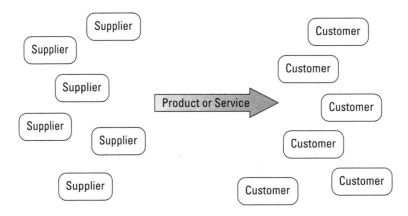

Figure 2-5   Adding Value

2.3.2   The Value Chain

The management of our enterprises should be focused on designing and maintaining coherent business processes. To be coherent, a business process must move raw materials from suppliers through several stages of production and then deliver the product (or service) to the customers. The viability of the business process depends on the degree to which value is added through these various stages. (See Figure 2-5.) If the added value is large, the enterprise enlarges its role in the marketplace. If the added value is small, the enterprise reduces its viability in the marketplace.

The process of adding value is best described as a *value chain* by Michael Porter of the Harvard Business School. The value chain focuses on the value contribution generated within the firm, thus determining the competitive advantage of the firm relative to other firms within its market segment.

> The value chain disaggregates a firm into its strategically relevant activities in order to understand the behavior of costs and the existing and potential sources of differentiation. A firm gains competitive advantage by performing these strategically important activities more cheaply or better than its competitors.[18]

A value chain, as defined by Porter, contrasts the firm's primary activities (inbound logistics, operations, outbound logistics, marketing, sales, and service) with its support activities (infrastructure, human resources, technology, and procurement). The *margin* for a firm is the perceived external values of its goods and services minus the cost of the primary and support activities, as shown in

---

18. Porter, 1985, 33–34.

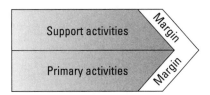

Figure 2-6 Generic Value Chain

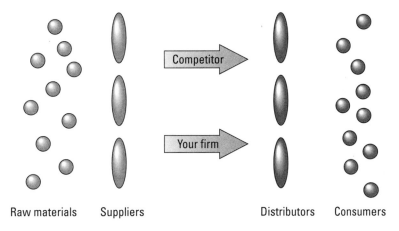

Figure 2-7 Generic Value System

Figure 2-6.[19] Porter distinguishes between the value chain of the firm and the *value system* in which the firm conducts its business. As in Figure 2-7, raw materials and suppliers are upstream, and distributors and consumers are downstream. According to Porter, competitive advantage within your value system comes from the ability of your firm to control costs and to differentiate your goods or services from those of other firms.

2.3.3 Redesigning Business Processes

The trend today is for enterprises to reexamine how they do their work. This implies the redesign (or reengineering) of critical business processes and the creative application of information technology to enable those processes in totally new ways.

> Reengineering is the *fundamental* rethinking and *radical* redesign of business *processes* to achieve *dramatic* improvements in critical, contemporary measures of performance.[20]

---

19. Porter, 1985, 37.
20. Hammer and Champy, 1993, 33.

A business process is "a collection of activities that takes one or more kinds of input and creates an output that is of value to the customer, " as stated by Hammer and Champy.[21]

The key objective is the *additional value you deliver to the customer* as compared with your suppliers (and your competitors). This requires a greater sensitivity and awareness of the business problems of the customer. Rather than survey the perceived requirements of the customer, enterprises are urged to join in partnership with the customer to understand the problem, jointly suggest solutions, and offer customized products or services that truly resolve the business problem. Working backward from this objective defines the business process.

Some writers (such as Michael Hammer) strongly assert that this redesign of business processes must be *radical,* implying a start-from-scratch attitude.

> It's basically taking an ax and a machine gun to your existing organization. One company said, "Through re-engineering we have saved the business and destroyed the organization." That just puts it perfectly.[22]

Some characteristics of redesigning business processes are as follows:[23]

1. Several jobs are integrated into one.
2. Processes have multiple versions to respond to variations in customer needs.
3. Work is performed where it makes sense.
4. Steps in a process are performed in a more natural order.

If an enterprise is successful, it can achieve dramatic improvements in product quality and service levels.

> It is not products but the processes that create products that bring companies long-term success. Good products don't make winners; winners make good products.[24]

The resulting world of work looks different.[25] Job responsibilities become multidimensional rather than simplistic; job preparation becomes education rather than training; performance is defined based on results rather than on activity; managers become coaches rather than supervisors; organizations become flattened rather than hierarchical.

---

21. Hammer and Champy, 1993, 35.
22. M. Hammer, Interview with Michael Hammer. *ComputerWorld.* January 24, 1994, 84–86.
23. Hammer and Champy, 1993, 50ff.
24. Hammer and Champy, 1993, 25.
25. Hammer and Champy, 1993, 65ff.

Figure 2-8   Five Competitive Forces

2.3.4 **Competitive Forces**

Every enterprise encounters competitive forces within its market. Some competitive forces are destructive to your enterprise and even to the market. Other competitive forces can be constructive, building your revenue stream amid a growing and healthy market. In any case, understanding the structure of competitive forces within your market is critical to understanding the positioning and effectiveness of your added value.

Porter suggests that there are five competitive forces in every market, as shown in Figure 2-8.[26] The first force is the *impacts from traditional competitors,* the ones that are visible to you and to your customers. In other words, traditional competitors are the ones that run full-page advertisements showing why your product is inferior to theirs with a contrived comparison chart. Factors that influence the competitive force of traditional competitors are market growth, cost structure, brand identity, customer switching pain, regional concentration, product differentiation, and exit barriers.

The second force is the *threat of new entrants* into a market that has low barriers to entry. This is especially true in the high technology markets. Small and innovative firms can quickly establish significant market share over bigger and older firms. Factors that influence the barrier to entry are economies of scale (which could be inverse), capital requirements, distribution channels, government regulations, and expected retaliation.

The third force is the *threat from substitutes* from the indirect competitors. For example, consider the railroad business of 50 years ago. Other railroad companies were the competitors, receiving your undivided attention. Trucking companies were not considered competitors, since they were in a different business. Yet the customers who needed to ship large volumes of goods increasingly used trucks instead of trains. Factors that influence the threat from substitutes are price/performance tradeoffs, switching costs, and propensity to substitute.

---

26. Porter, 1985, 4–8.

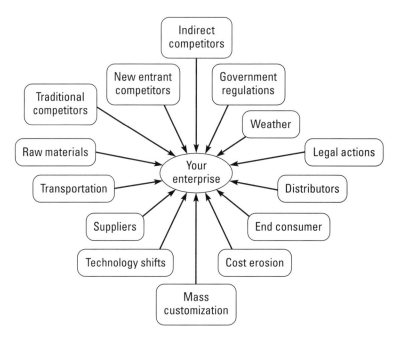

Figure 2-9   Overall Market Structure

The fourth force is the *bargaining power of suppliers.* If a supplier is dominant within a market, that supplier can determine pricing, delivery, and even restrictions on product use. Consider the situation of Microsoft in licensing its Windows operating systems to hardware vendors. As a hardware vendor, what are your alternatives? Factors that influence the bargaining power of suppliers are differentiation, supplier concentration, volume, switching cost, substitutability, and forward integration.

The fifth and last force is the *bargaining power of buyers.* In the long term, this force is the most powerful. Buyers convey the wealth to all those downstream in the value system. Turn off the flow, and everything downstream withers. Factors that influence the bargaining of buyers are price sensitivity, brand identity, seller concentration, volume, switching cost, and backward integration.

A broader perspective on your enterprise relative to your business environment is shown in Figure 2-9.

Porter's insights into competitive advantage are excellent. However, a focus on competitive forces is often too narrow to cope with today's market turbulence. External factors, such as government regulations, weather, and technology shifts, may have little relevance to competition, however defined. Further, a focus on competitive forces blinds an enterprise to a key determinant—a partnership with your customers, as explained in the next section.

Figure 2-10
The Dark Side of
Competitive
Advantage

2.3.5 The Dark Side of Competitive Advantage

The theme of competitive advantage has been a popular one for over a decade. Bolstered by popular management literature and confounded by industry chaos, many enterprises cling to this theme as the driving vision for their company.

An executive was said to have exclaimed, "Competitive advantage is our top and only priority in this company!" Our immediate reaction was that his company would soon "competitive advantage" itself out of business.

There is a dark side to competitive advantage that many are unwilling to face. The theme seems so simple and appealing. A typical reaction is, "Why not be the best in the marketplace?" It is certainly the case that stimulating the competitive juices of the troops does wonders for motivation and focus. However, looking over your shoulder at your competitors can divert your attention from strategic issues. Figure 2-10 shows the potential disaster of this situation. The problem is that the basic notion of competitive advantage can lead an enterprise into directions harmful to its long-term success. In other words, the theme is detrimental to your future when it is taken to extremes.

The very definition of firms as competitors will lock an enterprise into a static positioning—a positioning that may soon be obsolete within your marketplace. Attempts at product differentiation, conceived relative to the products of your competitors, are only incremental steps from current positioning. What is missing is the fertile ground for radical thinking that moves your company into an entirely different marketplace.

The IT marketplace is highly complex and dynamic. One day, a firm is a partner; the next, it is a competitor. One group in your enterprise views a firm as a partner; another group views the same firm as a competitor. For a market to be healthy, there should be a diversity of competing firms, all of which are enlarging the market with better products. Porter discusses the criteria for good and bad competitors: a good competitor is being a firm that increases "sustainable competitive advantage [for your firm] and improves the structure of the industry."[27]

The most important decision that affects your company's market positioning is the definition (or profile) of your customers. Once that decision is made, your sole focus should be on leveraging your resources to enhance the value chain of your customers. In other words, the recurring question should be "What can I do to make my customers successful in their marketplace?" If you have a product or service that will make your customers successful, your customers will not only have clear motivation to do business with you, but they will also have the funds.

In Figure 2-10, note that your customers (in the upper right) are really cheering for you. They have made a major commitment to your products and to your company. They want you to be successful. Pay attention to them. They just might help you avoid a major disaster.

Competitive advantage is not achieved through a slugfest over market share with known competitors. Rather, competitive advantage is being there for your customers through a keen awareness of their market and technology dynamics. If an enterprise has an honest concern for its customers, it should be in partnership alongside (or even a bit in front of) of each of its customers.

2.3.6 Missed Opportunities

In the everyday life of an enterprise, there are hundreds or thousands of opportunities to add value to your products or services from the perspective of your customer. Most of these opportunities are not fully exploited. In fact, most of them are often totally missed, resulting in a loss to the enterprise and to its customers.

As examples of missed opportunities, consider the following situations:

1. Fred overdrew his checking account and got a nasty letter from his bank. However, he had a savings account at the same bank with thousands of dollars in it!
2. Until last month, Chris flew to New York every week for six months. The airline never contacted him about his absence.
3. Over the past year, George has spent thousands of dollars on stereo equipment at a department store. Yet the store continually sends him ads for jewelry.
4. Steve defaulted on his house mortgage. A month later, his credit union sent him a special offer to lend him money for a new car at a low rate.

In every one of these situations, there is a failure by the enterprise to exploit the potential added value to the customer. In the first situation, it is a failure to recognize a customer as a whole person, rather than as two separate accounts. In the

---

27. Porter, 1985, 201ff.

second situation, it is a failure to recognize a continuing (and profitable) pattern. In the third situation, it is a failure to know the preferences of a customer and therefore to avoid unnecessary costs and annoying mass ads. Finally, it is a failure to avoid doing business with the wrong customer.

When the scale of a business is small, a given employee will come into contact with the same customer on numerous occasions. The ability (and motivation) to recognize such special situations and to exploit such business opportunities comes naturally. As we scale our enterprises to global proportions, our ability to exploit these opportunities increases in difficulty and relies heavily on the proper application of technology. Further, we often fail to motivate the employee to exploit such opportunities.

Let's explore this critical issue further by examining the moment of customer contact.

2.3.7 The Precious Moment of Customer Contact

The *moment of customer contact* is the greatest leverage point for adding value in your business processes. It is during those precious moments that customers (clients, prospects, etc.) communicate directly with someone in your enterprise about their concerns and requirements. The typical situations for customer contact are opening a new account, establishing a line of credit, submitting an order, complaining about problems, and so forth.

The leverage within this moment of customer contact is dependent on several factors. First, the degree to which the customer can control or customize the business transaction is an important factor. The objective should be that the customer defines who you are as an enterprise. The degree to which the enterprise molds its delivery mechanism to match the expectations of the customer is the degree to which the enterprise satisfies its customers.

The second factor is the quality of resources that the enterprise applies to the moment of customer contact. In particular, the people who come into contact with your customers are the ones who determine your added value. In many companies, and by tradition in many industries, the point of customer contact is usually staffed by the least skilled (and lowest-paid) employees, who have the least motivation for exploiting the customer contact.

This situation would probably seem odd to a visitor from another planet. Logic seems to dictate that the more resources (people being the most important) that are applied to the moment of customer contact, the more value is added to the business process, and the more successful the enterprise will be.

Michael Hammer captured this situation well:

> [There is] no element of customer service...no one is in charge...people involved in a process look inward toward their department and upward toward their boss, but no one looks outward toward the customer.[28]

---

28. Hammer and Champy, 1993, 27.

The third factor is the quality of the business transaction itself. The quality of the transaction can be improved if

- The requirements of the customer are anticipated.
- These requirements can be easily specified.
- Related requirements and solutions are suggested.
- Responses to variations in requirements are quickly customized.
- The product (or service) is immediately delivered.
- The product works the first time as advertised.
- Difficulties are quickly and painlessly resolved.
- The financial resolution is painless and mostly invisible.
- The entire product life cycle is managed for the customer.

...and so on. If we operated the corner store in a small town, the execution of the above list would come quite naturally. When we scale up our enterprise to serve thousands of customers spread across the globe, the simple reality of this list is lost.

The fourth factor in leveraging the moment of customer contact is the people who touch the product, the suppliers, and so on. If a person does not come in contact with the product in some way, that person is not contributing to the value-adding of the enterprise. In other words, that person is overhead! As IT is applied increasingly to business processes, middle management is now on the list of endangered species—for this very reason.

The final factor in leveraging the moment of customer contact is the information that describes the various aspects of the previous factors. More will be said about the process of disseminating information in later sections.

2.3.8 Automating and Enabling

A key factor in properly adding value to the business process is recognizing the strengths and weaknesses of automating and enabling. They form a continuum of business tactics from which we must select wisely.

To automate means to strive toward mass production through functional specialization. (See Figure 2-11.) It implies that we fully understand the business process, are able to control (or at least anticipate) its environment, and can achieve value through standardized products or services. If our assumptions are correct, automation is the most effective tactic for implementing this business process. The requirements for automation are top-down control through rules and procedures, and good planning and design.

In contrast, *to enable* means to strive toward *mass customization* through *process integration*. (See Figure 2-12.) It implies the opposite of automation. We do not fully understand the business process because it is (and should be) constantly changing. We cannot control its environment. And a standardized product has little value to the consumer. The key to effective enabling is to properly support the

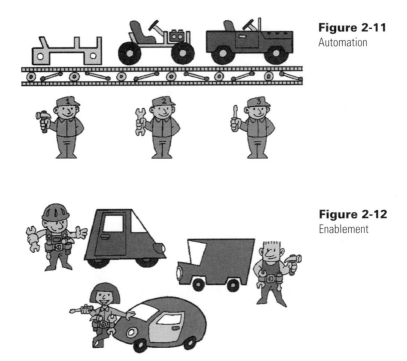

Figure 2-11
Automation

Figure 2-12
Enablement

people who come in contact with the customers and the products at the critical points of the business process. The requirements of enablement are bottom-up control via micro-decisions; powerful tools; and total information.

The strength of automation is that it makes a well-defined process more efficient. The procedure is in control. We can focus on batching transactions for efficiency (e.g., repetitive operations on small units) and control (e.g., load balancing). On the other hand, automation is difficult to change or customize. It is like a large ship that builds momentum, becoming difficult to turn. The uniqueness of the customer is lost, blended into the transaction batches.

The strength of enablement is that it makes an ill-defined process more effective. The human is in control, assisted and empowered by productive tools. The focus is on the processing of a discrete transaction, catering to its unique features. Exception processing is normal. The uniqueness of the customer is not lost. On the other hand, enablement is difficult to scale into large organizations that have larger customer bases. Finding and training the proper personnel and equipping them is a time-consuming and expensive endeavor.

In summary, automation is great for stable environments, and enablement is great for small organizations, as shown in Figure 2-13. How do we flex automation or scale enablement? In other words, can we have the best of both worlds, as shown in the upper right of Figure 2-13?

This is a misleading question, since we need to do both. Automation and enablement are part of the same continuum. The challenge is to design an organization

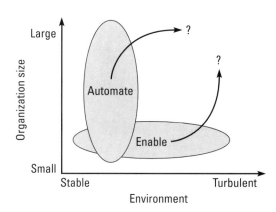

Figure 2-13
Organization Size
versus Environment

(and construct its information systems) so that there can be a dynamic tension across this automation-enablement (A-E) continuum. We need to move easily along this A-E continuum, as the business environment dictates.

To flex automation requires the following:

- Effective training in standardized skills
- Dynamic changes in the procedures manual
- A culture that accepts work changes as desirable
- The ability to manage the resulting complexity

To scale enablement requires a powerful work context that *informates* the person. Tom Peters makes a bold statement for total access to information concerning a customer:

> To informate is to use technology to invest people with enough knowledge and understanding of the process in which they're working to allow them to exercise, intelligently, the prerogatives normally reserved for management.[29]

2.4 Sharing Information

In the long term, the viability of an enterprise is directly related to its ability to facilitate information sharing (see Figure 2-14) and to promote organizational learning. Using Peters's terminology, we should *informate* the person and the entire organization by blending the soft side (social, cultural, political, leadership) with the hard side (technology, architecture, database design). Both aspects must be in balance.

---

29. Peters, 1994a, 75.

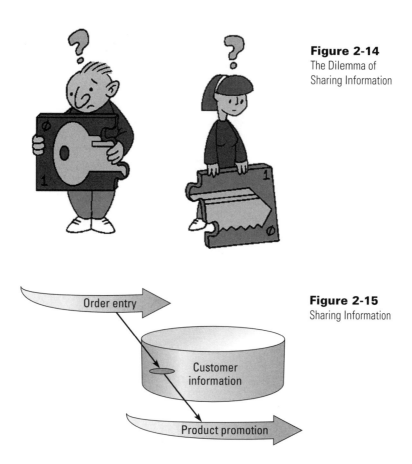

Figure 2-14
The Dilemma of
Sharing Information

Figure 2-15
Sharing Information

The best technology cannot overcome years of political dissension or authoritarian leadership. Moreover, the best leadership cannot overcome rigid legacy systems whose data is locked within undocumented flat files.

The ability to share information among business processes is the key to enhancing added value for business processes. At the heart of coordinating business processes and allocating resources is the sharing of information. In particular, it is the sharing of common business objects (in the sense of the object-oriented data model with the clustering of procedures and data).

Let's consider a simple example of the sharing of common business objects. In Figure 2-15, we have two business processes: one for order entry and another for product promotion (marketing). In order entry, we usually collect customer information to aid in shipping and inventory. As a first step in sharing customer information, product promotion can take this data and use it for a focused mailing to only those customers who have specific purchasing patterns. Note that this sharing is a significant value added to product promotion. Not only does it increase its effectiveness, but it also benefits the customers, who see only those products in which they are interested.

Figure 2-16
Sharing Information Among
Business Processes

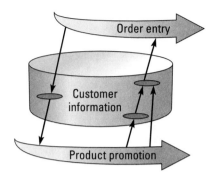

Continuing this example, let's consider an enhancement of the business process for order entry. If product promotion will share its information as to which products should be promoted (because of high appeal or large inventories), we can incorporate this information into the order entry process. As the customer is entering an order, related products can be suggested. In effect, the order entry process has become part of the product promotion. (See Figure 2-16.) And this integration through sharing common business objects has greatly enhanced both business processes.

Sharing of common business objects implies a managed environment in which objects are protected in terms of security, transaction integrity, concurrency controls, and so on. The viability of our enterprise systems depends on the degree to which they achieve this goal.

The sharing of information at an enterprise level carries with it an interesting set of principles. Unlike human resources or manufacturing facilities, information resources behave according to a different kind of physics and economics.

2.4.1 Information as a Unique Resource

Information is a unique resource. Data is information only when it hits its target precisely. If we are on target, other factors affect the perceived value and business impacts of data.

Once data is copied, we must maintain its currency to retain its business value. Is more data better? Within certain limits, it may be; however, there is also a strong need to aggregate or summarize data so that less is better. The cost of giving access to the data is changing rapidly as databases become commodity technology and the Internet becomes globally available. Instant and free access to data is a reality in some segments of society and industry. Is this better? What is the benefit of linking certain data to other data? The ability to interrelate data may have more value than any of the individual data items.

The most important virtue of information as an enterprise resource is the synergism of common data. If we couple business processes to common business objects, the coordination of those processes can be facilitated more effectively and the individuals involved can learn to manage those processes better.

2.4.2   Tyranny of Disparate Data

In contrast, the most important evil of information as an enterprise resource is the tyranny of disparate (or inconsistent) data.[30] Data that may be sufficient for a COBOL application is often totally inappropriate for decision support. Inaccurate or dirty data is a universal feature of operational systems. Ken Orr likens the data warehouse to a sewage treatment plant for the enterprise, allowing all kinds of disparate data to float to the surface.[31]

The evil of disparate data goes beyond the inconsistencies in the data collected and into the basic architectures of our systems. Centralized mainframes did give us a certain luxury in data integration and, thus, a handle on dealing with disparate data. Newer distributed architectures are increasing the difficulty of dealing with disparate data:

> Centralized mainframes are not a requirement for making a mess of enterprise data. Client-server systems have become very efficient at this task.[32]

The evil of disparate data also impacts the main objective of data warehousing—the constant struggle for a consistent model of the enterprise. Disparate data is not just the inconsistencies in the data values, but, more important, those in the structure and meaning of the data itself.

2.4.3   Toward an Information Ecology

The best way to view the implications of information sharing at an enterprise level is to see it as ecology, much like environmental ecology. As IT professionals, we need a deep understanding of information ecology and bear a major responsibility to teach others about it.

Information ecology is the understanding of

- Impacts of your "data actions" on the enterprise
- Interrelationships among various data contexts
- Maximizing information creation and sharing
- Minimizing resource consumption and delays

Every member of an enterprise creates, filters, and transforms data about various aspects of business (and many other) activities. Some of this data is captured within our information system; most is not. The ways in which data is interrelated

---

30. Brackett, 1994.
31. Inmon/Barnett Data Warehouse Conference, Washington, DC, April 1995.
32. *Bolder Report,* Insight #1, February 1995.

between one context and another are numerous and complex. The cost of these data activities is huge and spans a broad spectrum, from paper to electronic media.

The typical outcome of all this data activity is that we tend to focus on our personal data world with little concern for the data worlds of others and even less concern for the data world of the enterprise. Rather than thinking about our data world as blending together with others, we tend to maximize our personal data world, in isolation from others. We also tend to view enterprise data as belonging to management or to some other group, perceiving little potential benefit to us in sharing our personal data with the enterprise.

The control of information is and will always be power within the politics of the enterprise. Many feel, either rightly or wrongly, that sharing information is equivalent to sharing political power. If you share information, you give away some of your ability to influence others. In some cases, there may even be a sense of greed in hoarding data for oneself. In other cases, there may be a sense of fear and uncertainty. These emotions about information sharing are all very real.

As Davenport points out, information ecology requires a holistic approach to thinking about people and their behavior toward information within the enterprise.[33] As biological ecology thrives on diversity, information ecology too thrives on diversity, through the integration of many types of information. The inhibiting boundaries between structured and unstructured, text and images, audio and video, and so forth must be eliminated. Advances in technology are solving this integration problem technically. However, the greatest part of the problem lies simply in the way people conceive of and handle information, often in a careless and unthinking manner. Just as a person casually tosses out a pop can along the road, people casually create spreadsheets of valuable information, inconsistent with similar collections of information and inaccessible to other interested people.

Just as a person casually tosses out a pop can along the road,
people casually create spreadsheets of valuable information,
inconsistent with similar collections of information and inaccessible
to other interested people.

The positive side of information ecology is that there is an immense untapped potential in information sharing. The sharing of information is a prerequisite for effective organizational learning, which is a prerequisite for adaptability in changing markets. As we move our work style from automation to enablement, information sharing (see Figure 2-17) is the catalyst for mass customization.

In many enterprises, information is often a poorly utilized and grossly abused resource. Even with the ideal applications of IT, we have much to learn and appreciate about information ecology in our enterprise and in our society.

---

33. Davenport, 1997, 28ff.

Figure 2-17
The Key to Sharing
Information

2.5 Creating Information Markets

The next level of interaction within the enterprise is to explore new methods for coordination of business processes based on market mechanisms.[34] In fact, mechanisms that support publish-and-subscribe in distributed computing are actually the first stage in creating the electronic equivalent of a marketplace.

Market mechanisms are like a county fair—lots of diverse activity, a variety of products and services being exchanged. (See Figure 2-18.) Through wandering around, customers are informed of and have access to this diversity. However, at the enterprise level, markets are a method for coordinating business processes within and among self-directed teams. In traditional bureaucratic situations, coordination is handled through hierarchical authority and standardized procedures. As our enterprises move toward organizing around self-directed teams, we find little precedent in society for coordination methods at this high level of scale and flexibility. Electronic markets that support coordination in dynamic distributed architectures can be more dynamic and flexible than traditional (hard-wired) control hierarchies.

In general terms, there are four essential ingredients for a market:

1. A group of buyers (consumers) who need a solution to a problem
2. A group of sellers (producers) who offer a solution through a product or service
3. Information that is shared between the two groups
4. A mechanism to exchange items of economic value

---

34. Malone et al., 1987.

Figure 2-18
Information
Markets as a
County Fair

Figure 2-19
Publish-and-
Subscribe
Architecture

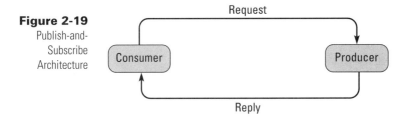

What is missing is the integrating mechanism that blends the ingredients. Such market mechanisms are described next in the paradigms of request-and-reply and publish-and-subscribe.

2.5.1 Basic Paradigms of Computing

For 30 years, the basic paradigm of computing has been *request-and-reply* (R&R). An application requests specific data or services, and a subroutine replies with them. As distributed processing has become popular, the paradigm has remained the same. A client requests some data via an SQL statement, and the server replies with a result set from the database. The R&R paradigm is summarized in Figure 2-19.[35]

The R&R paradigm is running out of gas. With mainframe systems, we could schedule the batch stream and predetermine the ordering of critical events. In the dynamic (and uncontrolled) environments of present-day enterprise systems, an application no longer has the luxury of knowing when and what to request. As our systems are scaled to global levels, R&R applications are reduced to inefficient polling for detecting critical business events.

---

35. R. Hackathorn, Publish or Perish, *BYTE,* September 1997, 65–72.

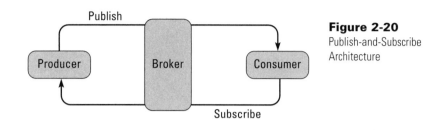

Figure 2-20
Publish-and-Subscribe
Architecture

*An application no longer has the luxury of knowing when
and what to request.*

2.5.2 Publish-and-Subscribe

An alternative technology, *publish-and-subscribe* (P&S), has emerged to coordinate the components of distributed applications. The general concept is quite old, starting hundreds of years ago with newspaper publishing. In recent times, the term has been applied to a variety of products that coordinate complex distributed applications or replicate diverse information content. Someone triggers an event in a business process; someone else should be notified so she can process that event. Someone generates content of a volatile nature; someone else is interested in that content on a continuing basis.

In whatever paradigm evolves from R&R and P&S, there must be a balance of power between producers and consumers. In R&R systems, the consumers (clients) drive the dynamics. In the initial P&S systems, the producers (servers) drive the dynamics. Both situations are extremes and need to be brought toward a balance.

In the complex distributed systems of the future, any element will need to cycle between the producer and the consumer. Attention must be given to the mechanism that consumers have to express their requirements and to the mechanism that producers have to listen to those requirements. To maximize the dynamics, producers must respond by publishing channels for which there will be a healthy market.

P&S is a connectivity paradigm that clearly separates the roles of producer and consumer using an intermediary, known as the *broker.* The broker manages the interactions so that neither the producer nor the consumer needs to know much about the other. In other words, the architecture is decoupled or loosely coupled, as shown in Figure 2-20.

With P&S, the broker maintains a relationship that couples producers with consumers, as contrasted with a momentary interaction of R&R. This relationship is called a *channel* (or *subscription, subject,* or *buffer*). Reversing the ordering from that of R&R, the producer initiates the interaction by publishing a message to the broker.

Figure 2-21
An Information Broker

The traditional way of linking data producers with data consumers is to design the system so that those links are static—hard-wired into module linkages and procedural calls. As we move into increasingly dynamic and complex environments, we no longer have the luxury of hard-wiring those links. Producers and consumers frequently appear and vanish.

A mechanism is required to efficiently match producers with consumers in a dynamic fashion. Adding flexibility and adaptation to system architectures is the role that P&S is fulfilling. If P&S is implemented properly, there is no centralized authority dictating design prior to operation, so all the elements of a system are leveraged dynamically.

*Adding flexibility and adaptation to system architectures
is the role that P&S is fulfilling.*

*There is no centralized authority dictating design prior to operation,
thereby leveraging all the elements of a system dynamically.*

The mechanism of publish-and-subscribe is not new; the publishing industry has used it for newspapers and magazines for over a hundred years. What is new is its emergence as an important coordination mechanism in distributed computing.

As we have described, the mechanism of publish-and-subscribe requires a third party, the broker, to mediate information among the parties that produce and consume information.[36] (See Figure 2-21.) The broker decouples producers from consumers so that limited information is shared between them. Producers are sometimes called *providers* or *publishers,* and consumers are sometimes called *subscribers.*

36. R. Hackathorn, Data Delivery When You Want It, *BYTE,* June 1997, 51.

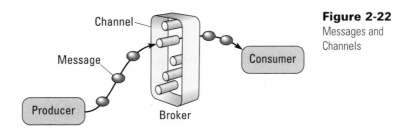

Figure 2-22
Messages and Channels

The broker establishes a *channel* to manage a stream of similar *messages*. The channel relieves both the producer and the consumer of the burden of maintaining currency. The broker maintains a channel as long as either a producer continues to publish or a consumer continues to subscribe. This time period may be a few seconds or a few years. The channels should have fine granularity to differentiate among the various types of messages. The architecture of a channel is shown in Figure 2-22.

When the producer-consumer relationship is decoupled, the security of both parties can be enhanced, allowing either party to participate anonymously. Producers could also share or transfer subscriptions to balance loads or to specialize in certain areas. Further, the P&S mechanism can form multilevel value-added chains in which a consumer can add value to the data and republish the result to another group of consumers.

A message describes a business event as it occurs. A message is usually divided into a *header* (structured data common to all message types) and a *body* (variable data specific to a certain message type). The body may contain free-form text, an HTML Web page, attribute-value pairs, and so on.

Finally, a market is formed when there is a high level of activity among a group of producers and consumers over one or more channels. Like those of normal markets in our society, the dynamics of markets within P&S systems are a major indicator for directions in which to evolve these systems.

In summary, the important elements of a P&S mechanism are as follows:

- A coordination mechanism is mediated by an independent broker.
- The broker establishes fine-grained channels, each of which manages a stream of messages of a similar type.
- A producer publishes a message to a channel. The message describes either a business event as it occurs or informational content as it changes.
- A consumer subscribes to a channel and asynchronously receives the message stream.
- A channel can have many producers and many consumers, each of whom has little knowledge of or control over the others.
- A market is the set of producers and consumers among whom there is significant activity over one or more channels.

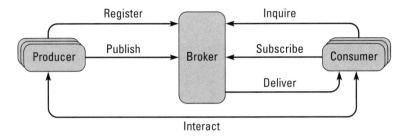

Figure 2-23   The P&S Interactions

The basic interactions of a P&S mechanism are shown in Figure 2-23. A producer first registers with the broker for a specific channel. This action may cause the broker to create the channel and establish its characteristics. Next, consumers can then *inquire* about available channels. If a desired channel is found, the consumer can *subscribe* to that channel. Later, the producer *publishes* a message to a channel, and the broker *delivers* the message to the proper set of consumers subscribing to that channel.

In some situations, direct interaction on the part of a producer-consumer pair is desirable, as shown with the *interact* link. Such a direct link is required for highly volatile or massive data, along with applications requiring efficient high-volume transactional semantics.

A final aspect of the interactions above is the possible financial exchange among producers, consumers, and the broker. As critical systems extend beyond the boundaries of a single company, an explicit financial incentive must be established to ensure stable operations. Although electronic commerce is rapidly increasing in various areas, no instances of financial exchange with P&S have occurred.

Several issues must be resolved for any practical application of P&S, such as

- Channels and namespace
- Level of service
- Pull versus push
- Privileges

The first issue is defining channels and, especially, the namespace of channels. A channel represents a stream of important business events or information resources. Defining your channels implies defining your business processes. Likewise, naming (or addressing) your channels implies the way the P&S applications will support your business processes. Most argue that the naming should be federated so that there is a shared responsibility among producers and the broker, similar to the treatment of domain names on the Internet.

The message header usually contains a structured field for a subject (or object type name). If the naming of messages uses this subject field, the P&S mechanism is said to be *subject-based.* If the naming is dependent on the content of the message body, it is said to be *content-based*. The subject-based mechanism is more efficient, while the content-based one allows more flexibility for the consumer to specify which messages are processed. Content-based naming may also imply that the message body has some self-defining format so that the broker can filter on various equivalence operators in addition to simple string matches.

The second issue is the level (or quality) of service, usually dependent on the reliability of message delivery. The typical levels of service are best-effort, reliable, guaranteed, and transactional. *Best-effort* implies that the broker uses some efficient (but lacking error correction) transport, such as UDP. *Reliable* implies that the broker uses a less efficient (but including error correction) transport, such as TCP. *Guaranteed* implies that the broker queues the message on permanent storage until it is certain that the consumer has received the message. Finally, *transactional* implies that the broker manages a transaction among the producers and consumers so that any actions by all parties are committed or aborted in unison. Among the various products, the scope of the transaction boundary is confusing and depends on whether the perspective is that of the producer or the consumer.

The third issue is "pull versus push" as used for P&S. The topic of push protocols has received much industry attention recently as the preferred alternative. The problem occurs when the broker sends a message to the set of consumers who have subscribed to that message. If the number of consumers is small, each consumer can pull its message from the broker via periodic polling, or the broker can send the message multiple times, once for each consumer. As the number of consumers rises from hundreds to millions, both of these approaches rapidly degrade network performance. In other words, approaches using pull and also simple push do not scale.

The essence of "true" push for P&S is twofold: First, the consumer receives its message asynchronously. In other words, an interrupt occurs at some level to switch the consumer's attention to the new message; there is no background polling by the consumer. Second, the message is multicast by the broker to many consumers. In other words, the broker initiates a single message that is efficiently distributed to the proper set of consumers. Efficient multicasting implies hardware assistance buried in network routers, and hence limits networks to homogeneous equipment. At the heart of the debate over efficient multicasting is IP multicasting for the TCP/IP protocol, as explained by Hurwicz.[37]

The fourth issue is specifying and managing the privileges of producers and consumers. As in a database system, it is necessary to have a secured environment in which all parties first are authenticated and then assume a set of "privileges" that limits their actions. Policies are required for determining who creates and controls channels and defines their characteristics (naming, typing, and granularity), who grants the privilege to publish, and to which channels, and who grants the privilege to subscribe, and to which channels.

---

37. For details, see Mike Hurwicz, Multicast to the Masses, *BYTE,* June 1997.

> *P&S technology has the potential to create global markets for information sharing, far beyond what we can imagine at present.*

As a coordination mechanism for information markets, P&S has a tremendous potential for flexibility, adaptation, and evolution. In complex, large-scale situations where requirements are constantly changing, P&S may provide the fertile soil in which the appropriate systems can be grown. Further, the standardization and commercialization of P&S technology has the potential to create global markets for information exchange and commerce, far beyond what we can imagine at present.

2.5.3 Virtual Organization

The culmination of using an open P&S mechanism for coordination within an enterprise is the *virtual organization*. An extreme definition of the virtual organization is an enterprise with no employees and no internal operations—only a legal and financial entity that outsources all business activity.

While this extreme is unlikely, the concept has to some extent become a reality in many companies. The trend toward outsourcing noncore activities is strong. This trend raises the question, "What is the core of an enterprise?" For some enterprises, the core competence may simply be the effective orchestrating of the proper mixture of activities.

Abbe Mowshowitz, a professor of computer science at the City College of New York, describes the virtual organization in a *CACM* article.[38] He describes the extreme flexibility in business processes that can be achieved through rapidly switching the assignments for performing those processes. When effort is concentrated on minimizing the delays and costs in this switching, the enterprise becomes more effective in making use of whatever resources are available. He notes that a negative side effect of these temporary, short-lived relationships is the decline in a person's loyalty to the enterprise. In effect, employees become independent contractors. Finally, Mowshowitz remarks that "out-sourcing is a precursor of meta-management," in which we specify the external parameters for an activity while ignoring its internal implementation—which is also a concise definition of object-oriented design.

Struggling with the role of the Internet in business strategy, Richard Gascoyne reaches similar conclusions about virtual organizations.[39] For success, it is necessary to refocus the enterprise externally by changing reward structures, rather than by streamlining internal units and tightening internal procedures. The primary goal should be the ability to act and adapt quickly, rather than the ability to attain dominance within a market niche.

---

38. A. Mowshowitz, Virtual Organization, *Comm of ACM,* vol. 40, no. 9, Sept. 1997, 30–37.
39. R. Gascoyne, Adapt to the Internet, *InformationWeek,* May 5, 1997, 89ff.

This chapter has examined the business perspective on Web farming—providing business intelligence to aid in decision making and in the creation of knowledge to enhance business processes. The next chapter describes the various disciplines for Web farming, from which we can gain valuable insights.

## Chapter Three

Foundations

For the farmer, the environment is constantly shifting, buffeted by the wind and rain. The really important things must be nailed down. Likewise, Web farming is constantly changing, week by week. Again, the really important things must be nailed down.

This chapter describes the reference disciplines that provide the foundation of Web farming. Like the three legs of a stool, the disciplines that support Web farming are Web technology, data warehousing, and information science.

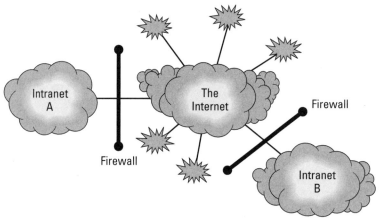

Figure 3-1   Internet, Intranet, and Extranet

3.1   Web Technology

This section is an introduction to web technology. Further details of Web technology are covered in Chapters 7, 8, and 9, which discuss Web standards, tools, and resources.

3.1.1   Internet, Intranet, and Extranet

Using TCP/IP as the basic communications transport, we can connect many computers (which are usually called hosts) into a physical network. Two networks can be interconnected with a gateway so that hosts on one network can communicate with a host on another network. If we continue to glue separate networks together with gateways, the collection of networks becomes one unified *internet* (with a lowercase *i*). Any host on that internet can interconnect with any other host, regardless of their physical configurations.

Web technology can be applied in several contexts. First, there is the (one and only) global *Internet* (with an uppercase *I*), which interconnects every major country and every major computer in the world. Second, there is the local *intranet,* which provides similar functionality, but only within the boundaries of an enterprise. Third, there is the *extranet,* which joins disparate intranets into one logical intranet using the Internet as a bridge. (See Figure 3-1.)

The differences among these three cases have to do with who can access which resources. Someone who connects directly into the Internet can access any Web page that is publicly available from anywhere in the world. From some parts of the world, this access may be slow, but it is possible. Someone who resides on intranet A can access any resources within that intranet, subject to the limitations of security policies. That same person can access any resources on the Internet, depending on the policies in force within the intranet's firewall. Usually, a firewall will prevent most traffic that originates outside the intranet, but will permit most traffic that originates inside the intranet.

If the firewalls of intranet A and intranet B are configured properly (using a virtual private network capability), then someone on either of the two intranets could access resources on the other intranet as if the two intranets were one. This is called an *extranet* between intranets A and B.

The Internet is highly dynamic and global in scale because new nodes can be attached daily with minimal central management. A user in any company or country can connect into the global Internet simply by connecting into the nearest node.

Throughout this text, we will refer simply to the Web, implying that we are using the global Internet to access Web sites external to your organization. All the concepts and techniques of Web farming can be applied within intranets and extranets. However, the focus of Web farming is on data external to the enterprise. The context of the global Internet will, therefore, be emphasized.

3.1.2   Web Browsers and Servers

Using your favorite Web browser, you request a Web page by entering its address. The address is usually in the form of a uniform resource locator (URL), such as http://www.bolder.com/. This URL refers to the "www" host at the domain named "bolder.com." Within a few seconds, you then expect to see the appropriate Web page appear on your screen. What really happens in those few seconds?

First, your browser uses a packet-switching network transport called *Transmission Control Protocol/Internet Protocol,* or *TCP/IP,* to make the proper connections (called *sockets*) with other nodes.[1]

The initial connection is made to resolve the URL address. A URL usually contains a domain name (such as bolder.com). TCP/IP uses a 36-bit binary address (called the *IP address*) that appears as a sequence of four numbers (e.g., 23.126.45.90). The conversion from the domain name to the proper IP address is performed using a domain name server (DNS), which contains a table that maps domain names to IP addresses.

Second, your browser makes a connection to the proper IP address and requests the specific Web page. This request uses the HyperText Transfer Protocol (HTTP), which is a protocol used over TCP/IP for requesting and retrieving Web pages.[2]

The overall architecture is shown in Figure 3-2. The browser receives the initial file, which is typically formatted in HyperText Markup Language (HTML). HTML is primarily a text presentation language, which specifies how the browser should render text and other images on the screen. The HTML specifications include numerous tags that specify fonts, bold/underline emphasis, paragraphs, headings, centering, indenting, outline items, tables, frames, and so forth—all the functions needed to make the text look pretty on the screen.

---

1. For more details, see the section on TCP/IP in Chapter 7, Standards.
2. For more details, see the section on HTTP in Chapter 7, Standards.

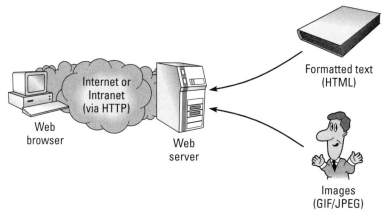

Figure 3-2   Web Servers

Another function of HTML (and one that some consider the most important) is its ability to refer to other Intranet objects, such as images to be displayed with the text. The typical HTML file refers to five to ten images that the browser must retrieve and display with the text.

Therefore, there is a distinction between a Web file and a Web page. A *Web file* is a single file on the Web server referred to by a URL and retrieved by a single HTTP GET operation. A *Web page* is actually a collection of Web files that are retrieved by a single user action.

When the user enters a URL address, the browser retrieves the Web file for that URL. This file is usually an HTML file and contains one or more HTML tags referring to images. The browser must retrieve each of those Web files and then render the image of that Web page on the screen.

In addition, Web pages can provide access to other Web pages by using another HTML tag. These anchor, or link, tags appear as blue underlined text on the screen. When the user clicks on this text, the browser retrieves and renders the specified Web page. Thus, a single Web page can consist of a large "web" of pages connected by the structure of links among those pages.

A *Web site* is the collection of Web pages managed by a particular Web server. Typically, there will be a *root Web page* that has a URL like http://www.domain.com/. Retrieving this URL implies the existence of a Web file called something like "index.html." This Web file then provides access to Web pages for the major sections of the Web site, such as corporate overview, products, services, support, what's new, and so on. Therefore, a Web site is also the collection of all Web pages within a domain stemming from the root page.

So far, we have described Web pages that are static files at a Web site. They are called *static* because the contents of the files reside on a directory, having been previously generated using an HTML editor or some other program. The trend in Web content is to move away from static Web pages and toward those that are dynamically generated from databases.

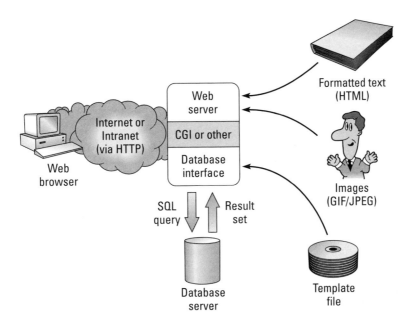

Figure 3-3   Web-Enabled Databases

3.1.3 Web-Enabled Databases

The future of Web content lies in *dynamic,* or *liquid,* pages whose content source is a database, as shown in Figure 3-3. When an HTTP request is received by the Web server, the Web server passes the request through a common gateway interface (CGI) or a similar interface to another program. This program is usually a database interface program that transforms the request into an SQL query and executes that query against a relational database. The result set is formatted into HTML and, in that format, is returned to the Web browser. Control of the result formatting is typically handled by a template (or macro) file that a programmer has configured.

Therefore, Web content can be generated directly from an active database, thus tracking the database's content in real time. The lengthy delay of manually editing content from a database into static files is eliminated. However, there is the additional complexity of handling dynamic content with the Web farming system.

3.1.4 Web Applets

Another development in web technology that has greatly expanded functionality is the creation of *applets*—small procedural modules that can be executed at the Web client (or at the Web server), as shown in Figure 3-4. The architecture works as follows: A user requests a Web page containing an HTML tag referencing the applet object. The browser downloads the applet and caches it in a local memory area. The

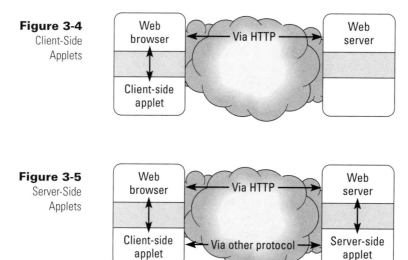

Figure 3-4
Client-Side
Applets

Figure 3-5
Server-Side
Applets

browser then executes the procedure, rather than rendering some image on the screen. This procedure can manipulate the screen image, sense the mouse/keyboard, invoke other procedures, and so forth. The procedure is usually executed within an interpreter shell so that security and code isolation are ensured.

The most conspicuous example of an applet is the Java applet, using the Java language. Sun, Netscape, IBM, and other companies are positioning this technology against that of Microsoft. These companies are promoting a thin client (using a generic browser with applets) as the alternative to the fat client (using Microsoft Windows). The Microsoft equivalent of Java applets (which Microsoft also supports, in its own manner) is the technology of ActiveX controls, although Microsoft does also support its own version of Java applets.

The other half of the applet story is often forgotten, but has importance for Web farming, as shown in Figure 3-5. Once a client-side applet is executing within the browser, this applet can invoke a sister procedure to execute as a server-side applet, sometimes called a *servlet*. The two applets can then establish communications using a more appropriate protocol than HTTP, such as the Internet Inter-ORB Protocol (IIOP) from OMG's Common Object Request Broker Architecture (CORBA). Note that the normal HTTP dialogue only initiates the applet-to-applet interaction and then ceases to be involved.

The combination of client-side and server-side applets enables Web technology to support robust, closely coupled client-server systems that are secure, reliable, and efficient. This type of architecture will be required for high-volume links to major content providers.

Initial Success on Finding Relevant Web Content

After just a few days, Alice found several Web sites containing useful information. For instance, WSJ Online offered detailed data on all of their top 10 customers, including investment patterns in buildings and equipment. By the end of the week, she had generated five documents and two spreadsheets from the analysis of these sites. The documents were distributed as hard-copy internal reports, while the XLS spreadsheets were placed in public folders on the finance server.

Next installment is on page 105.

3.2 Data Warehousing

Data warehousing (DW) has become a major IT driver, influencing system architectures and product directions across many industries globally. The popularity of DW has, unfortunately, obscured its basic objectives. Many people pursue the implementation of DW systems for simplistic reasons and with unrealistic expectations. DW systems often become "black holes" into which data is poured, never to be seen again.

Many people pursue the building of DW systems for simplistic reasons and with unrealistic expectations. DW systems often become "black holes" into which data is poured, never to be seen again.

Simplistic slogans (such as the ones suggested below) are often distorted to justify large purchases, long-term projects, and vague objectives.

- *More information is needed to better run our business!*
- *All that operational data must be very valuable, if only...*
- *Build the warehouse, and they will flock to it!*
- *Current technology is not sufficient. We need this new...*
- *A good query tool and clean relational tables are all that's required!*

The concepts behind DW are old and fundamental. They echo back to our earlier discussions of enablement and self-directed teams. Historically, DW is a variation of decision support systems (DSS) and executive information systems (EIS) that have been institutionalized at the enterprise level.[3]

---

3. Keen and Scott Morton, 1978.

Today, DW has been pushed out of the back room into highly visible mission-critical projects. Moreover, DW has transcended its traditional focus on the "decision makers" (i.e., management) to broadly affect people at all levels of the organization. In fact, some of the greatest business benefits of DW occur within call centers that assist personnel in support, order taking, and so on.

A Word About Terminology

In most situations, this text uses the phrase *data warehousing*, rather than *data warehouse*, to emphasize the overall process and architecture. The term *data warehouse* is reserved for the place for data storage, one component within a data warehousing system.

3.2.1 Consistent Image of Business Reality

Data warehousing is the creation, management, and dissemination of informational data, derived from various sources, to provide a consistent and accurate image of business reality. To return to our analogy of landing an airliner at a crowded urban airport, the data warehousing system provides the instrument panel in our enterprise's cockpit.

The quest of data warehousing to provide this image of business reality is a constant struggle of surfacing, refining, and integrating the various mental models of our enterprise. Among the various people who make up the enterprise, there are many valid models, each illuminating different aspects and each evolving to track the business environment. A single consistent image for the enterprise will always be difficult to achieve. The process of determining the image is complex and continuous, rather than a one-time event.

There are several challenges in seriously pursuing data warehousing:

- The challenge of properly understanding the data within the data warehousing from a business perspective. The ability to audit any data element is essential to instilling confidence in the data. "Drilling down" in both the value and the definition of any data element provides a deeper understanding of its nature.

- The challenge of consistency in the use of data. Two users may think they are debating about the same data elements when, in fact, their data elements indicate different aspects of the business because of either naming inconsistencies or timing nonsynchronization.

- The challenge of properly constructing SQL queries. Slight variations in SQL syntax may produce widely different results from the same set of data. Most SQL syntax is poorly understood and can be used properly only by an expert.

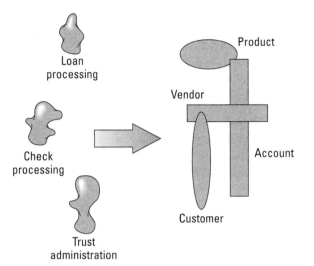

Figure 3-6
Application-Oriented
to Subject-Oriented

- The challenge of expanding access to the data warehouse or the data mart to people who may be unfamiliar with the precise business interpretation of a specific data element. Analyses based on that data element can easily lead to erroneous business decisions.

- The challenge of rapidly inventing new predefined queries and reports as business requirements change. Otherwise, each person dealing with these new requirements will develop ad hoc solutions, resulting in the duplication of effort and, worse, in a variety of business interpretations of the same data.

A complementary definition of data warehousing is Bill Inmon's classic definition of the data warehouse. It can be summarized in terms of four criteria.[4]

First, a data warehouse is *subject-oriented*. That is, the data organization is shifted from an application orientation to a subject orientation, as shown in Figure 3-6. Instead of being organized according to application or organizational functions, the data is organized on its natural subject areas. As shown in Figure 3-6, data about customers is integrated into a single database entity, rather than being classified as separate entities for loan processing and so on.

Second, a data warehouse is *integrated*. It consolidates data formats and encodings in a consistent manner so that comparisons and aggregations along various dimensions are valid.

Third, a data warehouse is *time-variant*. In other words, each row of data varies with time. Hence, each row typically contains one or more columns containing some type of time stamp.

---

4. Inmon, 1992; Inmon and Hackathorn, 1994.

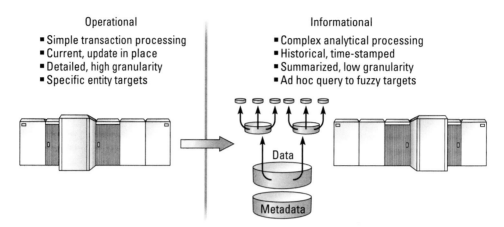

Figure 3-7 Operational to Informational

Finally, a data warehouse is *nonvolatile.* Data within the data warehouse is not deleted or updated, except for maintenance or error correction. Data is only loaded into the data warehouse or retrieved from the data warehouse.

3.2.2 Operational versus Informational

A fundamental distinction in DW is between *operational* and *informational* data. Operational data is data about the current status of the enterprise, to be used for current (direct) control. Informational data is data about the past status of the enterprise, to be used for future control in the support of decision processes. Informational data is heavily time-oriented, bearing a time stamp in each row. New rows are appended, rather than used to update existing rows.

The distinction between operational and informational is critical, as shown in Figure 3-7. A variation of the operational-information distinction is the Operational Data Store (ODS), shown in Figure 3-8.[5]

The ODS is an operational system that acts as a bridge into the data warehouse. The data of the Operation Data Store is volatile (meaning that a historical record is not maintained) and near-current (implying that update transactions are applied to the source legacy systems rather than to the ODS). However, the data has been consolidated into an integrated and subject-oriented view of the enterprise.

3.2.3 Architectures for Data Warehousing

Let's examine the evolving architectures for supporting data warehousing. Figure 3-9 continues the warehouse analogy by illustrating the data flow, through receiving and packaging, to customers. Several points about Figure 3-9 should be

5. Inmon, Imhoff, and Battas, 1996.

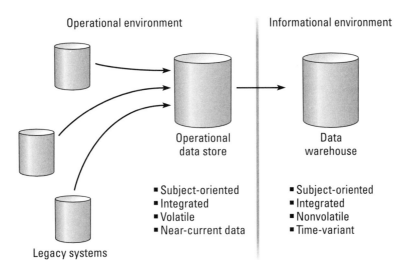

Figure 3-8 The Operational Data Store

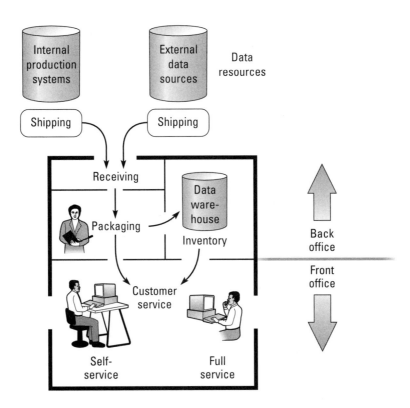

Figure 3-9 A Simple DW Architecture

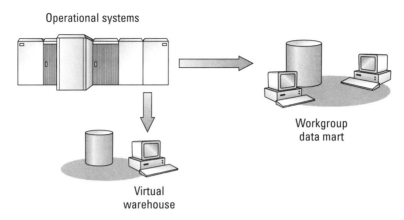

Operational systems

Workgroup
data mart

Virtual
warehouse

Figure 3-10   Virtual Warehouse and Data Mart

noted. First, data is received from both internal and external sources (such as the Web). Second, there are distinct shipping and receiving functions. Third, data can flow directly to the customer or flow into inventory (i.e., the data warehouse). Finally, DW operations can be separated into a front office and a back office.

Another perspective on DW is the flow from operational systems to work-stations and data marts, as in Figure 3-10.[6] The *virtual warehouse* is simply a work-station directly linking to operational systems, without a separate data warehouse. The advantage of the virtual warehouse is that it is a quick and inexpensive approach. However, this approach has limited usefulness. First, operational data is derived in its raw format, which can be misleading and confusing to the user. Second, data from multiple sources must be consolidated at the workstation using client-based transformations. Thirdly, the historical context of data is missed, since limited historical data is maintained by the operational systems. Finally, multiple virtual warehouses are not usually coordinated, and therefore confidence in using the underlying operational data is destroyed. In general, the virtual warehouse is an approach to be avoided, except for quick, short-term implementations.

The *data mart* is a data warehouse that focuses on a specific department function, such as marketing or finance. The advantage is that there is a specific and limited scope for the data warehouse. Resources can be effectively applied to solve critical business problems within a functional area of the company. The limitation of data marts is that the scope of the data is restricted to that which is useful for the specific business functions of the workgroup.

Data marts (and virtual warehouses) are seductive solutions because of their limited scope and the availability of inexpensive (yet powerful) technology. Fragmented enterprise data—a situation that DW was intended to resolve—is often a

---

6.   Taken from White & Hackathorn, DB/Expo Presentation, May 1995.

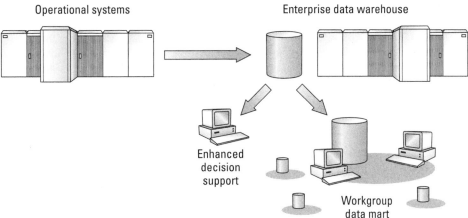

Operational systems   Enterprise data warehouse

Enhanced
decision
support

Workgroup
data mart

Figure 3-11   Enterprise Data Warehouse

side effect of data marts proliferating across the enterprise. As inconsistent data multiplies among data marts, long-term integration issues and reduced confidence in the data often result.

Yet a typical departmental manager usually has the budgetary resources and authority to acquire and operate a data mart. This data mart can often provide rapid answers to current business problems, justifying the expenditure within a short period. Hence, warnings of data chaos across the enterprise are ineffective in keeping companies from the evils of data marts. For better or for worse, data marts are now a major part of the DW landscape.

A mechanism is required to integrate and reconcile data among the increasing numbers of data marts so that we can regain the objective of a consistent image of business reality for the enterprise.

One solution to the inconsistencies among data marts is to focus attention and resources on the *enterprise data warehouse* (see Figure 3-11) and use it to support both individual and workgroup requirements. The current industry wisdom is that a company should create an enterprise-level model and construct an enterprise-level warehouse before data marts can be properly propagated through the organization. This approach constructs a unified information model of the enterprise and populates the database according to that model. From the enterprise data warehouse, individuals can query the enterprise data warehouse directly for enterprise-wide reporting, or it can be used to populate data marts for the various workgroups across the enterprise. The disadvantages of the enterprise data warehouse are the difficulty and the resources involved in building one that has the scope of the entire enterprise. Because of its size and complexity, the enterprise data warehouse tends to lag and be out of touch with the current set of critical business issues.

3.2.4 Flows in Data Warehousing

A different perspective on data warehousing is provided by examining the overall flow of data from creation to consumption. In fact, the real value of data warehousing lies in the establishment of an architecture that manages the flow of data and metadata, rather than just its processing. The following flows involve operational and informational systems, both data warehouses and various combinations of data marts.

---

*The real value of data warehousing
lies in the establishment of an architecture that
manages the flow of data and metadata.*

From this perspective, five flows can be described:[7]

- In-Flow
- Up-Flow
- Down-Flow
- Out-Flow
- Meta-Flow

The In-Flow, shown in Figure 3-12, is the data flow from data creation to the data warehouse. The primary source is the operational legacy systems that provide internal data on business operations. However, external sources and nontraditional unstructured data (text documents, electronic mail, images, etc.) are becoming more important. The In-Flow consists of a sequence of steps from data capture to validation (which may require data repair), to transformation, and then to application to the database. We can view the validation steps as resembling those of a customs agent at a border crossing. (See Figure 3-13.) In a similar manner, the validation and repair loop for data is like a data hospital (see Figure 3-14) in which unhealthy data is made healthy, rather than simply rejected.

The Up-Flow, shown in Figure 3-15, is the processing of the informational data to add value for its consumption through summarization (roll-up, aggregations), packaging (into OLE objects), and distribution (to data marts). This flow enhances the business value of the data.

The Down-Flow, shown in Figure 3-16, is the reverse of the Up-Flow process— "drilling down" into summaries or aggregations of interest to seek increasing levels of detail.

---

7. Hackathorn, 1995.

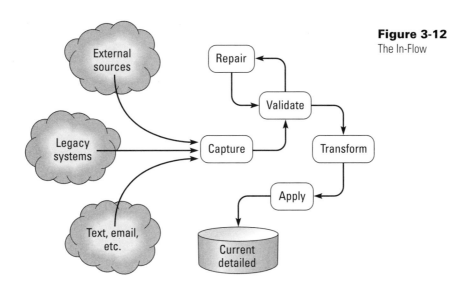

Figure 3-12
The In-Flow

Figure 3-13
Allowing Only the
Right Data In

Figure 3-14
Dealing with
Sick Data

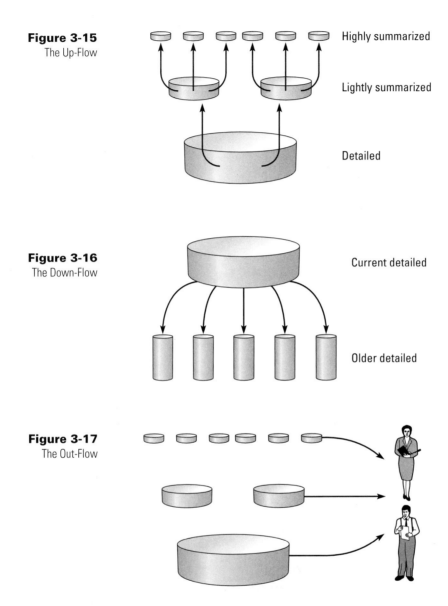

Figure 3-15
The Up-Flow

Figure 3-16
The Down-Flow

Figure 3-17
The Out-Flow

The Out-Flow, shown in Figure 3-17, is the delivery to consumers, either through ad hoc query or scheduled reporting. In the industry, the trend in Out-Flow is to be more proactive in the delivery of information, through mechanisms such as publish-and-subscribe.

Most DW information is passively delivered, since the system waits until the user requests the information. In contrast, traditional publishing industries, such as newspapers and magazines, take a proactive role by advertising and marketing their

Figure 3-18 Passive versus Active Delivery

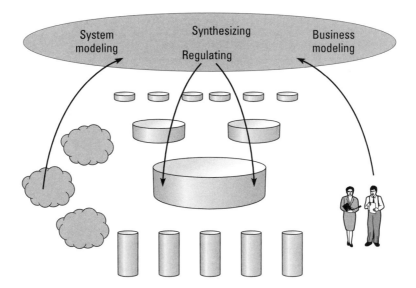

Figure 3-19 The Meta-Flow

publications. (See Figure 3-18.) Proponents of DW systems should consider adopting this more proactive role.

Most important, the Meta-Flow, shown in Figure 3-19, is the management of data descriptions concerning the other data flows. Meta-Flow is the set of rules governing the way the data is acquired, transformed, aggregated, and so on. It provides the basis for the proper "drill-down" during Down-Flow.

Many believe that after the data warehouse is designed, the metadata description does not change. This notion is wrong. These descriptions change almost to the same degree that data content changes. Hence, it is best to think of metadata as yet another flow to manage. Metadata deals with the following four areas:

- System modeling—technical analysis of operational systems, both internal and external to the enterprise
- Regulating—control of the other flows, such as the automatic creation of data acquisition modules
- Synthesizing—analysis of usage patterns to guide the design of information objects
- Business modeling—logical analysis of business processes, across the spectrum of the lines of business

Of the various flows, Meta-Flow is the least understood and the least exploited; yet it is the most important, because it is central to the success of data warehousing and the realization of its business value. System modeling is often overemphasized to the detriment of business modeling. Business modeling should lead the warehousing effort, driving the data requirements backward all the way to the In-Flow.

3.2.5 Web Warehousing

Web warehousing is defined as data warehousing that makes use of Web technology, primarily for publishing information from the data warehouse. Hence, Web warehousing should support the following:

- Access using a generic Web browser
- Connection via the Internet or an intranet
- Generation of contents dynamically from the database

First, access to the database is via a generic Web browser, such as Netscape Navigator or Microsoft Internet Explorer. (We assume that in your company, all client workstations will soon have such a tool available.) The function of a Web browser is similar to printing a page from a word processor. Text, various formatting instructions, and images are processed to display the information on a monitor (rather than print it).

Second, the client platform is connected to the Web server via the network. This network could be the global Internet, via an Internet service provider (ISP). Or this network could be your intranet—the internal corporate network, using the cabling throughout your building.

Third, the contents of the Web page should be generated directly from the contents of the database, as the contents are requested. Such Web pages are called dynamic (or liquid) pages, since the contents of the page are generated as needed for the specific request. In contrast, static pages are simply static files sitting on the disk waiting to be retrieved by a browser. Using dynamic pages ensures that only the current version of the database is retrieved.

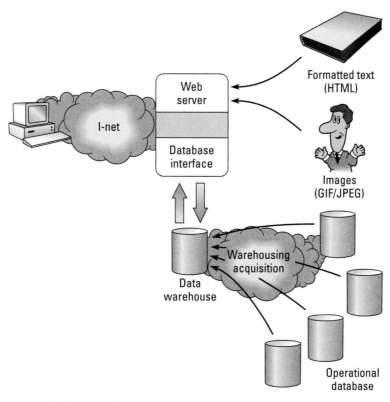

Figure 3-20 Web Warehousing

The architecture of Web warehousing is shown in Figure 3-20. If the Web-enabled database is used as the data warehouse, the delivery of information can be greatly enhanced, avoiding the development of special client applications.

3.3 Information Science

Personal Note

One of the pleasant surprises in writing this book was its close linkage to information science. The concepts and issues of this discipline echoed from the days of my graduate studies, bringing back old memories. As I spent time delving into the current state of library science, I was rewarded with useful insights from professional information brokers, special librarians, online database providers, corporate researchers, and even traditional librarians turned Webmasters.

In our fascination with technology, it is easy to forget that the traditional core for knowledge management has been the library. For centuries, librarians have had the responsibility of gathering, organizing, and disseminating information, and the purpose has been to accumulate the knowledge of humankind. We must exploit the fact that the basic objectives and discipline of information (or library) science are applicable to Web farming, lest we commit the gross sin of reinventing the wheel.

At a recent conference of research librarians, Bill Gates, CEO of Microsoft Corporation, stated that the corporate library should be the information hub for the company—quite a challenge for people who are often considered lowly support personnel:

> It is no exaggeration to say that in most industries the basis of competition will be on how a company deals with information. . . . Every company can have a specialized view of the Internet, of the parts that they really care about and it's up to the [corporate] library to build that. . . . The goal is really the same; it's to be the information hub of the company.[8]

On the other hand, a prominent academic (Thomas H. Davenport) argued that librarians have become too thoroughly seduced by information technology to evaluate information content properly:

> Even corporate librarians, perhaps the last bastion of these interested in information content, have increasingly become enchanted with technology while neglecting other sources of information. Many library and information science programs in universities have put computer-oriented training at the center of their curricula. Librarians perform more and more computer database searches; indeed, I have encountered many librarians and researchers who seem to have forgotten that some information can't be found—or trusted—in online databases.[9]

The point is that library science and associated disciplines offer a rich heritage of managing information. Structuring information (especially Web content) is much more than normalizing a relational database. The functional dependencies are numerous and indefinite. Yet the goal of Web farming is to discover and acquire this messy content for a star-schema warehouse. We need some assistance from the library folks!

3.3.1 Information Structuring

The task of information structuring captures an important dimension of information science. Information structuring is what is called *classification* or *categorization* by most librarians. In simple terms, where do you put the books? In the general sense,

---

8. W.H. Gates, Keynote Address to the 88th Annual Meeting of the Special Libraries Association, Seattle, June 9, 1997.
9. Davenport, 1997, 25.

Table 3-1 Traditional Classification Schemes

Dewey Decimal System	Library of Congress Classification
000 Generalities	A General Works
100 Philosophy	B Philosophy & Region
200 Religion	C History: Auxiliary
300 Social Sciences	D History: Old World
400 Language	EF American History
500 Science	G Geography
600 Technology	H Social Sciences
700 Arts	J Political Science
800 Literature	K Law
900 Geography & History	L Education
	M Music
	N Arts
	P Language & Literature
	Q Science
	R Medicine
	S Agriculture
	T Technology
	U Military Science
	V Naval Science
	Z Bibliography

information structuring is finding the "best" structure for knowledge representation, given a specific collection of material. For large libraries, that collection is the sum of all published material.

The most prominent schemes in use today in libraries are the Dewey Decimal System and the Library of Congress Classification. A comparison is given in Table 3-1. Both schemes came into use about a century ago, and now dominate the cataloging of books in most libraries. A book is classified into one (and only one) slot, and then placed on the shelf in its proper place. This system is known as "mark and park" among librarians. Public libraries prefer the Dewey Decimal System because it is simpler for the public. Research libraries prefer the Library of Congress Classification because it provides more detail for a large collection.

As we hurtle through cyberspace, what relevance does library classification have for us? Consider the huge task of classifying Web pages, performed by Yahoo! and the other directory services. Yahoo! now has over 20,000 categories, with daily changes. Adapted from one by Michael Lesk (and enhanced),[10] Table 3-2 is a comparison of the top levels of several Web directories.

Personal Note

I was amused by the attempts of my local bookstore to manage the rather volatile computer books. In frustration, they shelved the computer books alphabetically by publisher (not by subject, not by title, and not by author). The huge daily inflow of new computer books overloaded their ability to categorize by topic. Any such structuring would be valid for only a few months, and then another categorization scheme would be required. For their clientele, locating a book implied a linear scan of a wall of books. At least for some, this was a pleasant browsing experience. However, for those seeking a specific book, the experience was a painful one.

Table 3-2   Contemporary Classification Schemes

Yahoo!	Excite	Magellan	Librarian's Index*
Arts & Humanities	Arts	Arts	Arts
	Autos		Automobiles
Business & Economy	Business & Investing	Business	Business
			California
		Communications	
Computers & Internet	Computing	Computing	Computers
		Daily Living	
			Disabilities
		Economics	
Education	Careers & Education		
Entertainment	Entertainment	Entertainment	
		Environment	
			Families
		Food	Food
	Games		
			Gay, Lesbian, Bisexual
			Geography
Government			Government
Health	Health & Medicine	Health	Health & Medicine

*See http://sunsite.berkeley.edu/InternetIndex/.

---

10. Lesk, 1997.

Table 3-2   *(Continued)*

Yahoo!	Excite	Magellan	Librarian's Index
			History
	Hobbies		
		Humanities	
			Images, Graphics
		Internet	Internet Information
			Jobs
		Kid Zone	Kids
		Law	
	Lifestyle		
			Libraries
			Literature
		Mathematics	
			Media
			Men
	Money		
		Music	Music
News & Media	News & Reference	News	Current events
			Organizations
		.	People
			Philosophy
		Politics	Politics
		Pop Culture	
			Recreation
Reference			Reference
Regional			
		Spirituality	Religion
Science		Science	Science
	Shopping		
			Seniors
Social Science			
Society & Culture			Cultures (world)
Sports & Recreation	Sports	Sports	Sports
		Technology	
	Travel	Travel	Travel
			Women

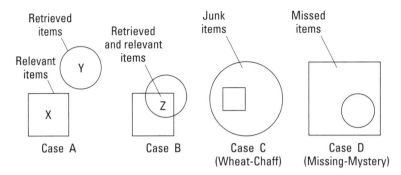

Figure 3-21   Cases of Recall versus Precision

3.3.2   Recall versus Precision

Another basic concept related to Web farming is the trade-off between recall and precision. These are terms used in library science to measure the effectiveness of information retrieval systems.

Let explore this trade-off, which we will call the *R-P trade-off*. The question is how well we performed our retrieval or filtering task. Suppose we wanted a collection of material consisting of X items (or megabytes), as shown in Figure 3-21. However, we retrieved Y items, of which only Z items were relevant to us.

To put this R-P trade-off into perspective, consider a simple database query. We want to retrieve the data on a specific customer (e.g., ID = 23498756). Normally, that query will generate a perfect recall (i.e., R = 100%) and perfect precision (i.e., P = 100%). We get what we wanted and only what we wanted.

In Case A, we did very poorly! We retrieved no items that were relevant (i.e., Z = 0), and all the items retrieved were junk. It would have been better to retrieve no items at all.

In Case B, we have the typical situation. Win some, lose some! Now we can define the terms of recall and precision. *Recall* is defined as the ratio of relevant items that we retrieved. In other words, R = Z / X. *Precision* is defined as the ratio of items retrieved that were relevant. In other words, P = Z / Y.

In Case C, we have great recall (i.e., we got all the relevant items), but lousy precision (i.e., plus a lot of junk). The problem is then to sort through the junk for the good stuff. In other words, the problem is separating the wheat from the chaff. We call this case the *wheat-chaff case*.

In Case D, we have great precision (i.e., all the stuff is good), but lousy recall (i.e., we are missing a lot of good stuff). The problem is then to assess how much we are missing and whether the missing items are significant to our task. We call this case the *missing-mystery case*.

In the context of Web farming, we often generate query results that are on the extremes. Sometimes, a query will retrieve thousands of items, of which the first 20 are shown. Now what? Do we brute force our way through several thousand items, 20 at a time? Do we quit in frustration? At other times, a query will retrieve zero or

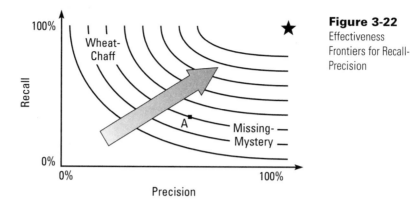

Figure 3-22

Effectiveness Frontiers for Recall-Precision

just a few items. Now what? Are we missing hundreds of good items? On this glorious World Wide Web, are there really no items that are important to us?

The overall situation is illustrated in Figure 3-22. Recall is plotted vertically, while precision is plotted horizontally. The star in the upper-right corner is our goal—a perfect retrieval, as with a simple database query. Given a specific set of technology and Web content, there is a specific *effectiveness frontier* along which we can trade off recall against precision. In other words, the desire for retrieving all the relevant items implies that many irrelevant items must be processed. Alternatively, the desire to process just a few items implies that many relevant items will probably be missing.

For instance, suppose we find ourselves at point A on some effectiveness frontier. If we want greater recall, we must accept less precision, and vice versa. The curves have been skewed to illustrate that in Web farming, greater recall often comes at a high price in the form of lost precision.

The challenge of Web farming is, therefore, one of both volume and effectiveness. We must push the processing volumes of Web farming to a higher level, while at the same time we should push the effectiveness boundary toward the upper-right corner of the figure.

3.3.3 Information Visualization

Information visualization has been a critical part of information science through the ages. Amid the dusty rows of books and card catalogs are the charts, diagrams, figures, and tables that summarize vast amounts of information into a single glance.

Edward Tufte, a professor at Cornell University, reminds us that effective information visualization existed hundreds of years before computers.[11] Charles Joseph Minard (1781–1870) showed the terrible fate of Napoleon's Russian campaign of 1812 in his classic chart, displayed in Figure 3-23. The combination of map and time series shows the losses suffered during the campaign. The width of the band

---

11. Tufte, 1983.

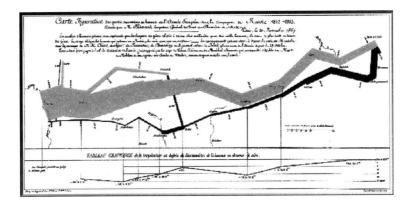

Figure 3-23 Napoleon's Russian Campaign of 1812

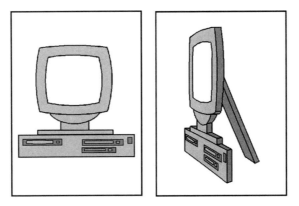

Figure 3-24 The Flatness of IT

indicates the size of the army, starting on the Russian-Polish border with 422,000 men. In September, the army reached Moscow, which had been sacked and deserted, with 100,000 men. The dark lower band indicates the path of Napoleon's retreat, which is linked to a temperature scale and dates at the bottom of the chart. Napoleon returns with only 10,000 men.

Visualizing is the primary means by which we analyze data and interact with the world. The most powerful processor in the world is between our two ears and connected to our eyeballs. Our inherent ability to recognize visual patterns is our strongest asset.

Yet the way information from enterprise systems is displayed seems to be decades behind other industries, such as the movies, the commercial arts, television, and so on. Tabular reports seem so weak when compared to the gigabytes of data within our databases. Our use of IT seems flat. (See Figure 3-24).

Figure 3-25
Seeing from a Different Perspective

Visualization is the arrangement of images in a presentation space. The factors that affect visualization the most are

- Eye scan
- Dimensions
- Density (i.e., numbers/bytes per square inch)
- Resolution (i.e., pixels/dots per inch plus color depth)

The concept of an eye scan is critical. An eye scan is the information that a person can view as a continuous whole. It is a single unit of data processed by our brains for useful patterns. Preserving the eye scan is an important design criterion for visualization. Dimensions are the number of separate variables (columns) that can be compared within an eye scan. Density is the raw amount of information displayed on a surface, measured roughly in bytes.[12] Finally, resolution is the ability to resolve data, again within an eye scan.

In the design of information displays, we seem to be limited to looking through a small keyhole into our vast databases. Consider Figure 3-25, which shows a party in progress in a room. Two people want to know what is going on; one is looking through a keyhole and the other is on a ladder looking down into the room. It seems

---

12. Assuming that one byte = one character; two bytes = one number.

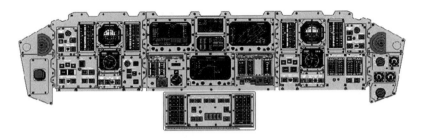

Figure 3-26   Instrument Panel of the Space Shuttle

that in our application of IT, we are like the person looking through the keyhole. We get brief glimpses of activity, with extreme difficulty in understanding the whole.

Industry wisdom dictates that we should design our systems to display only the data that is needed, and no more. Excess data will confuse and frustrate people. Some assumptions behind this wisdom are that

- The required data can be predetermined with confidence.
- It can communicate reliability without ambiguity.
- The person is not motivated to assimilate more data.
- The person is not capable of assimilating more data.

The alternative to information rationing is to offer well-designed, information-rich displays. An example is the instrument panel of the space shuttle, shown in Figure 3-26. Millions of hours of skilled design went into the arrangement of this information. And many thousands of hours of training are required to fully understand all of this information. Although this example may seem extreme, the information-richness of many enterprises is of the same magnitude as that of the instrument panel. Yet we take that information-richness and fragment it into thousands of reports and hundreds of SQL queries, such that there is no chance of preserving the eye scan.

Edward Tufte makes the point about information-rich displays succinctly:

> Visual displays rich with data are not only an appropriate and proper complement to human capabilities, but also such designs are frequently optimal. If the visual task is contrast, comparison, and choice—as so often it is—then the more relevant information within eye span, the better . . . .
>
> High-density designs also allow viewers to select, to narrate, to recast and personalize data for their own uses. Thus control of information is given over to viewers, not to editors, designers, and decorators.[13]

---

13. Tufte, 1990.

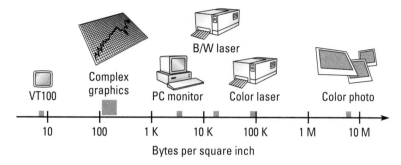

Figure 3-27 Limits of Information Density

The lack of effective information displays is a result of our lack of attention to and understanding of visualization—and possibly of our reluctance to share control of the information.

The potential of information-rich displays is immense. Figure 3-27 shows the spectrum of information density from simple tabular displays to full-color photographs. Good designs for soft or hard formats of complex graphs and illustrations fall in the range of 200 to 500 bytes per square inch. The limit of a typical VGA monitor is about 6,000 bytes per square inch and hard-copy printers output two to ten times that density. Therefore, we have plenty of room to improve using the technology available today.

As we add high-resolution monitors, sound, 3D virtual reality, and hypertext links, we can move beyond the limits of static images. Visualization can become an activity that moves a person beyond being an observer to being a participant in the unfolding of the information. If a person participates in the exploration of the information space, the time needed to learn can be reduced and the depth of understanding can be greatly enhanced. The person must be immersed in that space. The person must be able to "walk around" the space and interact with the objects in it.

The future of information delivery should focus on visualization, from the creation of information spaces to the design of information-rich displays. Visualization is one area of information science in which we have sufficient technology to do well, but for which we seem to lack the principles and practice to achieve its potential.

This chapter has covered the disciplines that make up the foundation of Web farming. The next three chapters delve into the details of designing, building, and managing a Web farming system.

## Part Two

Planting the Seeds

## Chapter Four

Methodology

The farmer learns the natural cycle of farming—preparing the land, planting the seed, cultivating the fields, and harvesting the crop. The lesson is that achieving any important goal requires an approach by stages, building on previous accomplishments. Likewise, you must approach Web farming in stages, learning new solutions and adopting new concepts along the way.

This chapter suggests a methodology of stages for evolving Web farming to a production-level function within the enterprise. The methodology starts with the external factors affecting the business and moves toward providing reliable input to the data warehouse.

Chapter 5, Architecture (for supporting infrastructure), and Chapter 10, Techniques (for specific skills), explain the technical details behind the methodology. This chapter concentrates on describing the intent and flow of the methodology through its stages. Amid the dynamics and complexity of the Web, the challenge is to stay focused on the business objectives.

Amid the dynamics and complexity of the Web,
the challenge of Web farming is to
stay focused upon the business objectives.

This methodology is a sequence of four stages. The first stage provides the foundation for the other three. The second builds on the first, the third on the second, and so on. By focusing on the important factors determining success for the enterprise, this first stage sets the direction that guides subsequent activities. The ultimate goal is to integrate the Web farming activity into the data warehousing system, and eventually into the knowledge management system, for the enterprise. Thus, the ultimate goal of Web farming is to disappear, as a distinct technology, into these other systems.

4.1   Stages of Growth

To better understand the flow of the Web farming methodology, consider a paradigm suggested in the late 1970s by Richard Nolan, a professor at the Harvard Business School and a major contributor to the MIS literature.[1] The paradigm explains the adoption of information technology in data processing departments as a sequence of *stages of growth*. To be used successfully by an enterprise, a technology must survive each of these stages in sequence. When a technology fails at any stage to deliver value to the enterprise, it is quickly discarded and forgotten.

In a simplification of Nolan's paradigm, Figure 4-1 shows the sequence of five stages of growth as an elongated S-shaped curve. For a technology to be successful, the level of its adoption increases over time, but not in a linear fashion. There are some ups and downs. Every successful technology must endure each stage in sequence. The only issues for debate are the length of time and the level of pain at each stage.

The five stages are as follows:

1. *Initiation,* in which adoption is slow and often frustrating for the people involved. There is usually considerable experimentation to make the technology work properly in the specific business situation. This stage is for the pioneers—people who exploit emerging technology in the hope of realizing huge gains but with the risk of receiving a few arrows in their backs.

2. *Contagion,* in which adoption is rapid and often chaotic. The specific technology is now generally accepted by most people, but is propelled forward by an overzealous "bandwagon" effect.

---

1.   R.L. Nolan, Managing Crises in Data Processing, *Harvard Business Review,* March/April 1979.

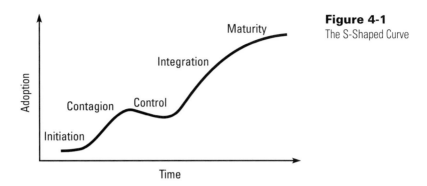

Figure 4-1
The S-Shaped Curve

3. *Control,* in which the enterprise tends to suppress adoption as it sorts out the appropriate application of the technology while exploiting its benefits. Management gets involved at this stage, usually to reduce spiraling costs.

4. *Integration,* in which the new technology is integrated within the overall infrastructure. If this integration work is successful, there is a slow upward incline in adoption. This stage is usually the longest and the hardest. However, the integration stage is when the technology finally pays off with productive and reliable performance.

5. *Maturity,* in which the technology has been integrated into the systems infrastructure. Maturity for a successful technology implies that it has become mundane (i.e., unrecognized as anything special), like transistors in transistor radios or jet engines in airplanes. The prize for a successful technology that makes it through all the stages is fading into the woodwork of the overall system.

These stages are quite generic and apply to a variety of situations involving technology adoption. For Web farming, the stages of growth can be illustrated in more detail as shown in Figure 4-2. The business objectives, in the context of the business environment, guide the discovery of content relevant to the enterprise. The discovery process generates a set of Web targets, which the acquisition process continuously probes and archives. The acquisition and structuring processes filter, validate, and transform the content into the data warehouse. The dissemination process packages the content and delivers it to the appropriate people.

The sequencing of the four stages is shown in the lower half of Figure 4-2, and again in Figure 4-3. The stages can be summarized as follows:

1. *Getting Started* (initiation) by establishing the business case based on the objectives and business environment of the enterprise

2. *Getting Serious* (contagion) by legitimizing the Web farming activity within the organization and by building infrastructure for production operations

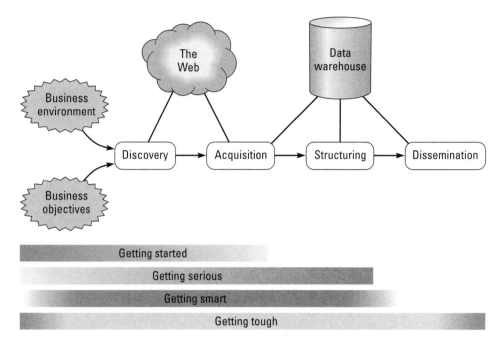

Figure 4-2   Sequencing of Methodology Stages

3. *Getting Smart* (control) by exploiting technology (especially for discovery and structuring of information) and by building pipelines to primary content providers

4. *Getting Tough* (integration) by structuring information for the data warehouse by revisiting the business objectives in light of the warehouse schema

The remainder of this chapter expands on each of these stages to describe a methodology for establishing Web farming as a business-relevant product-level function with the enterprise.

4.2   Stage One—Getting Started

The appropriate place to start is documenting the external factors that are critical to the success or failure of your enterprise. Whether your enterprise is a commercial concern, a nonprofit charity, or a government agency, there are many factors external to your organization that affect your success. Before you expend significant funds for the Web farming, these factors must be documented and organized in a format that can guide the subsequent stages.

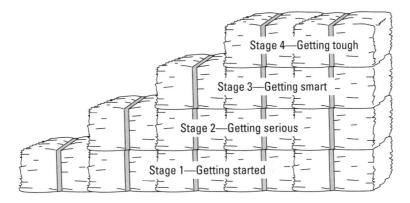

Figure 4-3   The Four Stages of Web Farming

The essential tasks in Getting Started are to

- Document the critical external factors
- Formulate a systematic discovery plan
- Identify important content providers
- Disseminate initial information to interested persons
- Compile a business case for Web farming

4.2.1 Document the Critical External Factors

The first task in Getting Started is the documentation of the external (or exogenous) factors that are important to the success of an enterprise. This type of factor is called a *Critical External Factor,* or *CEF.* By *external,* we mean that the factor is an entity outside the organization and its control, and hence the data about this factor is probably not available within the internal systems.

The focus of external factors has traditionally been on competitors and customers. However, doing business today is considerably more complex and involves many more external factors, such as pending legal actions, adverse weather in specific regions, shifts to alternative technologies, and so forth.

The activities involved in documenting the CEFs are listed below.

- Profile your company from annual reports and so on.
- Profile market segments using SIC (and NAICS) codes.
- Identify related trade publications, professional associations, shows, and so on.
- Work downstream in your value chain (distributors to end consumers).

- Work upstream in your value chain (suppliers to raw materials).
- Analyze current competition (traditional, indirect).
- Analyze future competition (new entrants).
- Analyze the various "partnering" relationships.
- Assess government regulations, potential legal actions, and politics.
- Assess impacts from technology shifts.
- Assess impacts from mass customization and cost erosion.
- Assess other exogenous factors, such as geography, weather, and so on.

Here are some suggestions for accomplishing these activities:

1. Profile your enterprise. Gather and compile data about your enterprise from
   - Annual report and other corporate reports
   - Confidential strategy documents about future directions
   - Press releases
   - Critiques by news and investment analysts
   - Interviews with sympathetic executives
   - Surveys of key customers
   - Direct observation of manufacturing floor and customer transactions
2. Supplement the above with any work done on an Information Architecture for the enterprise. In addition, examine the database schema from the data warehouse and key operational systems for clues about CEFs.
3. Work downstream in your value chain (i.e., distributors to end consumers). Determine the various ways that your product or service flows from your enterprise all the way to the end consumer of that product or service.
4. Work upstream in your value chain (i.e., suppliers to raw materials). Determine the various ways your enterprise receives the required raw materials (broadly defined). Realize that for knowledge-based firms, the recruitment and retention of personnel provide a critical "raw material."
5. Analyze current and future competition in terms of traditional competitors, new entrants (especially from a global perspective), and indirect competitors (who reduce your revenue stream while remaining invisible to you).
6. Analyze the various "partnering" relationships in terms of agreements for joint marketing, sales, distribution, supply, and so forth. A legal search of all contracts with other companies (other than normal sales) may provide insights.

7. Profile primary and related market segments. Determine the SIC (and new NAICS) codes for your enterprise and for other companies you have identified. Gather general census and market sizing data based on these codes.

8. Profile each company. For each of these companies, compile the parent/subsidiary relationships, SEC filings, financial history, key officers and employees, board members, large stockholders, and so on.

9. Identify related trade publications, professional associations, trade shows, Internet newsgroups, and so on. Determine the business community that associates (or should associate) with your enterprise.

10. Assess government regulations, potential legal actions, and general politics.

11. Assess the impacts from technology shifts in your manufacturing process, distribution channels, and core products. In other words, what changes in any of these technologies could affect your value-added chain? How should your enterprise take advantage of these shifts? In addition, how should your enterprise protect itself from the negative impacts of these shifts?

12. Assess the impacts of mass customization. Analyze the implications of delivering a customized product or service to *each* of your customers (all one million of them!). To what extent can your enterprise do this? To what extent can your competitor do this? What specific information about your customers is required?

13. Assess the impacts of cost erosion. Analyze the implications of delivering your product or service at one tenth the cost and in one tenth the time. To what extent can your enterprise do this? To what extent can your competitor do this? What specific information about your manufacturing and distribution processes is required?

14. Gather background information on the local region(s) in which your enterprise conducts business. In particular, note the characteristics of the labor force, general economics, transportation, and so on.

15. Assess other exogenous factors (such as geography and climate).

Complete documentation covering all of these factors can be a huge effort. You should manage this effort by lightly covering all the issues and then delving into more detail on selective issues as time permits. At all times, this documentation effort should be guided according to those factors deemed critical by management and the subjects that are (or will be) covered within the data warehousing system.

4.2.2 Formulate Discovery Plan

The second task in Getting Started is to formulate a systematic plan for acquiring relevant information from the Web. The discovery plan should be driven by the CEFs identified above. Unless we are systematic about this discovery process, the complexity of the Web will easily overwhelm us.

Almost any Web search will yield interesting and even useful information. There is a danger in considering the task finished with each such discovery. Web farming is not a "load-and-run" activity. Its value lies in the constant monitoring and historical accumulation of information.

The value of Web farming lies in the constant monitoring and historical accumulation of information.

For each such item, one must formulate a plan to acquire this item on a continuing basis and to discover similar items on a continuing basis. The plan is expressed in a schedule for monitoring and acquiring that specific Web document and in a search template to be periodically invoked for discovering similar information. Specific names (and phrases) for companies, individuals, government agencies, and other critical entities must be carefully noted. This is challenging work and is an essential component of Web farming.

4.2.3 Identify Content Providers

The third task in Getting Started is the identification of the major content providers relevant to the CEF list. It is expected that the bulk of Web content will be obtained from established content providers, such as the following:

- Online commercial databases (DIALOG, Disclosure, Dow Jones...)
- Industry-specific content providers (Pharmsearch, PaperChase...)
- General news services (CNN, *USA Today,* MSNBC, NetNews...)
- Trade publications (*ComputerWorld, InformationWeek, BYTE...*)
- Library services (LOC, various research libraries, corporate libraries...)
- Intelligence sources (Avert, Jane's...)
- U.S. government agencies (SEC, LOC, Census, PTO...)
- International agencies (United Nations, European Union...)

As we pursue the discovery plan outlined above, sites that specialize in relevant information should be documented and researched. For certain providers, service agreements and use fees are required. Read Chapter 9, Resources, for background about the major content providers.

Business Intelligence, Not Web Farming

"Alice, looks like you're stirring up some interest with this Web farming stuff," remarked Steve during a coffee break. "Let's continue the experiment for a few more weeks, and then document the experience in a joint memo." Steve paused to choose his words carefully, "But let's call this activity *business intelligence*, rather than *Web farming*. It will sound better to management, and it will distance us from that crazy guy in Colorado."

Next installment is on page 124.

4.2.4 Disseminate Information

The fourth task in Getting Started is to disseminate the initial information. When a useful item is found, package it into a convenient format (memo, report, spreadsheet, chart, presentation, or email). Distribute it to the people who should have a strong interest in it. Consider publishing a weekly bulletin summarizing important developments, as described in the Getting Started stage. Perhaps start an email forum for posting ideas and questions about the Web farming effort.

The most important aspect of this task is to track the reactions to this information. These reactions are valuable clues to defining the information communities that should be targeted by the Web farming effort.

4.2.5 Compile a Business Case

The final task in Getting Started is summarizing all of the above into a coherent business case for Web farming. In this first stage, the business case should concentrate on the benefit side, rather than the cost side. The plan should propose an incremental evolution for establishing the Web farming function within the enterprise, as the stages suggest. The business plan should be a well-written hard-copy report that will serve as an important milestone from which to measure subsequent developments in the Web farming implementation.

Consider the advice in Chapter 6, Management, about selling Web farming to a skeptical management. Start simple. Keep it focussed. Moreover, build for the longterm.

The result of this business plan should be a commitment by management to proceed with Getting Serious in Web farming. If it is not, honestly analyze whether Web farming is really of value to the enterprise, or whether the Getting Started stage lacks quality. If the former, toss this book and move on to a more productive area. If the latter, try again, concentrating more on the business benefits and on the political dynamics.

4.3   Stage Two—Getting Serious

As we move into the Getting Serious stage, we should have established a foundation on which we can build the infrastructure for Web farming. The foundation should be a clear business case documenting the critical external factors that are affecting our enterprise. Now we need to make a commitment to the Web farming effort. It is the proverbial "fish or cut bait" time! Either we have a clear mandate from management to proceed, or we do not.

The essential tasks in Getting Serious are to

- Legitimize Web farming within the organization.
- Build a stable infrastructure for long-term growth.
- Refine the CEF list into entities, indicators, and events.
- Maintain a historical context for all collected content.
- Establish an intranet web site to aid in information dissemination.

4.3.1   Legitimizing Web Farming

The first task of Getting Serious is to legitimize the Web farming effort as an official part of the enterprise. In the preceding stage, the Web farming effort is usually confined to a single individual. Such an effort was probably hidden from the radar scope of management, as the initiation of risky new technologies usually is.

In the Getting Serious stage, Web farming should be fully legitimized within the organization. In particular, Web farming should be legitimized by the following actions, tailored to the unique circumstances of the enterprise:

- Establishing a set of budget line items to support the effort
- Assigning specific full-time personnel to Web farming
- Defining a box on the organization chart for Web farming
- Identifying visible champions of Web farming among management
- Creating a general awareness of Web farming among the workforce
- Issuing periodic bulletins about progress (or the lack thereof)

The result of legitimizing Web farming is to make the benefits and costs of this activity officially accountable to management. Web farming must live (or die) by its accountability to the enterprise. Otherwise, the effort will likely dissipate into interesting and exciting areas, but these areas will be of little or no value to the enterprise.

Web farming must live (and die) by its
accountability to the enterprise.

4.3.2 Build the Infrastructure

The second task of Getting Serious is to build a stable long-term infrastructure for the Web farming function. The core processing for Web farming should be centralized and housed in a managed environment (i.e., the glass-house data center).

The critical areas in which to build infrastructure are the server environment, the IP connection, and the database management—which are discussed in Chapter 5, Architecture.

4.3.3 Refine the CEF List

The third task of Getting Serious is to refine the CEF list, as generated by the Getting Started stage. So far, the CEF list consists of various business factors about which a collection of semistructured information (i.e., text documents) has been gathered. This task should refine the CEF list by determining each of the following:

- *Entity* that identifies a person or organization for each CEF
- *Indicator* values that measure or characterize each CEF
- *Events* that signal significant changes in each CEF

First, specify one or more identifiers (such as a stock symbol for a publicly traded company) that uniquely distinguishes a person, an organization, a place, and so on. Individuals should be distinguished from organizations, with the proper mapping of their relationships. Then categorize both persons and organizations according to one or two general business dimensions (such as industry sector or geographical region). Any identifier that uniquely determines the CEF is called a *CEF entity* for that CEF.

Second, determine one or more indicators that best characterize each CEF. For instance, a CEF involving weather at a specific location may have several indicators based on wind chill, amount of precipitation, max/min temperatures, and so forth. A CEF indicator is a simple variable that describes some attribute of a CEF, such as interest rates, the price of a barrel of crude oil, or the predicted high temperature tomorrow for a given city. Any value that characterizes some attribute of a CEF is called a *CEF indicator.*

There are four types of indicators, depending on the nature of their values. Table 4-1 describes these types.

Third, determine one or more possible events involving a specific CEF and having a significant impact on the enterprise. For example, an event would be a new product introduction by a strong competitor. Significant changes in CEF indicators are possible events. Other events could be major stock fluctuations, press releases by partners of your competitors, a visible disaster involving your product, surprising quarterly earnings by a key supplier, public comments on your product by customers, a government investigation of your industry, federal legislation affecting your tax burden, and so on. By monitoring and anticipating events, you can design

Table 4-1 Types of Indicators

Indicator Type	Description
Nominal	Test for equality so that items can be categorized into groups, such as citizenship or sex.
Ordinal	Test for less than or greater than so that items can be ordered, such as the ratings of football teams.
Interval	Test for differences among items for numeric comparison, such as temperature or location.
Ratio	Test for differences from a zero point on the scale, such as length or weight.

mechanisms to detect them, acquire them, and integrate them into the data warehouse system. Any significant change related to a CEF is called a *CEF event*.

Once the CEF list has been expanded into CEF entities, indicators, and events, Web targets should be determined for each of those items. In other words, the source of each item should be specified as a search template containing the proper URL and its permissible variations. The mapping of targets to the CEF items is discussed further in the next chapter.

4.3.4 Maintain Historical Context

Web content is constantly changing, which is both its value for the enterprise and its burden for Web farming. Time is the dominant dimension in the analysis of CEFs. The assumption is that history is the best predictor of the future (albeit not in a linear fashion).

The volatility of Web content is a major factor in maintaining its historical context.[2] Content that is nonvolatile (such as federal statutes) should be treated differently than volatile content (such as stock prices). As the volatility increases, the burden of monitoring change also increases.

Web farming should maintain a historical context for every Web object that is collected. The change monitoring of Web content may be more important, business-wise, than the content itself. There are two methods for change monitoring of Web content—notify and poll.

*The change monitoring of Web content may be more important
than the content itself.*

---

2. See the section "Profiling Web Pages" in Chapter 10, Techniques, for details on measuring volatility of Web pages.

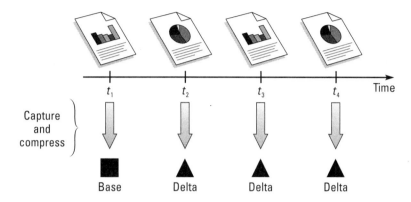

Figure 4-4 Recording the Historical Context

The notify method requires the author (or owner) of the source to notify any consumers that a change has occurred in the content and even to "push" the revised content to the consumer. Using the publish-and-subscribe framework (described in Chapter 2, Perspectives), this method is more effective, but it requires the network to support a true "push" capability (i.e., asynchronous notification and delivery).

The poll method requires that the consumer poll the source periodically to detect the occurrence of changes. Although this polling requires considerable overhead in processing and bandwidth, this method can be applied universally to any network, since all support a "pull" capability (i.e., simple retrieval and comparison).

Whatever combination of methods is employed, the requirement for Web farming is to obtain Web content and then to monitor changes to that content. At least initially, a complete audit trail of all Web content should be maintained. As storage and processing overhead becomes burdensome, portions should be offloaded to an archive. Criteria for selecting content to be archived should take into account the business value of the content, rather than just its age.

Since most changes to a Web page are small, the technique for recording the audit trail should exploit this fact, as shown in Figure 4-4. When a Web object is captured for the first time, it is compressed into a "base" representation. This compression consists of eliminating noncontent data (such as some HTML tags) and compressing the remaining data using some nonloss algorithm. When a change is detected in that Web object, it is also captured and compressed. However, only the changes (i.e., delta from base) are compressed. This approach is similar to that of MPEG with video stream compression.

An important aspect of capturing Web content is attaching the appropriate time to that content. The time dimension is of critical importance for maintaining the historical context. The first issue involved with the time dimension is whether time should be a point in time or a period of time. The second issue is the precision of the time value. For example, are the following time values equivalent: last month, September 1992, 199209010000 to 199209312359 (the ISO timestamp)?

And the third issue is when the time was noted, as in the following:

1. *Probe:* The time when the Web content was captured by probing the site. Probe time is an easily acquired by-product of the probing process and should be recorded.
2. *Transaction:* The time when the Web content was updated on its Web server. Transaction time may be available from the HTTP header, although some Web servers do not return this data, or the Web page could have been generated dynamically from a database.
3. *Valid:* The time when the event occurred as described by the Web content. Valid time may be embedded in the content and, if so, should be extracted.

For example, your major supplier filed for bankruptcy in federal court at 4:45 p.m. Wednesday afternoon in San Francisco. The WSJ Web site noted this event at 3:15 a.m. Thursday morning in New York. The Web farming system probed the WSJ Web site at 8:30 a.m. Friday morning from Denver. Which time should be attached to this event? How can that time be reliably obtained? Does it make a difference to your business? Determining and extracting the proper timestamp for each Web document is critical to maintaining the historical context.

4.3.5 Establish Intranet Site

The final task of Getting Serious is to establish an intranet web server. As part of disseminating information from the Web farming function, a structured Web site should be created, similar to that of a corporate research library. If such a Web site has already been established by the data warehousing group or another group, then collaborate in presenting a uniform image of corporate information, regardless of its source.

Once the basic flow of information from the Web farming function has been established, the Web site should be enhanced with the ability to alert specific groups of persons to specific events via browser "push" tools (e.g., PointCast), email, pagers, and the like.

4.4 Stage Three—Getting Smart

The stage of Getting Smart concentrates on extending the foundation established in Getting Started and the infrastructure built in Getting Serious. This stage focuses on exploiting technology to increase both the productivity and the volume of Web farming.

The essential tasks in Getting Smart are to

- Build the required selection and extraction filters
- Construct pipelines into primary content providers

- Analyze and structure content more efficiently
- Publish content more effectively

4.4.1 Build Selection and Extraction Filters

The first task of Getting Smart is to build a set of selection and extraction filters to support the periodic probing of Web pages. This building process will be an ongoing part of Web farming and will be aided by developments in metadata standards and Web agent tools.

The purpose of a selection filter is to identify and capture a specific Web page. The following methods of selection are available:

- *Static URL:* Identifies the Internet location of a stable Web page.
- *Static URL with client identifier* (e.g., extended URL or "cookie"): Identifies a Web page generated uniquely for the specific client browser.
- *Dynamic URL using CGI (or equivalent) parameters:* Identifies a specific set of data retrieved from a database and embedded into an HTML template.
- *Database Query:* Identifies a specific result set from a predefined database. The query specifications could be a standard such as ODMA URL extension[3] or an evolving standard using SQL syntax embedded within an RDF statement.[4]

The selection filter for the first method is a simple pass-through of the static URL to the Web probing procedure. The filter for the second method must manage a set of client identifiers and append them properly for the probing procedure. The filter for the last two methods is a technical challenge, because the value sets for one or more parameters must be managed.[5]

The purpose of the extraction filter is to pull data of interest from the Web pages. The following methods of extraction are available:

- *Simple Text Extraction:* Extract text from an HTML page by eliminating all HTML tags.
- *Enhanced Text Extraction:* Same as the first version, except that certain HTML tags (such as TITLE and META) are mapped as separate fields into the content database.

---

3. See the section "Open Document Management API" in Chapter 7, Standards.
4. See the section on "Resource Description Framework" in Chapter 7, Standards.
5. Further details are given in the section "Accessing Dynamic Pages" in Chapter 10, Techniques.

- *Manual copy and paste:* The least desirable but the most flexible! The Web analyst could use a generic word processor; however, the workbench for the analyst should display the incoming Web page to the analyst and assist in extracting selected fields into the content database.

- *HTML scrapper tool:* A variation on the 3270 Screen Scrapper tools of old. The Web analyst should specify the mapping of selected fields to the content database as above, but this mapping should be saved as an extraction template for subsequent probing of the same Web page.

- *MIME object:* Instead of an HTML Web page, a structured object in comma-delimited text, Microsoft Excel spreadsheet, dBASE, and so on. The Web analyst must specify a prior mapping of the incoming fields to tables in the content database.

- *RDL object:* A self-defined object using the Resource Description Framework in XML with a predetermined DTD schema.[6]

In the previous Getting Serious stage, selection used simple static URL references, and extraction used simple text extraction. In this Getting Smart stage, the challenge is to broaden selection and extraction methods.

4.4.2 Construct Pipelines to Primary Content Providers

The second task of Getting Smart is to construct pipelines to the primary content providers. By this third stage, there are probably one to three providers from which most of the required content can be obtained. Since most content providers emphasize interactive users as their main delivery mechanism, building pipelines may involve legal negotiation more than technical implementation.

A pipeline is a reliable communication channel for delivery of the required content. However, enhanced protocols using TCP/IP are available for reliable bulk data transfers over the Internet, such as OMG Internet Inter-ORB Protocol[7] and Secured Socket Layer.[8]

Another alternative is a "manual" pipeline via magnetic cartridge. The information provider generates one weekly or monthly and delivers it overnight for database loading. However, this alternative is not viable for volatile data.

4.4.3 Analyze and Structure Content

The third task of Getting Smart is to analyze and structure content more intelligently. The role of Web analyst should shift from the discovery of new Web resources to the transformation of existing content flow into more useful products.

---

6. See the "Resource Description Framework" section in Chapter 7, Standards.
7. See http://www.omg.org/corba/corbiiop.htm.
8. See http://www.netscape.com/newsref/std/SSL.html.

The emphasis should always be on maximizing business value amid the chaotic environment of the Internet.

There are two basic approaches to the task of analyzing and structuring content. First, you can specify a model of business dynamics and fit the content to that model. Or, second, you can detect patterns within the content and deduce a model of business dynamics. These approaches represent the classic distinction between theoretical (i.e., model infers data) and empirical (i.e., data deduces model) analysis. Both approaches are required to some degree. Synergism comes from the interactions involved in pursuing both approaches.

One type of model-based approach could use a well-conceived schema with an existing data warehousing system and augment it with content from the Web farming effort. This approach has been emphasized throughout this text. However, such a well-conceived schema may not exist. Then the task is to develop a model that will adequately guide the Web farming effort. This model should obviously be built on the business analysis performed in the previous stages and should always be directed toward maximizing business value.

An empirical-based approach is more difficult, especially in the absence of a model to guide the investigation. This approach is similar to that of data mining within the data warehousing context. The lessons learned from data mining attempts indicate that a firm model based on business objectives is essential. The disciplines of competitive intelligence, market research, and strategic forecasting would be useful in designing an appropriate empirical-based approach to analyzing and structuring content.[9]

4.4.4 Publishing Content

The final task of Getting Smart is to publish the content. A major contributor to the data warehousing field, Ralph Kimball, has stated,

> The responsibility to publish is at the very core of the data warehouse.[10]

As Web farming enhances the data warehousing function, this responsibility is also valid for Web farming. The purpose is twofold. First, information is valuable only when it is used, so the publishing of content is essential to reaping its business benefit. Second, the feedback from information consumers is also essential in guiding the Web farming effort into areas of greater business benefit. In fact, the viability of this feedback loop will be the critical factor in the success of the Web farming effort.

The viability of feedback from information consumers
will be the critical factor in the success of the Web farming effort.

---

9. See Chapter 3, Foundations.
10. Kimball, 1996, xxvi.

Once important business information has been obtained, it should be published through whatever mechanisms are effective. Such mechanisms may include the data warehouse (and its dissemination network). Other mechanisms may include an Internet Web site (as suggested in the Getting Serious stage), a weekly newsletter, an email flash to selected groups, Lotus Notes bulletins, pager alerts, and even personal one-on-one briefings. Be creative in making use of a variety of publishing mechanisms, as appropriate to the organization.

One suggestion is to publish a directory of important Web resources on a Web site so that people can quickly access those resources on demand. The directory should emphasize those resources with high importance and low volatility, organized by major business dimensions. Another suggestion is to provide a feedback mechanism for people using any Web content to indicate the importance of items and to request further information.

The publish-and-subscribe framework is an excellent approach for a production-level publishing function built around the data warehouse and Web farming system.[11] By separating data producers from data consumers, an information broker (i.e., people plus brokering system) can manage the information dissemination on an enterprise scale.

The P&S concept is discussed in Chapter 3, Foundations, and the architecture is discussed in Chapter 5, Architecture. Also, note the important discussion on the violation of copyright laws in Chapter 11, Society.

4.5 Stage Four—Getting Tough

As an activity of intelligence gathering and synthesis, Web farming is an enabling technology, requiring (never replacing) the unique skill and hard work of domain experts. People are required to structure Web content that is accurately interpreted to the business and properly integrated with the data warehouse. After the infrastructure has been developed in the previous stages, the Getting Tough stage culminates in this hard (and tough in a technical sense) work.

As an activity of intelligence gathering and synthesis,
Web farming is an enabling technology, requiring (never replacing)
the unique skill and hard work of domain experts.

---

11. See the section "Creating Information Markets" in Chapter 2, Perspectives.

The essential tasks in Getting Tough are to

- Rendezvous with the warehouse by extending schema and loading content
- Link to other enterprise-level systems
- Resolve entity mapping through matching of key values
- Establish credibility through various data checks

4.5.1 Rendezvous with the Warehouse

The first task of Getting Tough is to rendezvous with the data warehouse, which has been the ultimate objective of Web farming. The previous three stages are necessary to build the proper technical and organizational infrastructure for Web farming. Up to this point, the output generated by Web farming was not adequate in quality and reliability as input to the data warehouse.

There are several ways to rendezvous with the warehouse:

- Augment an existing dimension table. Since fact tables are usually business transactions (or aggregations thereof), the dimension tables add supplementary information about those transactions. Augmenting a dimension table implies that additional attributes are added to the table or a new table is added with a dependent relationship (as in a snowflake design). For example, augmenting a dimension table about branch stores with census data could generate insights into the incomes and cultural variables affecting customer buying patterns.
- Create new fact tables and associated dimensions. Creating new tables would require a significant extension of the warehouse schema, possibly adding an independent subject area. The creation of a new table consisting primarily of Web content may imply that the entity is external to the enterprise, focused on strategic forecasting or competitive analysis. For instance, a fact table about events related to competing companies (such as press releases, product introductions, and major contracts) could be used to forecast market trends.

Either way (or some combination thereof) requires coordination of schema design with the data warehousing group—a collaboration that should have begun in the earlier stages. Precise formats for structuring data and procedures for loading data must be specified and maintained on a production schedule.

Web farming has now entered the mission-critical ("beeper-on-the-belt") phase.

4.5.2 Link to Other Systems

The architecture for Web farming should support linkages to other enterprise-wide systems, such as enterprise resource planning and sales force automation. These systems both generate and consume data that potentially can have strong relationships with Web content. You should hope that there will be a vigorous integration of all these type of systems.

In addition, the rapid growth of corporate intranets has created specialized versions of the Web internal to the enterprise. The Web farming function should also target content sources on the corporate intranet as internal business documents become available. The same discovery and acquisition methodology can be applied to the intranet environment to acquire this information and integrate it into the data warehouse. However, you should remember that the greater potential for information on critical external factors affecting the enterprise does lie in the global Web.

4.5.3 Resolve Entity Mapping

The second task of Getting Tough is to resolve the mapping of Web content to the data warehouse at the data instance level. In other words, the database loading process must match the identifier of each content item with a key value in the warehouse table.

For example, the mapping of census data to a branch store is difficult. First, the address of each branch office must be converted to a longitude/latitude coordinate. Next, that coordinate has to be matched to the boundaries of a census district—a point-within-polygon equivalence operation. Finally, the district number must be added as a foreign key to the dimension table for branch stores.

This example is a simple one in that this mapping is performed only once for each branch store, since branch stores do not change their locations. If you are monitoring the weather for a trucking fleet, the mapping of locations is a continuous process.

Entity mapping is probably the toughest technical problem for Web farming. This problem cannot be resolved with better tools or refined data. It is a tough conceptual challenge for an analyst to determine the semantic equivalence of two complex clusters of data and to specify a mapping that relates those clusters. In addition, this mapping often involves policy decisions dependent on the business environment and objectives. Such decisions should be discussed within the context of an Enterprise (or Information) Architecture committee, which has this type of authority for data entities coming from internal sources.

The problem of entity mapping in data warehousing is not new. In retailing banking, the mapping of an individual customer to a household has been a struggle for 10 years, giving rise to a whole market niche.[12]

---

12. See the direct marketing services of Harte-Hanks at http://www.harte-hanks.com/.

4.5.4 Establish Credibility Checks

The final task of Getting Tough is to establish checks to ensure the credibility of the Web content. A situation that will occur with certainty is the questioning of the validity of Web content by a prominent member of management. The questioning will sound innocent: "These data just don't seem correct." However, the entire responsibility for proving the validity of those data will rest on the shoulders of the Web farming group. Without prior planning, shouldering that burden of proof can sabotage the entire Web farming effort. Trust in Web content as part of the data warehouse must be earned, item by item.

> *A situation that will occur with certainty is the questioning of the validity of Web content by a prominent member of management. How will you respond?*

The first step in establishing credibility is to build checks into the In-Flow processing. Whenever data is selected and extracted from a Web page, the following checks should be made:

- *Version:* Values are in the proper format and within the proper range.
- *Consistency:* Values have not varied unusually from earlier values.
- *Conformity:* Values can form joins with values in existing tables.
- *Completeness:* A complete set of values is obtained.

The second step is to periodically perform pattern analysis across several dimensions to detect unusual outlier values. When unusual patterns are detected, their validity should be investigated. Even if they are valid, those patterns may be useful in understanding significant changes in the business environment.

The final step is to implement a mechanism for performing a quick genealogy check on a specific data item. In other words, where did this data come from? A simple click of a menu should search the Web archive and print a complete audit trail about that data item from the point of capture through database loading. In some cases, viewing the original Web page will be invaluable in judging the validity of the data with a quick genealogy check. The inquiry can be deflected away from the Web farming group and into more constructive directions (for instance, toward the author of the original Web content).

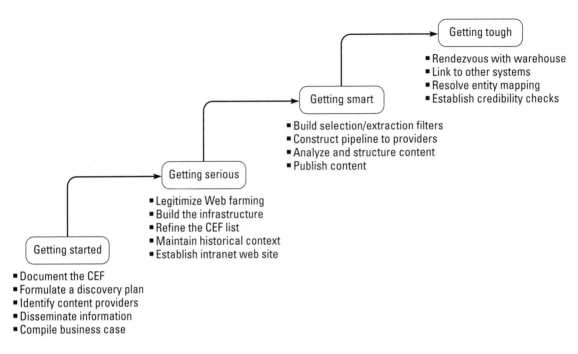

Getting tough
- Rendezvous with warehouse
- Link to other systems
- Resolve entity mapping
- Establish credibility checks

Getting smart
- Build selection/extraction filters
- Construct pipeline to providers
- Analyze and structure content
- Publish content

Getting serious
- Legitimize Web farming
- Build the infrastructure
- Refine the CEF list
- Maintain historical context
- Establish intranet web site

Getting started
- Document the CEF
- Formulate a discovery plan
- Identify content providers
- Disseminate information
- Compile business case

Figure 4-5 The Four Stages of Web Farming

4.6 Then What?

Figure 4-5 summarizes the four stages of Web farming, along with the tasks within each of the stages.

What happens in the fifth stage? The fifth stage is maturity. This implies that Web farming will eventually disappear as a separate and distinguishable technology. If successful, Web farming will blend into the architecture and procedures of the enterprise system, as many other information technologies have done over the years. In other words, Web farming is a transitional technology toward the larger goals of knowledge management in the enterprise.

The next chapter echoes the four stages for evolving Web farming by describing the architecture required to support this methodology.

## Chapter Five

Architecture

For the farmer, building a good stone wall is an exercise in skill and patience. The farmer must put the right pieces together in the right places so that the wall will stand the test of time. Likewise, Web farming requires the same kind of skills and patience, to build an architecture that will stand its own test of time.

This chapter complements the previous chapter by describing the architecture required to support the methodology for Web farming. The chapter follows the sequence of the four-stage methodology. For each of the stages, various tools are suggested as components in the architecture. A sampling of these tools is described in Chapter 8, Tools.

In particular, the components that are critical to Web farming are as follows:

- Extensible Web browser for the analyst
- Flexible database server for both content and control
- Intranet web server for an internal resource center
- Indexing server to parse and compile content
- Web crawler to acquire content
- Information analysis tools to discover patterns in massive content
- Publish-and-subscribe mechanism to disseminate information

In most cases, these tools are available as commercial off-the-shelf (COTS) products, minimizing the need for from-scratch software development. However, there will be many places where complex configuration and glue software will be required.

5.1   Stage One—Getting Started

The main objective of the Getting Started stage is to discover and document the external factors that are important to business success. This foundation should guide future investments in the Web farming function. Consider this stage an experiment, which should quickly yield insightful feedback on the relevance of Web farming to the enterprise.

The architecture for the Getting Started stage is simple, as shown in Figure 5-1. The architecture for this first stage emphasizes the support of a single skilled business analyst (also called an *information analyst* or a *Web analyst*).[1] This individual should have a thorough understanding of the business across a broad spectrum. Knowledge of Web technology and skills in effective Web search techniques are recommended. Some assistance may also be required from an Information Broker consultant (as defined in the membership lists of the Association of Independent Information Professionals and the Society for Competitive Information Professionals).

The two objectives for the business analyst are to conduct Web research and to disseminate the information. The Web research should be focused in the directions outlined in the methodology, resulting in a business plan for Web farming. The information dissemination should be focused on identifying topics critical to the enterprise and, especially, the groups interested in each of those topics.

---

1. See the position description of a Web analyst in Chapter 6, Management.

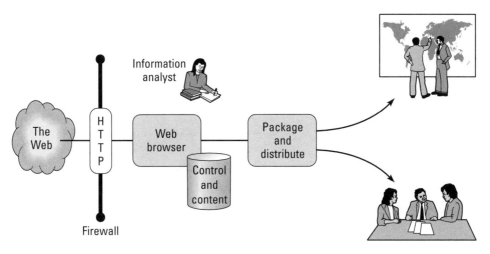

Figure 5-1 Stage One—Getting Started

Avoid purchasing new equipment or software at this stage. The danger of acquiring new technology is the diversion of attention from the business objectives. An inexpensive IP connection (e.g., 56 Kbps, unlimited time for approximately $20 per month), along with a generic browser, is all that is needed. Keep it simple and stay focused on defining the business objectives for Web farming.

> *Avoid purchasing new equipment or software.*
> *It will defocus your effort.*

5.2   Stage Two—Getting Serious

The main objectives of the Getting Serious stage are to legitimize the Web farming effort and to build the infrastructure. At this stage, a serious commitment should be made to pursue Web farming as an important means of expanding the functionality of the data warehouse. To accomplish this, a major change in the architecture to support Web farming must also be made. Taking Web farming seriously implies that adequate resources are dedicated to personnel and facilities to evolve eventually into a production-level system.

> *Taking Web farming seriously implies that adequate resources*
> *are dedicated to personnel and facilities to evolve eventually*
> *into a production-level system.*

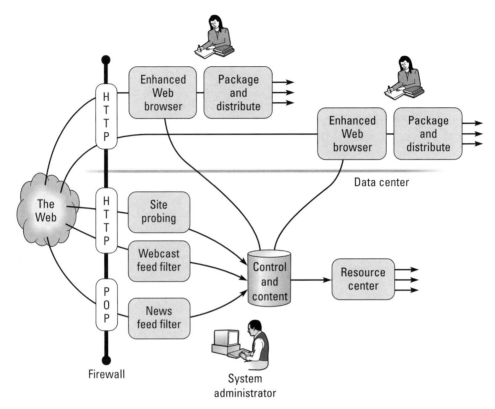

Figure 5-2 Stage Two—Getting Serious

Figure 5-2 shows the evolution of the architecture in the Getting Serious stage. The architecture evolves in the following directions:

- Transition of processing into a secured data center
- Control and content information on a common database server
- Content probing and feed filter software
- Intranet resource center
- New position for system administrator and possibly additional analysts

5.2.1 Transition into Data Center

The most important step of Getting Serious is to transition the Web farming function from various workstations scattered through the office into a secured data center environment. This environment should be managed as a production ("glass-house") facility with around-the-clock operation, full-time personnel, equipment maintenance, uninterruptible power source, controlled personnel access, disaster recovery, and so forth.

The critical components are the server platform and the IP connection.

The server platform should be similar to that of most client-server systems. The server platform should use an SMP processor under UNIX or NT with a RAID disk array, all of which are maintained within a data center. There are many off-the-shelf alternatives for such a platform. Unlike a typical Web server, the server supporting Web farming will externally appear to be a Web crawler (multiple clients intensely retrieving Web documents). Hence, the capacity for high transaction rates is not a major concern. Maintainability and recoverability are major criteria.

The IP (or Internet PPP) connection should be a dedicated ISDN or fractional T1 connection to a major Internet service provider. High bandwidth is probably not critical, especially in the beginning years of the Web farming effort. However, a separate IP connection for Web farming is recommended so that other Internet traffic (for email and the corporate Web site) is not affected.

5.2.2 Common Database Server

A shared database should manage the common content and control information for the Web farming function. This database could initially be a shared directory of favorite URL bookmarks, useful searches, and the like. Eventually, all content should flow through and be controlled by this common database. Likewise, Web browsers should be enhanced to work with this common database by caching Web objects, recording URL histories, noting search templates, and so on.

All content should flow through and be controlled by this common database.

The database server should be a full-function relational database with object-oriented extensions (especially in text and image processing). Most DBMS vendors now offer such products. The data exchange interface with the existing data warehouse is also critical. The database server should interface well with an intranet web server and small data mart as an interim configuration. The main objective is to support a common repository for both content and control of the entire Web farming function.

5.2.3 Content Probing and Feed Filters

The acquisition of Web content comes primarily from the periodic probing of specific Web pages. Through a table of targets in the control database, the content probing should maintain a current image of the Web page (i.e., the HTML base file along with associated image and other Web files). In addition, a complete audit trail of the changes occurring in that page should also be maintained, as discussed in Chapter 4, Methodology.

An email feed (stream) from content providers and newsgroups can supply considerable content that could be highly relevant to the data warehouse. Content from

---

Some Traditional Library Research

Driving to work one morning, Alice had one of those obvious ideas, making her feel guilty for not thinking of it sooner. "Is it okay if I spend a little time and some funds at our corporate research library?" she asked Steve that day. "They may have access to materials that are not on your typical Web site."

Alice scheduled an appointment with Helen, the head librarian, and explained the situation. Helen was very enthusiastic and asked a lot of questions about the material from Web sites. Helen decided to concentrate on the Dialog databases and to carefully formulate a search strategy by manually scanning the blue sheets. After a couple of Dialog sessions (and a few hundred dollars), 50 or 60 items about top customers were printed and reviewed by Alice.

"These are great!" Alice exclaimed to Helen. "But can you do the first two searches every week and give me the output on a diskette to place on the server?" Helen was a bit lost. The service from Dialog was undergoing extensive changes with a new "dialunit" costing method that was not obvious, licensing restrictions on content distribution, and a complex alerting scheme. Helen tried, but the group's interest for including the Dialog material gradually faded over the coming weeks.

Next installment is on page 135.

---

an email feed requires an extraction process different from that for Web content. Like an email client program, a filter for an email feed must periodically poll a mail server and retrieve the message using the Post Office Protocol (POP). Information in the header (i.e., TO, FROM, SUBJECT, and DATE fields) and message body should be parsed as if the object were a Web page.

As useful information becomes available through a subscription to a Webcasting channel, a similar set of filters should be built to acquire Webcasting content and format for the content database.

5.2.4   Intranet Resource Center

As a result of creating a full-function intranet web site, portions of the content database should serve as a resource center for the entire enterprise. The contents initially are mirrored images of Web pages and indexes to these pages, organized in a meaningful fashion. A continued effort to meaningfully organize this content has as its goal a shift from static content of indexes and mirrored pages to dynamic content generated from database tables.

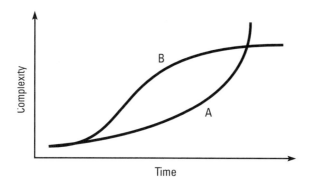

Figure 5-3   Time versus Complexity

5.2.5   New Position for System Administrator

A new position should be established for a system administrator, who will purchase, install, and maintain the required software within the data center. Additional business analysts should be hired if the hiring is justified by increased demand for packaged Web information.

5.2.6   Managing Complexity

In mathematics, it is a common occurrence for the results of a formula to increase at such a rate that its values seem to explode. Consider the formula x raised to the x power. For $x = 1,2,3,\ldots$ the results are 1, 4, 27, 256, 3125, 46656, 823543, and so forth. This is called a *combinatorial explosion.*

A similar situation occurs as we seriously pursue Web farming. In the Getting Started stage, the explosion was self-limiting because of the perseverance of the analyst and the deadlines of the project. As we move to a server-centric operation, the complexity of the Web farming will seem to explode, as Figure 5-3 illustrates.

A question to be investigated is whether, for the typical Web farming effort, complexity will level off or will continue to increase. In the figure, curve A indicates that the complexity will continue to increase at an ever-increasing rate. Curve B indicates that the complexity will eventually taper off. At any point in time, the content of the Web is finite, as the Internet Archive is finding. However, a typical WP effort may not have enough capacity to approach this limit.

The challenge of the complexity explosion is twofold. First, we need to be prepared for large volumes in bandwidth and storage. However, limitations to this preparation are usually imposed on us by budget constraints, so there is little to be done. Second, we need to predict the volume of information that will generate a sufficient business value. This prediction will be tricky at best, honed only through experience.

5.2.7 Being Web-Farming Friendly

Being an excellent Web site for the individual Web surfer is very different from being an excellent site for systematic Web farming. Flashy graphics, innovative page layouts, and unusual opinions often attract people. A Web farming system is looking for the facts—just the facts. For Web farming, the important characteristics are

- Quality
- Stability
- Programmability

The quality of information is usually a difficult characteristic to measure. Quality depends on some combination of accuracy, precision, coverage, currency, and organization. The essential question is whether you can trust the data as the basis for making business decisions. In many cases, the only true basis of trust is the domain name of the URL Web target. A domain name of sec.gov would be given a higher degree of trust than anydomain.com. The stability of information depends on accessibility, consistency, location dependence, and content volatility. The programmability of information depends upon an explicit metadata definition and ease of agent programming.

5.3 Stage Three—Getting Smart

The main objective of the Getting Smart stage is to increase the relevance of Web content to the business by extending the foundation established in Getting Started and the infrastructure built in Getting Serious.

Figure 5-4 shows the evolution of the architecture in the Getting Smart stage. The architecture evolves in the following directions:

- Enhanced control database to direct intelligent agent searching
- Integrated analyst workbench
- New position for programmer of Web agent processes
- Custom pipeline to content provider
- Delivery mechanism based on publish-and-subscribe
- New position for content broker

5.3.1 Enhanced Control Database

The database to control Web farming processing is a critical component in Getting Smart. This database should monitor each probe of Web content and relate it back to its CEF. A suggestion for such a database design is given in Figure 5-5.

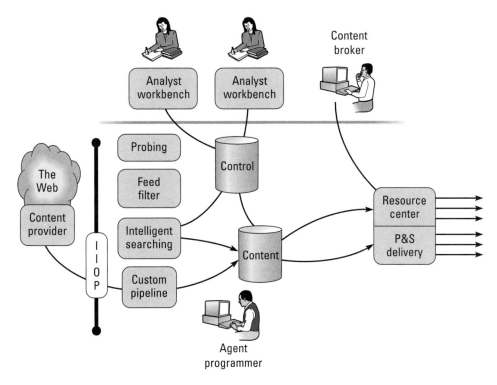

Figure 5-4 Stage Three—Getting Smart

> *The database to control Web farming processing is a critical component in Getting Smart.*

The CEF list is represented by the FACTOR entity, which is identified by a system-generated FACTOR ID, a TITLE (consisting of a well-chosen 100 characters or less), and an optional DESCRIPTION (of any length). The hierarchical structure in which a general factor is composed of several more specific factors is modeled by the relation PART OF.

The entities ENTITY, INDICATOR, and EVENT are subtypes of FACTOR. In other words, ENTITY specializes a CEF for a certain person, organization, or place. Likewise, INDICATOR specializes a CEF to a simple value to measure the degree of this factor. An INDICATOR can be a nominal, ordinal, interval, or ratio value, thus restricting the ways these values can be aggregated.[2] Finally, an EVENT specializes a

---

2. See the section "Refining the CEF List" in Chapter 4, Methodology, for an explanation of the indicator types.

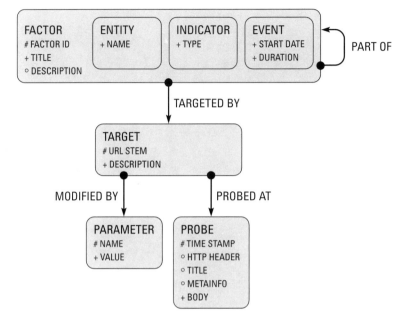

Figure 5-5   Schema for Control Database

CEF to a significant event having a START DATE and a DURATION (which could be zero).

The management of target references is explained in Chapter 10, Techniques.

5.3.2   Integrated Analyst Workbench

An integrated workbench environment should be created for the analysts. Sharing common control and context via the database server, the workbench enhances the browser with other tools, such as linguistic analysis and information visualization. Techniques for handling semistructured data are emerging, as in a project that adopted a "wrapper" approach for parsing a Web page into a structured field by exploiting HTML formatting tags.[3]

The goal is a major increase in the productivity of the analysts to discover relevant information and to acquire that information on a routine basis.

---

3.   See the section "Parsing Semistructured Data" in Chapter 10, Techniques.

5.3.3 New Position for Agent Programmer

A new position for a programmer should be established, and the programmer supervised, by the system administrator. The programmer should concentrate on programming server-side agents that perform the analyst-guided searching of specific resource sites and periodic probing of Web targets.

5.3.4 Custom Pipeline to Content Provider

A custom pipeline is a reliable communication channel used to deliver data from a content provider. Initially, this channel can be a magnetic cartridge (or similar removable storage) that is mounted on the server platform and loaded into the database. As the frequency and variety of content providers matures, it will be highly desirable to automate delivery of this content via the Internet. Through reliable and secure protocols (e.g., OMG IIOP) layered on TCP/IP, pipelines can be activated with hourly updates for volatile content.

5.3.5 Publish-and-Subscribe Delivery

The goal is to create an information market driven by the data warehousing and Web farming functions.[4] As the analyst specifies how to locate a data item and its mapping into the content database, she should also specify its view in business terms to potential consumers in the enterprise.

In the P&S framework, this action is called publishing; it allows the information broker to announce the existence of this information and to accept subscriptions for its delivery to specific consumers. The subscriptions can consist of one-time, periodic, or continuous delivery of information in a variety of packaged formats.

5.3.6 New Position for Content Broker

A new position for a content broker should also be established. The responsibility of this person is to be the information broker within the P&S framework. In other words, this person should organize and publicize specific channels of information related to important business factors.

The broker must maintain close coordination with the analysts so that discovery and acquisition are continuously aligned with business needs. In particular, a major role of the broker is to understand the needs of various information communities within the enterprise and communicate these needs to the analysts.

---

4. See the section "Creating Information Markets" in Chapter 2, Perspectives.

5.4   Stage Four—Getting Tough

The main objective of the Getting Tough stage is to fulfill the promise of providing reliable input to the data warehouse. Now comes the hard (and tough) work of structuring information properly for the warehouse schema.

Figure 5-6 shows the evolution of the architecture in the Getting Tough stage. The architecture evolves in the following directions:

1. The content database becomes a staging area for the warehouse.
2. Validating, transforming, and loading procedures are performed.
3. A new position is established for a data administrator.
4. The data warehouse becomes the resource center.

5.4.1   Staging Area for the Warehouse

The content database for Web farming shifts its role to the staging of content for loading into the data warehouse. In the previous stage, the content database could be accessed directly by users within the enterprise. In this stage, the database is used to transform data so that its structure is appropriate for the data warehouse by aggregating data across time periods and joining data across sources.

5.4.2   The Validating and Loading Procedures

The procedures for validating and loading data are important links to the data warehouse. Besides the technical requirements of data movement, these procedures perform the essential role of establishing and maintaining credibility for the data warehouse.[5] The burden of proof that data is valid rests on these procedures, which check version, consistency, conformity, and completeness.

5.4.3   New Position for a Data Administrator

A new position, for a data administrator, should be established. This person should maintain close coordination with the warehouse design group and may even be a member of that group. The required skill set is the same as that for warehouse (database) design, with the addition of expertise about the unique aspects of diverse Web content and emerging metadata standards.

---

5.   See the section "Establish Credibility Checks" in Chapter 4, Methodology.

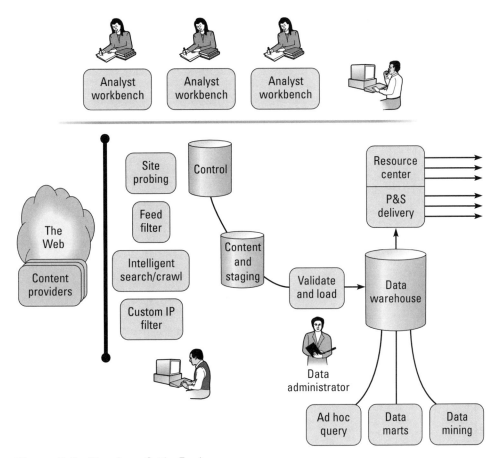

Figure 5-6   Stage Four—Getting Tough

5.4.4   The Data Warehouse as the Resource Center

The data warehouse should now become the resource center, as described in earlier stages. Instead of being a collection of interesting business data farmed from the Web, the resource center should take on the greater role of managing and disseminating business information regardless of its source. As the resource center evolves into multimedia and semistructured data, the data warehouse will, ideally, be its foundation.

This chapter has sketched the evolution of the architecture as we moved through the four stages. Remember that the ultimate goal of web farming is to blend into a single system for data warehousing and knowledge management. Web farming should fade into the background as the integration of these systems rises in importance.

The next chapter outlines the management considerations underlying the methodology and architecture discussed in this chapter and the preceding one.

## Chapter Six

Management

Managing Web farming is like managing any farming enterprise. Sitting at the table in the evening, the farmer must make a close accounting of each penny expended, along with each one received. The process can be tedious, but is very rewarding in the end.

This chapter explores the management issues related to implementing a Web farming function within the enterprise and within the marketplace. It gives some practical advice on selling Web farming to a skeptical management, describes the position of Web analysts, and offers a few alternatives for organizing the Web farming function within the enterprise. The chapter concludes by suggesting a few ways to make money with Web farming.

6.1 Selling Web Farming to a Skeptical Management

This section discusses ways to position and promote the idea of Web farming within a management climate that may be a bit skeptical. The assumption is that a firm business justification for Web farming has been completed, as suggested in the Getting Started stage.

The second chapter, Perspectives, provides a good background for this part of the book. Chapter 2 deals not with a business justification for Web farming but more with a conceptual justification. In other words, it helps us to point our heads in the right direction...to think the right vision.

The fourth chapter is called Methodology, and the first stage of our methodology is Getting Started. The purpose of the Getting Started stage is to construct a business justification (unique to your enterprise) for Web farming. This justification must deal with the important business issues as perceived by management, which provide the starting point for the discussion in this chapter.

Here is some practical advice.

6.1.1 Deal with the Skepticism

Skepticism about Web farming, or about any new technology, is healthy. Do not be defensive. Consider the skepticism an ally that is imposing some necessary testing. Remember that in general, most new technologies are dumb ideas and should be quickly discarded.

In general, most new technologies are dumb ideas
and should be quickly discarded.

Methodically raise the skeptical questions, then attempt to resolve them quickly and honestly. If a question remains unresolved, keep that question in front of everyone, and consider it yet another risk factor that you must manage.

6.1.2 Focus on Business Issues

The greatest danger is being sidetracked into areas that consume considerable resources and deliver little business value. You should constantly question whether your current efforts in Web farming are delivering real business value to the enterprise.

The primary question is whether the information is being used in ways that are making a difference in the enterprise. The only way of investigating this question is to be very close to the people receiving the Web farming information. A vigorous give-and-take in this dissemination function is critical.

Getting Serious with a Formal Plan

After just two months, Susan, the CIO, deemed the experiment a success. People had started asking the DW staff to schedule Alice's reports on a regular basis and to enlarge the scope of the subject areas. Several key executives were frequent users and were vying among themselves to take credit for the experiment.

Steve convened a meeting to decide the next steps and establish a formal plan for establishing business intelligence as a unit within the Data Warehouse group. Alice was assigned full time, and a position announcement was approved for an assistant to her. Tom, the Webmaster for the corporate site, was commissioned to outline the equipment, software, and personnel requirements for an intranet web site.

Next installment is on page 151.

The secondary question is whether the Web content processed by your web farming effort actually illuminates the major factors that are affecting the enterprise now and over the next few years. Perhaps a monthly assessment meeting would be healthy.

6.1.3 Avoid the Technology Hype

Do not use the term *Web farming* with management. Although this term may enhance the sales of a technical book, it lacks a certain professional sound. Your closest colleagues will circulate the worst agricultural jokes, and management detractors will dismiss your proposals with a single guttural groan. Use phrases such as "strategic information on industry trends from external sources," which will contrast nicely with "tactical data on operational systems from internal sources."

For similar reasons, do not use the terms *the Web* or *the Internet;* avoid any association with unbusinesslike Web sites and "flaky-free" content from questionable sources. The Web has been so overhyped that it is difficult for even the most astute to separate fact from fiction. Use instead such phases as "reliable governmental databases accessed via electronic means."

The Web has been so overhyped
that it is difficult for even the most astute
to separate fact from fiction.

Also, avoid using terms such as

- *Knowledge management:* As if we knew how to do such a thing.
- *Collaborative filtering:* As if we knew what it meant.
- *Information visualization:* As if we knew where it leads us.

For any technical jargon used with management, apply the mother-in-law test: imagine the bizarre facial expression of your mother-in-law if you used such a term during dinner conversation.

The point is that the technology of Web farming should be invisible to management. The aspects of Web farming that *should* be visible to management are the business justification at initiation and the business benefits at every stage of evolution.

6.1.4 Deal with Data Quality

Suppose you hear the statement, "Buy IBM stock because it will double in the next six months." Your reaction should depend on whether that suggestion came from a conversation overheard on the subway, from a chat with a friend over dinner, or from a phone call from a trusted financial advisor. The same is true of the Web.

Most people have a lowly "flaky-free" image of Web content. As mentioned earlier, in reality, the Web is a global bulletin board where both the wise and the foolish have equal space. The fact that content is acquired from the Web should not reflect positively or negatively on its quality. There must be a mechanism to track the sources of all content and a method for an analyst to judge the quality of that content. These requirements are part of designing a Web farming system.

---

*The Web is a global bulletin board
where both the wise and the foolish have equal space.*

6.1.5 Keep It Simple

The first stage of Web farming, Getting Started, embodies lots of common sense in the task of finding the critical business factors. In general, this stage should require one to three person-months of effort, preferably by one or two persons with adequate support.

The qualifications of each of these persons are critical. Here are a few suggestions: The person should be an employee with several years of experience. Avoid outside consultants. The person should have solid business and people skills, along with a broad range of system analysis skills. It will even be healthy if this person is skeptical (but fully motivated) about the project. Some skills for information discovery on the Web may be useful, although these can be quickly learned. Good connections with the corporate library (if there is one) or with a nearby research library are desirable.

A possible schedule for the first month could be as follows:

- *First week:* Formulate detailed action plan; arrange training; schedule interviews; design a list of 10 to 30 interview questions. The questions should profile your enterprise by covering its basic business objectives and trends. Some suggested topics are:
  - Annual report and other external reports
  - Confidential strategy documents about future directions
  - Press releases
  - Critiques by news and investment analysts
  - Interviews with sympathetic executives
  - Survey of key customers
  - Direct observation of manufacturing floor and customer transactions
- *Second week:* Interview people, as many and as varied as possible; take good notes; summarize each interview immediately after it ends.
- *Third week:* Compile and organize materials from research libraries and pertinent Web sites, giving specific illustrations of useful Web resources and key information providers.
- *Fourth week:* Write a 20-page summary report; create a crisp 30-minute presentation to explain the report; distribute the report to management and to the persons interviewed; offer to present and discuss the findings in a one-hour session.

A possible outline for the summary report could be as follows:

- Critical factors that are affecting our business
- Information that is available about these factors
- Mechanism for discovering, acquiring, and disseminating this information
- Expected business results over the short term and the long term

Discussion of Web farming and related technology should be minimal. Detailed cost analysis should come later, based on a tentative decision to proceed. Concentrate on the concepts and issues that are related to the business before fiddling with the numbers.

Finally, remember to avoid the purchase of any new technology. An existing workstation and a simple modem connection to the Internet should suffice.

6.1.6   Build for the Long Term

Within the data warehousing arena, there is considerable debate on the balance between enterprise warehouses and data marts. This debate embodies the classical opposition between building for the long term and doing something in the short term. Most agree that building for the long term is desirable, if moderated by budget limitations and survival crises.

A heavy burden will fall on the shoulders of a few individuals leading your Web farming effort. Much of this burden is the constant trade-off between the long term and the short term. Years later, people will review the current Web farming effort positively if

- The current leaders have kept the effort alive and produced tangible benefits.
- A legacy has been established that can be integrated smoothly into later systems.

Remember that the ultimate objective is for Web farming to fade into the background—to disappear as a distinct technology!

> *Remember that the ultimate objective is for Web farming to fade into the background—to disappear as a distinct technology!*

6.2   Organizational Designs

This section contrasts a few ways of organizing the Web farming function within the corporation. In general, there are two designs: one that is more conventional, with an emphasis on the current IT organization, and one that is more contemporary, with an emphasis on knowledge management.

The more conventional organizational design focuses on the IT organization as managed by a Chief Information Officer (CIO), as shown in Figure 6-1. The CIO moderates an IT Strategy Committee with members from various lines of business. This committee can be invaluable in setting the direction for Web farming, because the strategic business issues can be clarified and prioritized within this committee.

The IT Architecture and Planning group, which reports to the CIO, researches and advises on information technology adoption. Ideally, it is this group that will advocate Web farming and guide the effort through the Getting Started stage. As Web farming enters the next stages, its operational management is placed under the Data Warehouse group, which may be part of Systems Development or Systems Operation. A close liaison with the Database Administration group is required to ensure smooth integration during the later stages.

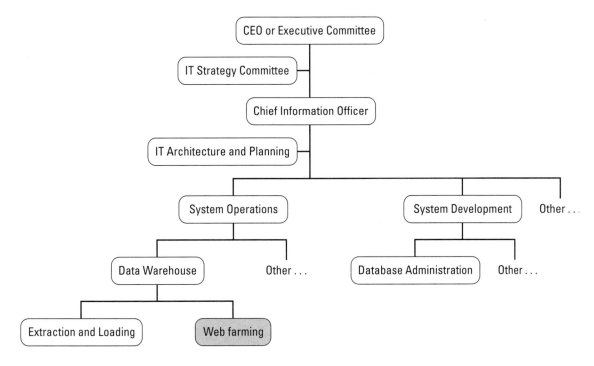

Figure 6-1 CIO-centric Organizational Design

The more contemporary organizational design focuses on the Web farming function as managed by the Chief Knowledge Officer (CKO), as shown in Figure 6-2. The IT Strategy Committee plays the same role as it does in the first model, except that this committee advises both the CIO and the CKO functions from the perspective of the lines of business. The Knowledge Exploitation group is an R&D staff function for the CKO to explore new opportunities. This group should have a close liaison with the IT Architecture and Planning group under the CIO. The Knowledge Acquisition and Knowledge Application groups manage the knowledge resources of the enterprise and apply these resources to specific business processes. From this perspective, the Web Farming function is part of the Knowledge Acquisition function and provides content to the Data Warehousing Systems.

In some enterprises, the role of the CIO is subordinated to or even subsumed by that of the CEO, rather than maintaining a peer relationship. In either case, the traditional IT organization then becomes a peer group to the Knowledge Acquisition and Knowledge Application groups. This variation would be preferred if the enterprise were highly dependent on intellectual resources, like a consulting or system integration firm.

There are many variations on the above organizational designs for managing the Web farming function. In one design, which is not suggested, Web farming is part of a Web site management, either Internet or intranet or both. This design

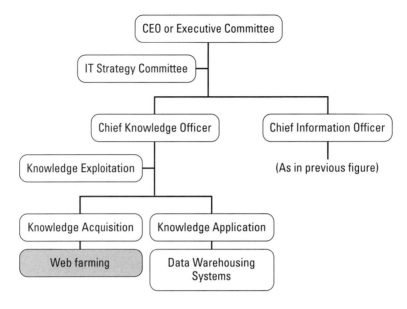

Figure 6-2   CKO-centric Organization Design

focuses too much on the Web technology aspects, rather than on the business benefits of structuring information for the data warehousing systems.

Do not manage Web farming as part of Web site management!

6.3 The Position of Information Analyst

Throughout previous discussions, we have described the work involved with Web
farming as substantial (i.e., requiring specialized skills and broad business knowledge) and as full-time (i.e., supporting a production facility). A new position should
be defined for an information analyst or *Web analyst*.[1] This position should be complementary to the existing positions of warehouse designer, database administrator,
Web site master, intranet manager, in-house publications reporter, corporate librarian, LAN administrator, and similar positions.

---

1.   Or should it be *Web farmer?*

6.3.1 Qualifications

Some suggested qualifications for the information analyst position are as follows:

1. Ability to understand the business objectives of the enterprise and to translate those objectives into the technical context of the data warehouse
2. Ability to communicate the results of Web farming to managers and nontechnical persons in business-related terms
3. Information structuring skills similar to those required in the information (or library) science field
4. Web-searching skills, with proficiency in advanced query facilities of key discovery resources
5. Relational database design and implementation skills, sufficient to create and populate a single-user desktop database
6. Medium-level programming skills, including knowledge of desktop GUI development tools
7. Other skills as required, cultivated through a healthy curiosity about the technology and guided firmly by a sense of business priorities

Given these requirements, the position of information analyst should be a highly paid one, possibly supplemented with incentives based on real business savings. This person should report to the group responsible for the data warehouse.

6.3.2 Career Opportunities for Research Librarians

People experienced in the traditional library science field have an opportunity to apply their skills in Web farming. This is especially true of research librarians (who can brave the turbulent business environment) and information brokers (who can scale their activities to an enterprise context).

6.3.3 Career Opportunities for Intelligence Analysts

In a similar fashion, people experienced in the traditional intelligence fields have an opportunity to apply their skills in Web farming. A creative analyst with several years of experience in political or military intelligence would be an excellent candidate for a Web analyst position. These individuals bring an acute sense for probing beneath the surface and for linking together diverse facts. At a conference for intelligence analysts, this opportunity did not escape the attention of the conference organizers:

> INTELLIGENCE ANALYSTS = INFORMATION ANALYSTS...
> whose functional role is no different than analysts in any large services industry. They must rapidly gather, manipulate, understand, and use large volumes of information, just as information workers do in, for example, banking, finance, health, real estate, insurance, education, travel, etc. All these information analysts live in a revolutionary world of technological progress that enables the processing, storing, retrieving and communicating of information, in whatever form, unconstrained by distance, time, and volume. It is this progress that adds huge new capacities to information production, and, paradoxically, makes the job of analysis much more difficult. In this new world, information analysts are expected to match the pace and scope of their analysis and production to the dynamics of the business they are in, or in the case of the information analysts in the intelligence community, to the pace of the policymakers' and warfighters' needs. [2]

6.4 Business Opportunities with Web Farming

Until now, our discussion of Web farming has been from the perspective of a technical group performing this service for its organization. This section takes a different perspective. If you believe that Web farming will be a significant market driver, what are the business opportunities that will emerge with this new technology direction? In other words, how can you make money in the emerging Web farming business?

If we survey the spectrum of activities involved with a successful Web farming implementation, we see that the following roles are critical:

- Content provider
- System integrator
- Tool developer
- Education provider

---

2. See http://www.odci.gov/ic/aipa97/aipa.htm; from an Advanced Information Processing and Analysis Symposium in 1997.

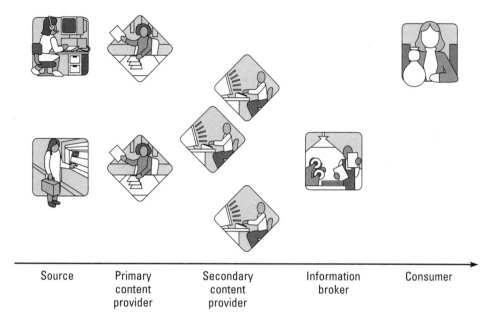

Source   Primary   Secondary   Information   Consumer
          content   content   broker
          provider   provider

Figure 6-3 Types of Content Providers

6.4.1 Content Provider

The first thing required for successful Web farming is a solid network of content providers. If information about a critical external factor is unavailable, out of date, usually inaccurate, not sufficiently detailed, and so forth, the Web farming system will be infected with the classic "Garbage In, Garbage Out" syndrome.

There is a complex network through which content flows from source to consumer, as shown in Figure 6-3. In this network, there are three types of content providers:

1. *Primary content providers:* Collect and distribute source data.
2. *Secondary content providers:* Integrate and resell data from primary providers.
3. *Information brokers:* Analyze and compile data on request.

Figure 6-3 shows the value chain for content providers, from the business transactions that generate source data to the consumer of data. On the left, data is collected from various sources. In most business transactions today, there are point-of-sale devices that are capturing data at a detailed level. From banking to grocery stores, detailed data is being collected, moment by moment, every business day. The classic story of the SABRE system of American Airlines echoes the fact that information

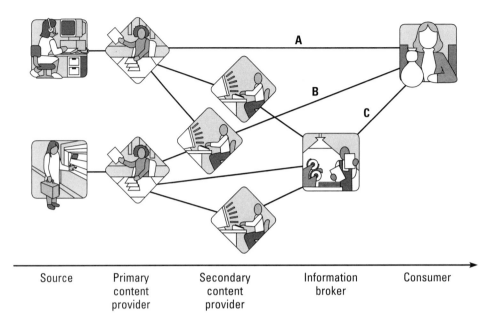

| Source | Primary content provider | Secondary content provider | Information broker | Consumer |

Figure 6-4   Value-Added Chain for Content Providers

collected in the course of doing business may become more valuable than the core business itself.

The *primary content provider* is a vendor that collects source data directly from its operations and resells the data. In the past, this organization kept this data to itself; however, with Web technology and growing information consumerism, there is a business opportunity to become a provider of this source data. Current examples are newspapers and magazines that consider their printed materials to be their core business. Most are now offering their content via Web sites, using various business models (e.g., free with ads, subscription, or fee for use).

The future of primary content providers is very favorable, because every business generates source data and marketing and distributing the data becomes easier every month.

The *secondary content provider* is a vendor that collects and integrates data from other content providers. Online database providers, such as DIALOG,[3] are classic examples of secondary content providers offering access to hundreds of databases dating back 10 years or more. This group of providers are rapidly redesigning their business with Web technology for global access. However, they are struggling against sacrificing their current revenue streams by launching themselves into new business models.

The *information broker* is a service provider that understands the business problem for a client and gathers data on a customized basis for that problem.

---

3.   See http://www.dialog.com/.

Except for service bureaus of the larger online database providers, the business of information broker has been a cottage industry composed of independent consultants. The service is usually performed on a one-time basis, by request. From the Web farming perspective, the business of the information broker can be greatly enlarged. From warehouse schema design to catalogs of monitored Web targets to continuous data pipes, information brokers have an opportunity to contribute to the Web farming effort.

Figure 6-4 shows three ways of delivering content to the consumer. The **A** path is for the consumer to obtain it directly from the primary content provider. For instance, you can access the EDGAR database[4] of the SEC to find quarterly financials on a specific company. The **B** path is for the consumer to obtain information from a secondary content provider that has added value to the original source data. For example, you can access EDGAR-Online[5] for a structured report with comparison and trend graphics of the same quarterly financials. The **C** path is for the consumer to work through an information broker, who taps into several sources to compile a customized report on the same company's financial performance.

6.4.2 System Integrator

The *system integrator* is a service provider who integrates the diverse set of technologies required for Web farming and delivers an integrated system to the client. The traditional system integrators (such as EDS, Arthur Anderson, CTP, IBM, and Lockheed Martin) are stressing data warehousing as a growth area. It would be a small conceptual step for them to expand into Web farming.

A side business for some system integrators is the outsourcing of information processing. In the cases in which their current outsourcing contracts involve data warehousing, these firms can enlarge their responsibilities to provide Web farming for their clients as well.

6.4.3 Tool Developer

The *tool developer* is a software vendor who develops and markets tools for Web farming. A critical problem in implementing Web farming today is the lack of tools that integrate the various functions. In particular, the following tools for Web farming are needed:

- *Integrated discovery environment:* Common workbench (i.e., enhanced browsers) to share control and content data among a group of Web analysts
- *Acquisition server:* Variation of a well-designed Web crawler whose acquisition patterns are controlled by a common database of Web targets

---

4. See http://www.sec.gov/edgarhp.htm.
5. See http://www.edgar-online.com/.

- *Selection/Extraction agent:* Background process that periodically selects content from Web targets, extracts specific fields, and validates the results
- *Information visualizer:* Tool that analyzes a collection of hypertext objects and displays the results in a well-conceived visual representation

6.4.4 Education Provider

Finally, the Education Provider designs and delivers educational or training materials and events related to Web farming. This market has become quite profitable owing to the rapid turnover in technology skills. The renewal of your technical concepts and skills is essential to remaining viable in today's IT industry. Certainly, Web farming is a technology that introduces new concepts and skills, requiring educational services beyond the ordinary.

This chapter has dealt with the management issues involved with Web farming, from selling the idea to suggesting organizational designs and then to defining the Web analyst position. The chapter concluded with the business opportunities that arise from Web farming, ranging from the role of content providers to that of tool developers.

## Part Three

Cultivating the Plants

## Chapter Seven

Standards

It is important for the farmer to set standards and then measure his produce by those standards. Those standards can guide his work and enhance his ability to collaborate with others. Likewise, Web farming is highly dependent on an emerging set of standards. Web farmers must know those standards and be involved with their evolution.

This chapter discusses the various standards that support the infrastructure for Web farming. The first section covers the TCP/IP protocols and the markup languages (with sample code) that make up the core of Web technology. The next section deals with the messy issues of standardizing metadata—a critical concern for Web farming. The last section discusses the standards groups that influenced the previous Web standards.

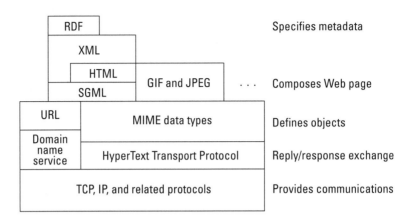

Figure 7-1   Layers (and Layers) of Protocols

7.1 Web Protocols

This section covers the various Web protocols that are of special interest for Web farming.[1] We start at the bottom, with the basic communication protocols, and move toward higher-level protocols, as shown in Figure 7-1.

The Transmission Control Protocol (TCP), the Internet Protocol (IP), and other related protocols form the foundation. The HyperText Transport Protocol (HTTP) and the Multipurpose Internet Mail Extensions (MIME) data types define the data formats that flow between a client and a server. The Uniform Resource Locator (URL) and its associated domain-name service provide unique identification of Web resources. The HyperText Markup Language (HTML, which is based on SGML), along with graphical images (in GIF and JPEG encodings), composes a Web page to be rendered by a Web browser on the screen in all its glory. Finally, the Extensible Markup Language (XML) and the Resource Definition Framework (RDF, also based on SGML) are emerging protocols for defining the structure of data.

Note that the diagram in Figure 7-1 resembles the Open Systems Interconnection (OSI) Seven-Layer Architecture and, in fact, can be mapped in part to that architecture.

7.1.1 TCP/IP Protocol Suite

It seems ironic that with all the current fuss about the Web, it owes its existence to a U.S. military project in the mid-1970s. The Defense Advanced Research Projects Agency (DARPA) funded packet-switched networking, resulting in the original ARPANET around 1979. Primarily through free university involvement (and on the

---

1. For further information on Web protocols, see Yahoo:Data Formats for a current listing of Web resources.

Frustration with 24 x 7 Processing

Mark joined the group as the system administrator for business intelligence. With some help from the networking people, Mark installed an NT server with BackOffice and connected it directly into a dedicated ISDN line to a local ISP. He was careful to configure the proxy firewall to allow only TCP/IP traffic generated by specific NT services. By configuring the Verify search engine, Mark also initiated periodic probing of 20 to 30 hot Web sites, along with an email news feed from Quote.Com on 20 key companies. It took a full month (and considerable frustration) to get the operation stabilized. "It's funny how hundreds of little things bite you when you least expect it," lamented Mark.

Next installment is on page 195.

---

backs of many graduate-student slaves), the networking protocol and its ARPANET implementation grew in coverage and robustness, resulting in TCP/IP. Among technology historians, a study that contrasts TCP/IP evolution with the ISO Open Systems Interconnect (OSI) protocol (which has not been commercially successful) can stimulate intense debates.

TCP/IP is actually a broad suite of protocols dominated by the Transmission Control Protocol (TCP) and the Internet Protocol (IP). The shorthand term TCP/IP combines their designations.

The TCP protocol provides the base of a packet-switched (or connectionless) delivery of packets. It is full-duplex, meaning that data can flow in both directions at the same time. In addition, the delivery of a packet is reliable in that transmission errors are automatically detected and corrected without program (or user) involvement.

The IP protocol provides the ability to interconnect "universally" any pair of computers, even though the computers may not be on the same physical network. IP enables the routing of packets from one network to another that eventually arrive at the destination computer. This universal interconnection is the essential capability that has allowed the Internet to expand to a global scale. Each new computer that is connected somewhere to the Internet now has the ability to communicate with any of the millions of other computers on the Internet.

The addressing scheme of IP is the key to this global scale. A 32-bit binary value uniquely identifies each computer (or host) connected to the Internet; it is called an *IP address.* This address is usually displayed as four integers separated by periods (e.g., 123.34.45.2). The integers represent the four bytes of the IP address and thus each has a value between 0 to 255. A clever scheme is used to partition the IP address into a specific net identifier (NETID) and an identifier for a specific host on that net (HOSTID). Gateways that route packets from one network to another use the net identifier to efficiently perform this routing.

As amazing as it may seem, we are running out of IP addresses on the Internet. One would think that 4,294,967,296 (or 2^{32}) unique addresses would be enough for the entire planet. However, the partitioning scheme, along with expanded functions for multicasting and the like, is creating pressure for a movement to a new form of IP addressing (known as *IPv6I*) that is based on a longer address field.

7.1.2 HyperText Transfer Protocol

HyperText Transfer Protocol or (HTTP)[2] is described in the RFC recommendation as

> an application-level protocol for distributed, collaborative, hypermedia information systems. It is a generic, stateless, object-oriented protocol which can be used for many tasks, such as name servers and distributed object management systems, through extension of its request methods. A feature of HTTP is the typing and negotiation of data representation, allowing systems to be built independently of the data being transferred.[3]

In other words, HTTP is a simple protocol, layered on TCP/IP, that supports a rich hypertext (with graphics) exchange of data between a Web server and a Web browser. Without HTTP, there would be no World Wide Web. HTTP is a recent addition to Internet protocols, joining its older cousins such as electronic mail (SMTP), discussion groups (the Usenet), file transfer (FTP), and information search (ARCHIE, GOPHER, WAIS).

HTTP is a simple protocol in that it has only three methods (or verbs) for requesting a Web object, along with the appropriate responses to those methods. The main methods are:

1. GET: To retrieve a Web page
2. HEAD: To retrieve header information about a page
3. POST: To send bulk data to be stored on the server

When a browser requests a Web page, the browser opens a TCP connection (or socket) to the Web server on the proper port (usually 80). Then the browser issues the following HTTP command:

```
GET /pub/MyProject/status.html HTTP/1.0
```

---

2. See http://www.w3.org/pub/WWW/Protocols/.
3. See http://www.ics.uci.edu/pub/ietf/http/rfc2068.txt.

It is interesting to note that this command passes as plain text to the Web server, in the tradition of UNIX architecture. The Web server then returns a response containing an error code and Web content (if successful), such as the following:

```
HTTP/1.0 200 OK
Date: Fri, 23 Sep 1998 13:34:56 GMT
Content-Type: text/html
Content-Length: 2345

<html>
```

... and so on.

The various HTTP response codes (including the one shown in the first line) are given in Table 7-1. You may have seen a few 403 and 404 responses in the course of your Web browsing. For further details, see the RFC specification[4] for HTTP/1.0 and an informative HTTP guide.[5]

A little-known secret is that Telnet (a standard UNIX program) allows you to interact "manually" with a Web server. You don't need a fancy Web browser after all!

Table 7-1 HTTP Response Codes

Code	Explanation
200	OK
201	Created
202	Accepted
204	No Content
301	Moved Permanently
302	Moved Temporarily
304	Not Modified
400	Bad Request
401	Unauthorized
403	Forbidden
404	Not Found
500	Internal Server Error
501	Not Implemented
502	Bad Gateway
503	Service Unavailable

---

4. See http://www.ics.uci.edu/pub/ietf/http/rfc1945.html.
5. See http://www.jmarshall.com/easy/http/.

For instance, following the hyperlink telnet://www.bolder.com:80/ will invoke the Telnet program and open a socket to the Bolder Technology Web site. You should enable local echoing to display your typing. You can now enter some HTTP statements, followed by a blank line. Try "HEAD /index.html HTTP/1.0" to obtain the header information on the main Web page.

The art of using HTTP to explore the Web is amazingly complex. Web crawlers (as discussed in Chapter 8, Tools) are programs that efficiently and politely explore the Web hyperlink structure, gathering content related to specific criteria. These programs are enough to keep most egocentric programmers quite humble.

It is important to note that HTTP is a stateless protocol, implying that each request is considered to be the same "state" as any other by the Web server. In other words, each Web request is treated as the first and only one, independent of any other request from the same person. For simple informational browsing, this limitation is not a problem. However, it is a problem for a complex series of actions that must be treated as a single unit (e.g., a business transaction for electronic commerce). Various mechanisms (such as the use of "cookies") are used to add state-tracking functionality on top of the HTTP exchange.

7.1.3 Uniform Resource Locator

The basic element for linking together Web objects is the *Uniform Resource Locator,*[6] or *URL.* The URL is an address (pointer or link) for any Web resource, based on the location of that resource. A resource can be a Web page, an image file, a section within a Web page, or many other types of Web object.[7]

The URL is one type of *Uniform Resource Identifier* (URI), which is based on specifying the location. For instance, using a URL is like saying "the occupant of 123 South Main Street, Anytown, Colorado 80345 USA," rather than saying "John Q. Smith, Jr." Both identifiers may refer to the same person at some point in time. However, if Mr. Smith moves his residence, the postal address may then refer to a vacant house or to a different occupant. The location dependence of the URL is both its strength and its weakness for retrieving Web resources. As we will discuss in a later section, the Uniform Resource Name (URN) is another type of URI that attempts to overcome this potential problem of location dependence.

The general format[8] for a URL is

```
<scheme>:<scheme specification>
```

where `<scheme>` is the protocol used to locate the resource and `<scheme specification>` is the way to retrieve the resource using that protocol.

---

6. *Universal* is sometimes incorrectly substituted for *Uniform,* and *Link* is sometimes substituted for *Locator.* However, everyone uses the abbreviation URL in any case.

7. See the later section on MIME types.

8. For details, see Web Naming and Addressing at http://www.w3.org/pub/WWW/Addressing/, Key Specifications of the World Wide Web at http://www.w3.org/Journal/2/, or RFC 1738 (dated December 1994) at http://ds.internic.net/rfc/rfc1738.txt.

The most popular protocol is HTTP to access Web pages, as we will explain later. Other schemes used on the Internet are FTP for file transfers, NEWS for Usenet discussion groups, TELNET to initiate an interactive terminal session, GOPHER for information retrieval, and MAILTO to send email.

For Web pages using HTTP, there are four formats for a URL:

Full

1. `http://<host>.<domain>:<port>/<path>/<filename>`

Relative

2. `<path>/<filename>`

Fragment

3. `http://<host>.<domain>:<port>/<path>/<filename>#<anchor>`

Search

4. `http://<host>.<domain>:<port>/<path>/<procname>?<parms>`

The `<host>` field refers to the specific Web server for the site and is usually WWW for a site that has only one Web server.[9] The `<domain>` field refers to the domain name of the Web site and is described further in the next section. The `<port>` field is the specific TCP/IP socket on which a socket connection should be established. In general, the `<port>` is omitted and assumed to be 80 for HTTP connections. The `<path>` field refers to a subdirectory at the Web site containing the specified Web page. And the `<filename>` field refers to the specific Web page requested and usually has the file extension of HTML.

The first format (Full) is a fully qualified URL for a single Web page. If the path is omitted, the default is the initial (or root) directory of the Web site. If the filename is omitted, the default is the file index.html. Therefore, a URL of http://www.anydomain.com/ actually refers to the index.html file in the root directory of that Web server, while http://www.anydomain.com/docs/new.html refers to the new.html page in the docs subdirectory.

The second format (Relative) is a relative URL that refers to a Web page within the same Web site. It assumes that a base URL was previously specified. For example, a URL of /docs/new.html refers to the same Web page, assuming that the base was properly set to http://www.anydomain.com/.

The third format (Fragment) is a URL that refers to a fragment (or specific section) contained within a Web page. When the browser retrieves that page, it will position the display at the beginning of that fragment. Within the Web page, the HTML A tag with the NAME attribute is used to set the anchor at the proper place. This URL can also use the relative format (the second format). For example, a URL of /docs/new.html#section3 refers to a specific section of the Web page.

---

9. However, larger Web sites may divide their subject matter into subsites using different host names. There is also a growing tendency to omit the host name entirely, as being redundant.

The fourth format (Search) is a URL that is searching a database. It is the same as the first, except for the addition of the dollar sign and <parms>. This format will invoke a procedure <procname> with the parameters <parms> to process a search against some database. Hence, this URL returns a dynamic Web page rather than a static page. In other words, the HTML that is returned to the browser is custom-generated by the procedure for this specific request. So a URL of http://www.anydomain.com/search.cgi?name=hackathorn will invoke the search procedure to find an entry indexed on the name of hackathorn.

This fourth format is particularly important for handling dynamic pages and will be discussed further in the Forms section on the HTML specifications and in Chapter 10, Techniques.

7.1.4 Domain Naming

For Web farming, the critical part of the URL is the domain name. The <domain> field within the URL refers to the name of the organization responsible for the Web site. Technically, the domain name is simply a convenient character string (e.g., bolder.com) that is converted into an IP address (e.g., 205.245.81.159) whenever a browser retrieves a Web page. An elaborate globally distributed database does the matching between domain name and IP address.

The critical part of the URL is the domain name.

A domain name consists of two parts separated by a period. The right-hand portion is the top-level (or root) name and is strictly controlled by the Internet Assigned Numbers Authority. The top-level name is usually a three-letter suffix indicating the type of organization, such as

- COM for commercial companies
- ORG for nonprofit companies
- EDU for educational institutes in North America
- GOV for U.S. government agencies
- INT for international organizations
- MIL for U.S. military organizations
- NET for networking providers

Almost 90% of the registered domain names have COM as their top level. In addition, the top-level domains for countries are

- AD for Andorra
- AE for United Arab Emirates
- AF for Afghanistan

- AG for Antigua and Barbuda
- AI for Anguilla
- AL for Albania
- ... and so forth for a total of 243 countries[10]

For each of these top-level domains, a specific organization is responsible for assigning the second-level domain.[11] The major authorities in the U.S. are InterNIC (through Network Services, Inc.) for the COM, EDU, and NET roots and the Information Sciences Institute[12] of the University of Southern California for U.S. top-level domains.[13] A globally shared domain name registry, called the Internet Council of Registrars[14] (CORE), administers seven new generic top-level domains: FIRM, SHOP, WEB, ARTS, REC, INFO, and NOM. CORE is based in Switzerland and has 89 registrars in 23 countries.

> *Web farmers should watch carefully how the new* INFO
> *top-level domains are administered by CORE.*

7.1.5 Uniform Resource Name

A Uniform Resource Name (URN) is the second type of Uniform Resource Identifier, the first being the URL described above. In contrast to a URL, a URN is an identifier for a Web resource for which there is an "institutional commitment to persistence and availability."[15] The URN specification is still evolving, although all agree on its importance.

The disadvantage of URL addressing is that it is based on the location of a Web object, rather than its content. Remember the postal example, in which a person was *located* by an address, rather than *identified* by a Social Security Number. There is no guarantee that a specific Web object will be there (or that the same version of it will be there) when you need it in the future. In fact, the prevalence of broken URL links is probably the greatest challenge to storing Web content within a database. It forces the hard choice between storing a URL link to a Web object or storing the entire content of the Web object. In particular, this book contains many URL links. How many of these will be valid just a few months after publication?

---

10. See http://www.ics.uci.edu/pub/websoft/wwwstat/country-codes.txt for a complete listing of top-level country codes.
11. See http://www.uninett.no/navn/domreg.html for the organization responsible for assigning a specific top-level domain.
12. See http://www.isi.edu/.
13. See http://www.isi.edu/in-notes/usdnr/ for information on U.S. top-level domains.
14. See http://www.core.gtld-mou.org/. Also see http://www.gtld-mou.org/ for a general explanation of the Generic Top-Level Domain Memorandum of Understanding.
15. See http://www.w3.org/Addressing/ for general information on Web naming and addressing.

An article by Michael Mealling[16] highlights the tough problem of "naming" Web objects, as opposed to specifying their locations. This is especially true of objects that are time-dependent, such as weather maps or stock prices.

The syntax for a URN is

```
URN:<UID>:<qualifying string>
```

where <UID> is the name-space controlled by some authorized organization. For example, consider the identification of a published work (which has not been standardized yet) as

```
URN:ISBN:1-23456-789-0
```

This URN would be interpreted by the authority assigning ISBN numbers. The interpretation could be a bibliographic citation, or the contents of a specific book, or the procedure for obtaining the book, and so on.

Compatible with the evolving URN specifications, the Online Computer Library Center (OCLC) has supported a free service for a Persistent Uniform Resource Locator (PURL).[17] Instead of pointing directly to a Web resource, a PURL (which is actually a normal URL) points to a resolution service that returns the real URL as a standard HTTP redirect.

The emergence of the URN specification is an important area to monitor for Web farming. The best resource centers are the IEFT working group for URN[18] and the InterNIC News.[19]

7.1.6   MIME Data Types

Multipurpose Internet Mail Extensions, or MIME, were created to specify the characteristics of email attachments and has been broadened for use with Web pages. Each Web file is described by a specific MIME content type. The initial file for a Web page is of MIME type text/html, implying that it is plain text containing HTML. Most of the visual content of a Web page is supplied by separate graphics files of MIME type image/gif or image/jpeg.

The major MIME types are text, image, audio, video, and application. When combined with a subtype, a variety of MIME types are in use on the Web. Examples of the popular MIME types are shown in Table 7-2.

The assignment of MIME types is controlled by the Internet Assigned Numbers Authority (IANA) to avoid conflicts. MIME subtypes beginning with *x-* are not registered with IANA, and their interpretation is dependent upon the browser.

---

16. M. Mealling, Where in the World Is That Resource?, *InterNIC News,* December 1997, http://rs.internic.net/nic-support/nicnews/dec97/urn.html.
17. See http://purl.oclc.org/.
18. See http://www.ietf.org/html.charters/urn-charter.html.
19. See http://rs.internic.net/nic-support/nicnews.

Table 7-2 MIME Types

MIME Type	File Extension	Description
text/html	html,htm	HyperText Markup Language
text/plain	txt,text	plain ASCII text
image/gif	gif	CompuServe graphic interchange format
image/jpeg	jpeg,jpg	Joint Photographic Experts Group (ISO/IEC 10918)
image/tiff	tif,tiff	Tagged Image File Format
audio/au	au,snd	Sun/Next sound format
audio/x-pn-realaudio	ra,ram	Progressive Networks' Real-Audio format
video/mpeg	mpg,mpeg	Motion Picture Experts Group (another ISO group)
video/quicktime	mov	Apple Quicktime
application/postscript	ps	Adobe Postscript
application/rtf	rtf	Microsoft Rich Text Format
application/pdf	pdf	Adobe Portable Document Format for Acrobat
application/msword	doc	Microsoft Word format
application/zip	zip	PkWare compression format for PKUNZIP
application/wav	wav	Microsoft Windows sound for Media Player

MIME content types for Web files are rapidly proliferating, especially within the application/x category. Browsers now support an open-ended capability to invoke the proper "helper" or plug-in application to view and process the specific content type.

7.1.7 HyperText Markup Language

HyperText Markup Language, or HTML, is the language used for constructing Web pages. The initial idea was quite simple. Take some text, intersperse a few formatting commands, add some graphics, and then display (or render) the Web page on the screen.

The formatting commands, called *tags*, use angle brackets as delimiters and resemble some ancient cryptic computer language. Actually, HTML does come from such a heritage. HTML is a greatly simplified subset of the Standard Generalized Markup Language (SGML).[20] Derived from the Graphic Communication Association's (GCA) GenCode and IBM's Generalized Markup Language in the 1960s, SGML was conceived for production editing and printing of complex documents. SGML became ISO Standard 8879 in 1986 and has a strong international following.

---

20. See The SGML Web Page and ISO 8879:1986.

In the early days of HTML, we used a simple text editor to create a Web page, as shown below. Save this text file with an HTML extension, load it onto a Web server, and a new Web site has come into existence.

```
<HTML>

<HEAD>
<TITLE>A Good Descriptive Title</TITLE>
... other head elements
</HEAD>

<BODY>
... a document body that is rendered on the screen
</BODY>

</HTML>
```

The structure of a typical Web page consists of a HEAD section followed by a BODY section, both of which are bracketed between matching HTML tags. The HEAD section describes the page—its base location, keywords, author, and so on. The BODY section conveys the content of the pages, with text, images, and links arranged in some fashion. Various formatting tags specify the layout, such as header lines, spacing, fonts, type sizes, paragraph breaks, and so forth. Further descriptions of HTML can be found in numerous books and at the World Wide Web Consortium (W3C) site.[21]

Over the past few years, this language has evolved in complexity. A wide spectrum of tools is now used to edit HTML. The language specification is entering the HTML 4.0 version[22] by recommendation of W3C. This version includes advanced forms, in-line frames, enhanced tables, object support, scripts, style sheets, and multilingual markup. In addition, Microsoft and others have proposed extensions (called *dynamic HTML*) to allow direct control of HTML tag parameters through a common object model.

For Web farming, most of the HTML specifications are of little interest, since their emphasis is on rendering a Web page on the screen. In Web farming, we just want the facts—nothing pretty!

The areas of HTML that are important to Web farming are

- Hyperlink anchor using the A tag
- Form template using the FORM, INPUT, SELECT, and related tags
- Document meta-information using the META tag

---

21. Basic specifications for HTML can be retrieved from
    http://www.ncsa.uiuc.edu/General/Internet/WWW/HTMLPrimer.html, and detailed specifications
    are located at http://www.w3.org/MarkUp/.
22. See http://www.w3.org/TR/REC-html40 for the full HTML 4.0 specifications.

7.1.8 HTML Anchor Tags

The anchor (or A) tag refers to other Web pages, thus supporting the important hypertext, or "webbing," capability. A person browsing through a Web page can link to a variety of other Web sites by clicking on the anchor tags on that page.

An example of the anchor tag is the following:

```
<A HREF="http://www.anydomain.com/chapter5.html">Chapter Five</A>
```

When rendered by a browser, the text *Chapter Five* will be displayed in a different color and underlined. A single click on this text will take you to the `chapter5.html` Web page at the anydomain.com site. The URL as the value for the `HREF` attribute can be in any of the formats described above.

7.1.9 HTML FORM Templates

The form template uses the FORM tag along with several other tags. As an example, consider the welcome page for Yahoo! Finance,[23] shown here.

Embedded in the source of this Web page are the following HTML statements:

begins the FORM tag
```
<form method=get action="/q">
```

specifies a text field
```
<input type=text size=25 name=s>
```

specifies a push button
```
<input type=submit value="Get Quotes">
```

specifies a pull-down list containing these values
```
<select name=d>
<option value=f selected>Basic
<option value=t>Detailed
<option value=1y>Chart
<option value=r>Research
```

---

23. See http://quote.yahoo.com/.

ends pull-down list
```
</select>
```
ends the FORM tag
```
</form>
```

The initial FORM tag specifies a method of GET implying a simple retrieval (rather than an update) from a database. The action is /q, implying that the procedure invoked is the Q procedure. The first INPUT tag specifies the parameter S, which is a text field with a maximum of 25 characters. The second INPUT tag displays a button with the label *Get Quotes*. The SELECT and OPTION tags display a pull-down list specifying a second parameter, D, that is limited to a set of four values (*f, t, 1y,* or *r*).

If the user enters **intc** to retrieve the Intel stock price and pushes the Get Quotes button, the URL http://quote.yahoo.com/q?s=intc&d=f is generated, resulting in the display shown here:

Wed Oct 29 10:53AM Eastern U.S. Time -- U.S. Markets close in 5 hours 7 minutes.

Symbol	Last Trade		Change		Volume	More Info
INTC	10:37AM	$82\,^1/_4$	$2\,^{11}/_{16}$	-3.16%	13,209,900	Chart, News, Profile, Research, SEC Filings

7.1.10   HTML META Tags

The document meta-information uses the META tag to specify characteristics of the Web page, such as author, keywords, copyright, expiration, language, and so on. An example[24] from the HTML 4.0 specifications is as follows:

```
<HEAD profile="http://www.acme.com/profiles/core">
  <TITLE>How to complete Memorandum cover sheets</TITLE>
  <META name="author" content="John Doe">
  <META name="copyright" content="&copy; 1997 Acme Corp.">
  <META name="keywords" content="corporate,guidelines,cataloging">
  <META name="date" content="1994-11-06T08:49:37+00:00">
  <META scheme="ISBN" name="identifier" content="1-23456-789-0">
</HEAD>
```

The last META tag uses the SCHEME attribute to further qualify the name/content pair, as we described in the discussion of URNs.

7.1.11   Extensible Markup Language

The *Extensible Markup Language* (*XML*) is an emerging standard of the W3C for structuring data on the Web. The objective of XML is to give a context for exchanging data that has not been predefined between the parties involved. It is like

---

24. See the META specification at http://www.w3.org/TR/REC-html40/.

exchanging information about your alphabet and vocabulary before conversing with a person who speaks a different language.

An Example

Remember the scene from the movie *Close Encounters of the Third Kind* in which the problem was to find a language in which to communicate with aliens? In that situation, a series of musical notes was used. If they had agreed to XML, the data exchange would have been much easier...

XML is a cousin of HTML and is based on a simplified subset of SGML (less than one tenth the size). However, XML retains the rigor of SGML for extensibility, structuring, and validation. Each Document Type Definition (DTD) file defines the names of its unique tags, their structures, and their contents. The structure of each XML file is based on a complementary DTD like that in SGML. One can think of the DTD as functioning like an Interface Definition Language (IDL) specification or a relational database schema. Each XML file must specify a separate DTD file in its header or include the entire DTD within itself, so that self-description is enforced.

Several firms (such as ArborText with ADEPT,[25] Inso with DynaBase,[26] and Microsoft) are already offering tools to validate and generate XML as extensions of HTML development environments. As XML comes into widespread use, the market for XML tools will rapidly grow.

By using XML as the context, communities of organizations or individuals who are interested in exchanging the same kind of data can agree on the set of required and optional tags for their particular XML vocabulary or dialects. Several vertical industries (such as automobile manufacturing, pharmaceuticals, telecommunications, and aerospace) are designing XML vocabularies. Examples of XML vocabularies for other information-exchange communities are

- Open Financial Exchange (OFE) for transactions using personal finance software
- Microsoft Channel Definition Format (CDF) for describing content of Web sites
- Netscape's Meta-Content Format (MCF)
- Chemical Markup Language (CML)
- Mathematical Markup Language (MathML)
- Open Software Description (OSD) for delivering and maintaining software applications via the Web
- Resource Description Framework (RDF), described in the next section

---

25. See http://www.arbortext.com/70rlease2.html.
26. See http://www.inso.com/frames/consumer/db/index.htm.

An example of XML used for defining a Web channel (in CDF) is given in a document by Michael Edwards, "XML: Data the Way You Want It."[27] It shows the paired tags that define various subattributes of the CHANNEL object, such as a schedule for updating its contents.

```
<?XML version="1.0"?>
<CHANNEL HREF="http://www.microsoft.com/xml/sample/homepage.htm"
    BASE="http://www.microsoft.com/xml/sample/">
    <TITLE>Sample "Color" Channel</TITLE>
    <ABSTRACT>This channel contains a red, green,
        and blue page for viewing.</ABSTRACT>
    <LOGO HREF="logo_big.gif" STYLE="IMAGE-WIDE"/>
    <LOGO HREF="logo_med.gif" STYLE="IMAGE"/>
    <SCHEDULE STARTDATE="1997-09-23">
        <INTERVALTIME DAY="1" />
        <EARLIESTTIME HOUR="2" />
        <LATESTTIME HOUR="6" />
    </SCHEDULE>
    <ITEM HREF="page1.htm">
        <LOGO HREF="red.gif" STYLE="ICON"/>
        <TITLE>The Red Page</TITLE>
        <ABSTRACT>This is the abstract description for the red page.</ABSTRACT>
    </ITEM>
 . . .
    <ITEM HREF="scrnsave.htm">
        <USAGE VALUE="ScreenSaver"></USAGE>
    </ITEM>
</CHANNEL>
```

Currently, W3C is moving XML through its standards process as a W3C recommendation. The motivation to reach closure on the formal XML specifications is very strong. Connolly and others wrote, in "The Evolution of Web Documents: The Ascent of XML," the following assessment of XML's presence in the marketplace:

> If it seems that XML is moving very fast, look again. The community is moving very fast to exploit XML, but the momentum against changes to XML itself is tremendous. XML is not a collection of new ideas; it is a selection of tried-and-true ideas.[28]

The use of XML in Web farming can enable analysts in their role as "data archaeologists," as Khare and Rifkin muse in "Capturing the State of Distributed Systems with XML":

> "Data Archaeologist" smacks of postmodernism gone awry, but the business of rummaging through now-forgotten tapes of healthcare

---

27. See http://www.microsoft.com/xml/xmldata.htm.
28. D. Connolly et al., "The Evolution of Web Documents: The Ascent of XML" in XML: Principles, Tools, and Techniques, *World Wide Web Journal*, vol. 2, issue 4, Fall 1997. Collection of papers on XML from O'Reilly, http://www.w3j.com/.

records or satellite observations for archival data is already a viable industry.[29]

Our discussion of XML will continue in the section "Resource Description Framework," below.

7.2 Metadata Standards

Metadata is data that describes other data. The distinction is relative. As a popular saying goes, "one application's metadata is another application's data"—a situation often repeated in many areas of computer science. Therefore, the content of data and the description of data should have the same uniform representation. If a standard for exchanging metadata existed, dissimilar programs could exchange complex sets of data—as in Web farming. Note that this is unlike the relational data model, which has two distinct levels for data description and data instances.

This section continues the discussion of standards for Web farming by looking at ways of specifying metadata about Web resources. The ability to handle metadata is critical to Web farming. Further evolution and widespread use of the conventions described in this section can elevate Web resources from being *machine-readable* to being *machine-understandable.*[30] Web farming requires a mechanism for attaching precise meanings to Web resources, both for information discovery and for information commerce.

For more information on current work involving metadata standards, check the following:

- IFLA Metadata Resources for Digital Libraries[31]—excellent!
- Judy and Magda's List of Metadata Initiatives at the University of Michigan[32]
- IEEE Metadata Information Sources,[33] hosted at the Lawrence Livermore National Laboratory
- EPA Scientific Metadata Standards Project[34]

---

29. R. Khare and A. Rifkin, "Capturing the State of Distributed Systems with XML" in XML: Principles, Tools, and Techniques, *World Wide Web Journal,* vol. 2, issue 4, Fall 1997. Collection of papers on XML from O'Reilly, http://www.w3j.com/.
30. Quote taken from Introduction to RDF Metadata at http://www.w3.org/TR/NOTE-rdf-simple-intro.
31. See http://www.nlc-bnc.ca/ifla/II/metadata.htm.
32. See http://www-personal.umich.edu/~jaheim/alcts/bibacces.htm.
33. See http://www.llnl.gov/liv_comp/metadata/.
34. See http://www.lbl.gov/~olken/epa.html.

7.2.1 ANSI/NISO Z39.50-1995

The Z39.50 Information Retrieval standard is not well known outside the library science field. As a reaction to the growing incompatibility of retrieval systems for library card categories, an effort was started in the 1970s to allow a researcher to query text databases and process the results in a standard manner. The main contribution of Z39.50 is its content semantics, based on the legacy of the library science discipline of managing bibliographic references.

Z39.50 went through a series of approved standards with ANSI and NISO, the National Information Standards Organization, which is accredited by ANSI to manage standards for libraries and publishers. The latest standard is officially the ANSI/NISO Z39.50-1995 Information Retrieval (Z39.50): Application Service Definition and Protocol Specification, or simply Z39.50 Version 3. An effort is being made to secure ISO approval of an international Z39.50 standard, but progress is slow because of language issues.

The Library of Congress is the "maintenance agency" and maintains a resource site on the Z39.50 standard, containing the specification document, changes, implementations, articles, tutorials, and so on.[35] For more details on the evolution of Z39.50, see the "Strategic View" article by Clifford Lynch in *D-Lib.*[36]

The standard is a simple client-server architecture in which a researcher at the client (Origin) enters a query through some (undefined) user interface. The query is translated into the Z39.50 protocol, and a connection is established to the server (Target). The results are returned in a standard protocol and displayed to the researcher in an appropriate format. The Z39.50 specification covers only a single connection from one Origin (client) to one Target (server).

The Z39.50 standard was initially created on the OSI framework and assumed an OSI network implementation. OSI is a well-conceived (though voluminous) international standard, but it never achieved market viability; TCP/IP now dominates the field. A Z39.50 variation is defined for use over TCP/IP as RFC 1729,[37] but this use is not part of the ANSI standard.

The Wide Area Information System (WAIS) supports a variant of the Z39.50 protocol. To get a feeling for Z39.50 usage, try a few bibliography queries via telnet to a WAIS server.

7.2.2 Dublin Core and Warwick Framework

The Dublin Core[38] is an evolving specification for a 15-element set that is roughly equivalent to a catalog card for electronic resources. Its purpose is to facilitate discovery of Web resources across various disciplines globally by improving descriptions of

---

35. See http://lcweb.loc.gov/z3950/agency.
36. C.A. Lynch, The Z39.50 Information Retrieval Standard—Part I: A Strategic View of Its Past, Present and Future, *D-Lib Magazine,* April 1997, http://www.dlib.org/dlib/apr97/04lynch.html.
37. See http://www.internic.net/rfc/rfc1729.txt.
38. See http://purl.oclc.org/metadata/dublin_core/.

those resources by authors and library professionals. Building on the MARC[39] specifications for machine-readable bibliographic catalog, the Dublin Core is a selected subset focused on Web resources, rather than printed materials.

Through a series of annual workshops, experts from multiple disciplines and from multiple countries have refined the Dublin Core over the years. In fact, the name *Dublin Core* came from the location of the first workshop, in 1995, in Dublin, Ohio, where OCLC is located.

The focus of the Dublin Core initially is to extend the META tag in the HTML header section (which is greatly enhanced in HTML 4.0). Here is an example of a META tag:

```
<META name="DC.creator" lang="fr" content="Arnaud Le Hors">
<META name="DC.subject" scheme="DDC" content="541.34">
```

The first statement uses the CREATOR element to specify the author, who is writing in French. The second statement uses the SUBJECT element to specify the subject category according to the scheme of the Dewey Decimal Code. A list of the Dublin Core elements is given in Table 7-3.

An effort is also being made to merge the Dublin Core with the Z39.50 standard of ISO and the emerging RDF recommendations of W3C. The ultimate goal of the Dublin Core has been stated as follows:

> In the Internet Commons, disparate description models interfere with the ability to search across discipline boundaries. Promoting a commonly understood set of descriptors that helps to unify other data content standards increases the possibility of semantic interoperability across disciplines. The Dublin Core is the leading candidate as a lingua franca for resource discovery on the Internet.[40]

The 15 elements of the Dublin Core[41] are as shown in Table 7-3. As you may notice, there are active discussions about the formal specifications of several of the elements.

The Warwick Framework, which emerged from the Dublin Core workshops, derived its name from the workshop site in Warwick, U.K. It is an attempt to extend the Dublin Core by nesting a collection of simpler objects (called *packages*) into a larger *container*. This arrangement is shown in Figure 7-2. This nesting mechanism permits the creation of arbitrarily complex objects built from simpler ones. This mechanism evolved into the notion of embedded resources in the RDF specifications, which we will discuss later.

---

39. See http://www.loc.gov/marc/.
40. See http://purl.oclc.org/metadata/dublin_core/.
41. See http://purl.oclc.org/metadata/dublin_core_elements

Table 7-3 Elements of the Dublin Core

Title	The name given to the resource by the creator or publisher.
Creator	The person or organization primarily responsible for creating the intellectual content of the resource. For example, authors in the case of written documents; artists, photographers, or illustrators in the case of visual resources.
Subject	The topic of the resource. Typically, the subject will be expressed in keywords or phrases that describe the subject or content of the resource. The use of controlled vocabularies and formal classification schemas is encouraged.
Description	A textual description of the content of the resource, including abstracts in the case of document-like objects or content descriptions in the case of visual resources.
Publisher	The entity responsible for making the resource available in its present form, such as a publishing house, a university department, or a corporate entity.
Contributor	A person or organization not specified in a creator element who has made significant intellectual contributions to the resource but whose contribution is secondary to that of any person or organization specified in a creator element (for example, editor, transcriber, and illustrator).
Date	The date the resource was made available in its present form. Recommended best practice is an eight-digit number in the form YYYY-MM-DD as defined in the profile of ISO 8601.[*]
Type	The category of the resource, such as home page, novel, poem, working paper, technical report, essay, dictionary. A specific set of values is being formulated, similar to that of the MIME types discussed earlier.[†]
Format	The data format of the resource, used to identify the software and possibly the hardware that might be needed to display or operate the resource. For the sake of interoperability, format should be selected from a list that is under development in the workshop series at the time of publication of this document.
Identifier	String or number used to uniquely identify the resource. Examples for networked resources include URLs and URNs (when implemented). Other globally unique identifiers, such as International Standard Book Numbers (ISBN) or other formal names, would also be candidates for this element in the case of off-line resources.
Source	A string or number used to uniquely identify the work from which this resource was derived, if applicable. For example, a PDF version of a novel might have a source element containing an ISBN number for the physical book.
Language	Language(s) of the intellectual content of the resource. Where practical, the content of this field should coincide with RFC 1766.[‡]

[*]See http://www.w3.org/TR/NOTE-datetime.
[†]See http://sunsite.berkeley.edu/Metadata/types.html.
[‡]See http://ds.internic.net/rfc/rfc1766.txt.

Table 7-3   *(Continued)*

Relation	The relationship of this resource to other resources. The intent of this element is to provide a means to express relationships among resources that have formal relationships to others, but exist as discrete resources themselves—for example, images in a document, chapters in a book, or items in a collection. Formal specification of relation is currently under development.
Coverage	The spatial and/or temporal characteristics of the resource. Formal specification of coverage is currently under development.
Rights	A link to a copyright notice, to a rights-management statement, or to a service that would provide information about terms of access to the resource. Formal specification of rights is currently under development.

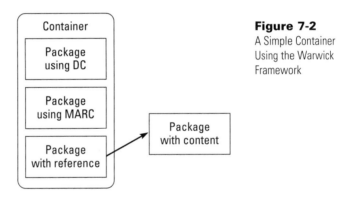

Figure 7-2
A Simple Container Using the Warwick Framework

7.2.3   Metadata Interchange Specifications

Metadata Interchange Specifications (MDIS)[42] is a set of format specifications for the access and interchange of metadata files between data warehousing tools (both for design and for analysis). MDIS was defined by the Metadata Coalition,[43] an industrial consortium founded in October 1995. The Metadata Council, the group's steering committee, includes Arbor Software, Business Objects, Cognos, Evolutionary Technologies International, Platinum Technology, and Intellidex. Membership is open both to vendors and to end users.

As data warehousing becomes a critical function for most enterprises, integrating the variety of tools supporting a common warehouse becomes a major problem.

---

42. See http://www.he.net/~metadata/standards/.
43. See http://www.he.net/~metadata/.

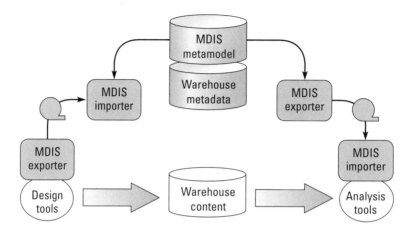

Figure 7-3 Information Flow Using MDIS

MDIS alleviates this problem by providing a common format for exchanging meta-data about the warehouse among tools from various vendors. By adopting the approach of using a simple text file, MDIS specifies a format for file importing and exporting, similar to that of the CASE Data Interchange Format[44] of EIA. Figure 7-3 illustrates the role of the MDIS metamodel: to control the import and export processes. As a demonstration of MDIS, a project was completed using MDIS to import and export typical DW metadata into and out of the Microsoft Repository[45] (which uses the Open Information Model based upon the OMG Unified Modeling Language).[46] The Open Information Model has been extended to describe DW objects.

7.2.4 Open Document Management API

Open Document Management API (ODMA)[47] is a standard developed by the Association for Information and Image Management International (AIIM). Its objective is to provide a common interface for document management systems, thus reducing the effort required to access public and private document stores. The primary creators of this standard are Activedoc Corporation, Adobe Systems, Inc., Arbortext, Inc., Corel, Inc., FileNet Corporation, Lava Systems, Inc., and Motiva Software Corporation.

ODMA is a set of over thirty programming (C++-like) specifications, such as ODMActivate, ODMCloseDoc, ODMGetDMS, ODMGetDMSInfo, ODMGet-

---

44. See http://www.cdif.org/.
45. See http://www.microsoft.com/repository/.
46. See ftp://ftp.omg.org/pub/docs/ad/97-08-02.pdf or use the search engine on the OMG site for all documents related to UML.
47. See http://www.aiim.org/odma/odma.htm.

DMSList, ODMGetDocInfo, and so on. The document identifiers, which are based on a MIME-like concept, are of interest to Web farmers.

An extension to ODMA is an evolving specification for interfacing a document management system to a Web server using the CGI interface.[48] An example of a dynamic URL using this extension is as follows:

```
http://www.foo.com/cgibin/ODMA?METHOD=ODMQueryDMS&ODM_AUTHOR=Mark+Twain
   &ODM_TYPE=Story&MAX_SIZE=300
```

This query retrieves up to 300 document references to stories by Mark Twain. The URL syntax is awkward, but a good FORM design or Java applet could smooth the rough spots.

7.2.5 Resource Description Framework

The Resource Description Framework (RDF)[49] is part of the W3C Metadata Activity.[50] The objective of RDF is to provide interoperability to exchange Web content that is understandable by programs. RDF uses a refined XML vocabulary and leverages the various tools being built around XML.

RDF allows different application communities to define the metadata property set that best serves the needs of each community. As described in a W3C press release,[51] RDF metadata can be used in a variety of application areas:

- In resource discovery to provide better search engine capabilities
- In cataloging for describing the content and content relationships available at a particular Web site, page, or digital library
- By intelligent software agents to facilitate knowledge sharing and exchange
- In content rating for child protection and privacy protection
- In describing collections of pages that represent a single logical "document"
- For describing intellectual property rights related to Web content
- For building webs of trust for electronic commerce using digital signatures

The W3C RDF Working Group consists of major industry players including DVL, Grif, IBM, KnowledgeCite, LANL, Microsoft, Netscape, Nokia, OCLC, Reuters, SoftQuad, and the University of Michigan. The collaborative design effort for RDF originated as an extension on the PICS content description technology.

48. See http://www.aiim.org/odma/interspc.htm.
49. See http://www.w3.org/Metadata/RDF.
50. See http://www.w3.org/Metadata/Activity.html.
51. See http://www.w3.org/Press/RDF.

RDF draws upon the XML design as well as[52]

- XML-Data,[53] CDF,[54] and OSD[55] work by Microsoft
- Meta-Content Framework[56] work by Netscape (formerly by Apple Research)
- Dublin Core and the Warwick Framework (discussed previously)

So what is RDF?

RDF consists of nodes with attached pairs of attribute (or property) and value. A node is any Web resource (as identified by a URI). In other words, a metadata statement in RDF is a labeled directed graph, and RDF is best expressed as such.

In Figure 7-4,[57] nodes as resources are shown as ovals, the arcs are labeled with the attributes, and boxes are simple values. This illustration shows two ways of specifying the author of a Web resource. The top statement indicates that the author is some person identified by the string "Dave Smith"—whether that string is a name, a Social Security Number, or a street address. To express this statement in XML, the directed graph would be "serialized" into the following XML statements:

```
<ASSERTIONS href="http://www. . .">
   <author>Dave Smith</author>
</ASSERTIONS>
```

The RDF statement at the bottom of Figure 7-4 illustrates how the metadata can be extended by adding resources within resources. This process is known as *nesting* or as *containing,* as in the Warwick Framework. The statement states that the author is some resource whose name is "Dave Smith," whose email address is "ds@dom.com," and whose phone number is "123-456-6789." Not only do we know more about the author of the Web resource, we can continue this nesting to add as much information about the author as needed.

This bottom RDF statement would be serialized into XML as follows:

```
<ASSERTIONS href="http://www. . .">
   <author>
     <RESOURCE>
       <name>Dave Smith</name>
       <email>ds@dom.com</email>
       <phone>123-456-6789</phone>
     </RESOURCE>
   </author>
</ASSERTIONS>
```

---

52. See http://www.oclc.org/oclc/press/971107a.htm.
53. See http://www.microsoft.com/standards/xml/xmldata.htm.
54. See http://www.microsoft.com/standards/cdf-f.htm.
55. See http://www.microsoft.com/standards/osd/.
56. See http://www.textuality.com/mcf/MCF-tutorial.html and http://www.textuality.com/mcf/NOTE-MCF-XML.html, both edited by Tim Bray of Textuality based on the HotSauce work of Ramanathan V. Guha at Apple Research (he is now with Netscape).
57. Adapted from http://www.w3.org/TR/WD-rdf.syntax.

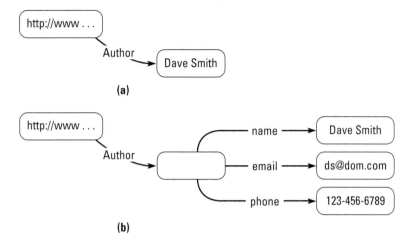

Figure 7-4 Two Simple RDF Statements

The specifications for RDF are under discussion. For the latest status, check the RDF home page[58] at W3C.

To illustrate the extension of RDF into e-commerce and other areas, consider an earlier example from the Microsoft XML-Data document[59] for a sales order:

```
<ORDER>
  <SOLD-TO>
    <PERSON><LASTNAME>Layman</LASTNAME>
            <FIRSTNAME>Andrew</FIRSTNAME>
    </PERSON>
  </SOLD-TO>
  <SOLD-ON>19970317</SOLD-ON>
  <ITEM>
    <PRICE>5.95</PRICE>
    <BOOK>
      <TITLE>Number, the Language of Science</TITLE>
      <AUTHOR>Dantzig, Tobias</AUTHOR>
    </BOOK>
  </ITEM>
  <ITEM>
    <PRICE>12.95</PRICE>
    <BOOK>
      <TITLE>Introduction to Objectivist Epistemology</TITLE>
      <AUTHOR>Rand, Ayn</AUTHOR>
    </BOOK>
  </ITEM>
    . . .
</ORDER>
```

Although this example is now out of date with respect to current RDF work, it is interesting to see how nesting is used to create a complex object (such as ORDER).

---

58. See http://www.w3.org/Metadata/RDF/.
59. See http://www.microsoft.com/standards/xml/xmldata.htm.

By agreeing on an RDF schema, a community of producers and consumers can create a market in which specific types of information can be reliably exchanged. In particular, this community must specify for each attribute its meaning, whether it is required or optional, and its allowable values.

> *By agreeing on an RDF schema, a community of producers and consumers can create a market in which specific types of information can be reliably exchanged.*

7.3 Standards Groups

Many organizations are involved with standards in the Internet arena. The primary ones are IEFT and W3C, with ISOC backing, although the traditional governmental organizations (such as ISO, ANSI, and NIST) play a major role. Finally, the professional societies and industry consortiums also play a role in formulating standards for Web farming.

An article in *Wired* mapped the various standards groups involved with domain naming.[60] Figure 7-5 is a simplification of that article that helps shows how these groups fit together. The point of the figure is the lack of formal relationships among the various standards groups involved with the Web. Although informal cooperation has been excellent in the past, the international and commercial implications will test the viability of these relationships. The current issue is the proper authority for domain naming.

7.3.1 American National Standards Institute

The American National Standards Institute (ANSI)[61] coordinates the U.S. private-sector standardization efforts. ANSI was founded in 1918 by five engineering societies and three government agencies, and remains "a private, nonprofit membership organization supported by a diverse constituency of private and public sector organizations."

7.3.2 Internet Assigned Numbers Authority

The Internet Assigned Numbers Authority (IANA)[62] is the "central coordinator for the assignment of unique parameter values for Internet protocols." IANA is chartered by the Internet Society and the Federal Network Council (FNC) to "act as the

---

60. D. Diamond, Whose Internet Is It, Anyway? *Wired,* April 1998, 172–195.
61. See http://www.ansi.org/.
62. See http://www.isi.edu/div7/iana/.

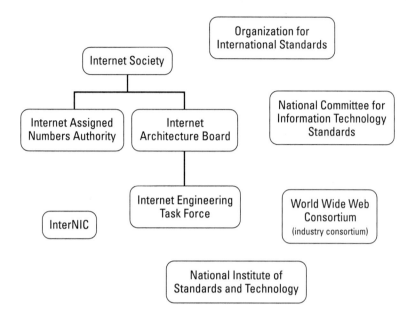

Figure 7-5 Relationships (or Lack Thereof) Among Standards Groups

clearinghouse to assign and coordinate the use of numerous Internet protocol parameters." IANA is located at and operated by the Information Sciences Institute of the University of Southern California.[63] IANA is especially involved with controlling the top-level domains (COM, ORG, etc.) and assigning the U.S. second-level domains (e.g., boulder.co.us).

7.3.3 Internet Engineering Task Force

The Internet Engineering Task Force (IETF)[64] is the development agency responsible for Internet protocols. The IETF is "an open international community of network designers, service providers, vendors, and researchers" concerned with "the evolution of the Internet architecture and the smooth operation of the Internet."

The actual technical work of the IETF is done in its working groups, which are organized by topic into several areas (e.g., routing, transport, and security). The IETF working groups are managed by Area Directors (AD), who are members of the Internet Engineering Steering Group (IESG).[65] The RFC Editor[66] is responsible for preparing and organizing the standards in their final form. Providing architectural oversight is the Internet Architecture Board (IAB),[67] which handles appeals

---

63. See http://www.isi.edu/.
64. See http://www.ietf.org/.
65. See http://www.ietf.org/iesg.html.
66. See http://www.isi.edu/rfc-editor/.

when someone complains that the IESG has failed in its duties. The IAB and IESG are chartered by the Internet Society (ISOC), which promotes the specifications as international standards. The standards may be found at numerous sites distributed throughout the world, such as InterNIC.[68]

7.3.4 Internet Society

The Internet Society (ISOC)[69] is not actually a generator of Web standards. However, ISOC is the major international authority that charters many of the global standards organizations, such as IETF and IANA. See "Professional Societies" section of Chapter 9, Resources, for a more complete description.

7.3.5 InterNIC

InterNIC[70] was established in 1993 as a collaborative project of AT&T, General Atomics, and Network Solutions, Inc. and supported by the U.S. National Science Foundation. The most visible functions of InterNIC are domain name registration and IP network number assignment, as administered by Network Solutions. This role and the execution of this function have been controversial, and a number of proposals are being considered to spread this authority across other organizations. The *InterNIC News*[71] has especially informative material on current Internet standards.

7.3.6 National Committee for Information Technology Standards

The National Committee for Information Technology Standards (NCITS)[72] was formerly known as the Accredited Standards Committee X3, Information Technology, or simply X3. Its objectives are to develop standards for the U.S. and to participate on behalf of the U.S. in the international standards activities of ISO/IEC JTC 1 (Information Technology). This is the group responsible for the standards for SQL3 and C++, among other technology delights.

7.3.7 National Institute of Standards and Technology

The National Institute of Standards and Technology (NIST)[73] was established by Congress "to assist industry in the development of technology . . . needed to improve product quality, to modernize manufacturing processes, to ensure product reliability

---

67. See http://www.iab.org/iab/.
68. See http://ds.internic.net/ds/dspg1intdoc.html.
69. See http://www.isoc.org/.
70. See http://www.internic.net/.
71. See http://rs.internic.net/nic-support/nicnews/.
72. See http://www.x3.org/.
73. See http://www.nist.gov/.

...and to facilitate rapid commercialization...of products based on new scientific discoveries."

The Information Technology Laboratory (ITL)[74] provides "industry with objective, neutral tests of various types of information technology," including high-performance computing and communications systems; emerging network technologies; access to, exchange, and retrieval of complex information; computational and statistical methods; information security; and testing tools and methods to improve the quality of software." See the NIST Computer and Network Security Facility for advances in network security.

7.3.8 Organization for International Standards

The Organization for International Standards (ISO),[75] established in 1947, is "a worldwide non-governmental federation of national standards bodies from some 100 countries, one from each country." The mission of ISO is "to promote the development of standardization and related activities in the world with a view to facilitating the international exchange of goods and services, and to developing cooperation in the spheres of intellectual, scientific, technological and economic activity." The subjects covered are quite diverse, from nuclear reactors to metal fasteners. For Web farming, pay attention to the work of the Joint Technical Committee on Information Technology (JTC-1),[76] which has authority over more than 500 international IT standards. In particular, the JTC1/SC32 area is working with over 30 standards that involve SQL, EDI, RIDS, and so on.[77] There is even an ISO standard for representing codes for human sex (ISO 5218:1977).

7.3.9 World Wide Web Consortium

The World Wide Web Consortium (W3C)[78] was created to develop common protocols that enhance interoperability and promote the evolution of the World Wide Web. It is an industry consortium jointly hosted by the MIT Laboratory for Computer Science,[79] the National Institute for Research in Computer Science and Control[80] in France, and Keio University[81] in Japan. Services provided by the Consortium include a repository of information about the World Wide Web for developers and users; reference code implementations to embody and promote standards; and various prototype and sample applications to demonstrate the use of new technology. To date, over 210 organizations are members of W3C.

---

74. See http://www.itl.nist.gov/.
75. See http://www.iso.ch/.
76. See http://www.iso.ch/meme/JTC1.html.
77. See http://www.iso.ch/liste/JTC1SC32.html.
78. See http://www.w3.org/.
79. See http://www.lcs.mit.edu/.
80. See http://www.inria.fr/.
81. See http://www.keio.ac.jp/.

7.3.10 Professional Societies and Industry Consortiums

Standards for Web farming are also influenced by various professional societies and industry consortiums. ACM, IEEE, and similar professional societies in the U.S. and other countries have contributed to and support many of the activities of these standards organizations.

Web Farmers

Band together to develop standards for structured data exchange to enhance the effectiveness of Web farming systems.

An industrial consortium is a group of companies (mainly vendors) with varying interests that collaborate on technical specifications to bring maturity to a market. The resulting standards are ad hoc and quickly developed. Often, little is accomplished. However, a sudden shift in industry attention can signal the widespread adoption of a standard that will eventually be submitted to a formal standards body for consideration.

Web Farmers

Watch for important industry consortiums within your industry! Become involved.

Some examples of consortiums are

- Association for Information and Image Management International (AIIM), with its development of the Open Document Management API standard for document management systems (we discussed this in an earlier section)
- Meta-Data Coalition, with its development of the Metadata Interchange Specifications for data warehousing systems (we discussed this in an earlier section)
- Electronic Industries Association, with its development of the CASE Data Interchange Format
- Object Management Group, with its Unified Modeling Language[82]
- OLAP Council
- Web Enterprise Management Initiative (WEBM)

---

82. See http://www.omg.org/ with the PDF document ftp://ftp.omg.org/pub/docs/ad/97-08-02.pdf that gives an overview of UML.

For more information, scan the following resources to obtain a current list of standards organizations:

- Yahoo:Reference:Standards[83]
- Yahoo:Computers and Internet:Standards[84]
- List of Standards and Standardization Bodies of the World Wide Web Virtual Library as maintained by ISO.[85] It has excellent coverage of international organizations.

7.4 Where To Now?

The discussion above describes several standardization efforts for extending current Web technology to handle the difficult problems of discovery, acquisition, and structuring of Web resources. Over the next few years, an important part of Web farming will be monitoring and participating in the evolution of theses standards, especially for the practical implementation of metadata standards in information e-commerce.

---

83. See http://www.yahoo.com/Reference/Standards/. The format of *yahoo* followed by one or more words refers to Yahoo!'s hierarchical directory structure—a structure with over 50,000 entries!
84. See http://www.yahoo.com/Computers_and_Internet/Standards/.
85. See http://www.iso.ch/VL/Standards.html.

Chapter Eight

Tools

A farmer is only as good as his tools and his ability to use those tools. The same is true for Web farming. The moral: Know thy tools and continually look for better ones!

This chapter is a survey of tools that assist in various aspects of Web farming. Most of these tools are commercially available products from established vendors; however, several are research projects (e.g., WEBSOM from Helsinki University), and a few are only OEM-licensed components (e.g., VizControls from InXight).

This survey is not inclusive; it is a sampling of relevant tools. The product descriptions have been distilled from an enormous amount of marketing fluff. Details of pricing and so on are omitted to highlight basic approaches and functions relevant to Web farming. You should reevaluate for yourself a selected subset of these products when you have determined your requirements for Web farming.

Table 8-1 Categories of Web Farming Tools

Category	Discovery	Acquisition	Structuring	Dissemination
Generic Web Browsers	◆			
Web Agents	◆	◆◆		
Hypertext Analysis and Transformation	◆	◆◆	◆◆◆	◆
Information Visualization	◆◆			◆
Extended Relational Databases			◆◆	◆
Data Marts		◆	◆	◆◆
Knowledge Management Systems		◆	◆◆◆	◆◆

The chapter starts with the generic browser, followed by Web agents, hypertext analysis, information visualization, extended relational databases, data marts, and knowledge management systems. The chapter concludes with a summary listing and suitability ratings of the various tools.

You should first glance quickly through the tool descriptions and then concentrate on the summaries at the start of each section and at the end of the chapter.

To evaluate the various tools, we will use the following phases of information refinement for Web farming—discovery, acquisition, structuring, and dissemination—as described in the first chapter. The tools are classified into seven categories, as shown in Table 8-1. The columns at the right indicate a rough rating of suitability for the activities of discovery, acquisition, structuring, and dissemination. The diamonds indicate the degree to which a tool is suitable for a particular function. One diamond implies that the tool has some (but limited) functionality, requiring additional tools or extensive programming. Two diamonds imply that the tool has most (but not all) functionality, requiring some programming and extension. Three diamonds imply that the tool has complete functionality, requiring only installation and configuration.

8.1 Generic Web Browsers

The first essential tool for Web farming is a Web browser that is generic in its ability to render properly the HTML encoding of Web pages. However, the rendering (or presentation) of a Web page is only a portion of the required functionality.

Some of the desired extensions for a browser are

- Management and organization of massive numbers of URL links
- Search assistance in creating complex queries and distilling massive result sets

- Capture of text, links, and images into a database as a single object
- Pattern recognition and template construction of textual analysis
- Easy OCR on images to extract textual content
- GUI macro language for specifying complex Web procedures
- Interface to server agents to perform procedures upon schedule or event
- Ability to easily extend functionality as new needs are discovered

The *browser wars* between Netscape Navigator and Microsoft Internet Explorer have produced two excellent and inexpensive browsers in a relatively short time. That is the good news. The bad news is that the wars have eliminated all other competing products from the marketplace. For Web farming, the assumption is that one or both of these browsers are used.

Web Farmers

Become familiar with both Netscape Navigator and Microsoft Internet Explorer, along with their respective enhancements and extensions. Note especially the ability to customize the browser interface as a component within a large application.

We will not describe either of these browser products, since they are rapidly changing and other books adequately cover the functional details and product use.[1]

8.2 Web Agents

Web agents are programs that perform some specific procedure involving the Web while executing independently of manual intervention. More precisely, agents are autonomous, goal-directed processes that react (with some intelligence) to a variety of factors in the Web environment. A summary of Web agent tools is given in Table 8-2. Other Web agent tools that are not described are KnowItAll from Grasp Information[2] and Zoot from Zoot Software.[3]

One aspect to note is the execution platform for the Web agent. Most agent products execute only on the user's workstation. Mobile agents (as described by General Magic) can select their execution site and migrate with their code and data to that site—a scary thought! Missing is the explicit ability to manage a set of agents that execute only on the server platform.

---

1. Scan Amazon.Com on the keywords "web browser" for a current list of such books.
2. See http://www.grasp.com/.
3. See http://www.zootsoftware.com/.

For Further Information

Excellent resource centers for software agents are maintained by the UMBC Laboratory for Advanced Information Technology[4] and the Agent Society.[5]

Another interesting resource center is the BotSpot (at www.botspot.com), which contains descriptions and background information on intelligent agents, or 'bots.

The name ['bot] comes from *robot,* of course, but that word comes from Karel Capek's 1921 play *R.U.R.,* for Rossum's Universal Robots, *robota* being Czech for *work.*

Many Web agent products are enhancements to the popular Windows 95 browsers, running within or alongside them as toolbars. For current information on similar browser enhancements, scan the WinFiles.Com listing for browser enhancements.[6] Each week, there are usually several new and innovative products listed here, at reasonable prices.

The ability to program an agent is another important aspect of Web agents. Most agent programs offer a range of procedures depending on a predetermined set of parameters. More desirable is the ability to program Web agents in Java (or a similar language), thus handling unusual situations in more mature systems.

Table 8-2   Web Agent Tools

Tool	Vendor/Developer	Description
Web Agents		
Alexa	Alexa Internet	Internet surf engine
Copernic	Agents Technologies Corp	Meta-search utility
LiveAgent Pro	AgentSoft Ltd.	Agent script builder in Java
NetGetIt	Crossproduct Solutions	Specialized search utility for GoldMine
Odyssey	General Magic	Mobile agent builder in Java
Smart Bookmarks	FirstFloor	URL manager
WebCompass	QuarterDeck	Meta-search utility
WebWhacker	Blue Squirrel	Download utility
Who's Talking	Software Solutions	Specialized search utility

4. See http://www.cs.umbc.edu/agents/.
5. See http://www.agent.org/.
6. See http://www.winfiles.com/apps/webtools.html.

Figure 8-1   The Alexa Toolbar

8.2.1   Alexa from Alexa Internet

Alexa Internet[7] is a free service that "helps you surf smarter, faster, and easier." Founded in April 1996 by Brewster Kahle and Bruce Gilliat, Alexa Internet had the novel vision of Web navigation that learns and improves over time with the collective participation of fellow Web surfers.

One way of understanding Alexa is through personal observation. I visited a new university whose campus was just being constructed. The architects, in their wisdom, did not pave the sidewalks during the first year. As students wandered from class to class, they etched unusual trails in the mud. During the next summer, those mud trails were paved in concrete. That is the principle behind Alexa.

Displayed as a toolbar on the user's desktop, Alexa works in cooperation with the browser and interacts with the Alexa Server over the same IP connection.

From left to right, as shown in Figure 8-1, the Alexa toolbar displays

- Information about the current site via a pop-up that displays additional site statistics
- Vote of one's preference for this site
- List of other sites associated with this site
- An ad supposedly tailored to your surfing habits
- A query to a Merriam-Webster's Online Dictionary and Thesaurus Britannia Online

The following passage summarizes the method and intention of the Alexa.

> Whenever your browser goes to a Web page, the Alexa service requests information about that page from Alexa's servers. We then record that an Alexa user has spent time at that site as a kind of vote—we don't know who passed through this site, but we know how many have passed this way. We can even learn from the fact that users visit several related sites as they browse the Web, and tend to spend more time at the sites that give them more of what they are looking for. We also learn from users by letting them explicitly make related links. They do this by selecting "Add a link to this list" in the "Where to Go Next" pop-up on the Alexa Toolbar.... The more people use Alexa, the more we all benefit.

---

7.   See http://www.alexa.com/.

Closely associated with Alexa, the Internet Archive[8] is collecting and storing public materials from the Web to provide historians, researchers, and other scholars with access to this vast collection of data (reaching 12 terabytes), and to ensure the longevity of this information.

8.2.2   Copernic from Agents Technologies (MEB) Corp.

Copernic[9] is a meta–search agent with the following features:

- Duplicate matches are automatically removed.
- Invalid and unreachable URL links are eliminated.
- Matching documents can be downloaded for offline browsing.
- Documents can be submitted to local subsearches.
- Search reports can be generated in Web page format for easy browsing.
- Selector toolbar allows you to switch quickly between the matching documents.
- Searches can be updated and grouped into folders.

Figure 8-2 shows a typical search for pictures from the Mars Pathfinder.

8.2.3   LiveAgent Pro from AgentSoft Ltd.

LiveAgent Pro[10] is an agent builder to assist in personal web browsing. As you browse through the Web, a script is created that can be used to direct a Java-based agent to replicate your browsing procedures. Agents can perform routine tasks and generate user-defined browsing reports.

> Scripts provide full programming power to the serious developer. Scripts can include variables, react to conditions found at runtime, loop through multiple pages of information, and fully interact with HTML pages and forms. The MasterAgent tool allows multiple agents to run in parallel and return data from multiple sources for integration and comparison.

One interesting aspect of LiveAgent is its HTML Position Definition (HPD) Language, which locates specific elements within the HTML page (even when the page changes). Functionality can be extended through the creation of custom Java classes that are integrated into the program's architecture.

---

8. See http://www.archive.org/.
9. See http://www.agents-tech.com/ or http://www.copernic.com/.
10. See http://www.agentsoft.com/.

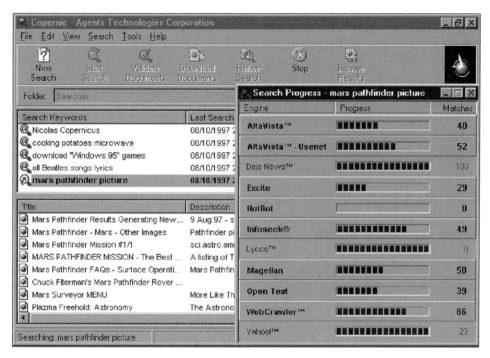

Figure 8-2 Sample Screen Shot from Copernic

AgentSoft has pursued the XML specifications and has a demo of LiveAgent with several XML files. The files are mostly CDF formats of news channels, but also included is a query of Shakespeare's *Julius Caesar* in XML format.

8.2.4 NetGetIt from Crossproduct Solutions

NetGetIt[11] is a specialized search agent that searches and monitors current Web data about your prospects, customers, and competitors, for import into the Gold-Mine contact management software.

> Using the public search engines and business information sites as a starting point, NetGetIt finds related information and then digs deeper into the referenced web sites to find the best information. It pulls everything in, ranks it, and delivers the best results right to your desktop. NetGetIt can research your contacts automatically, and alert you in GoldMine to new information.

This product is a good example of an embedded search procedure specialized for a specific target database.

---

11. See http://www.crossproduct.com/ngiinfo.htm.

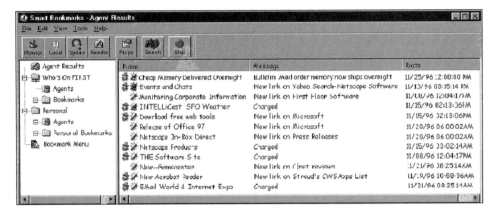

Figure 8-3   Screen Shot of Smart Bookmarks

8.2.5   Odyssey from General Magic

General Magic[12] is recognized as a pioneer in agent technology, particularly in the area of mobile agents. Odyssey[13] is the result of redirecting their previous work with its Telescript language to Java and ActiveX platforms. Odyssey currently runs on any platform that supports the JDK toolkit and uses the Remote Method Invocation (RMI) and the Java class libraries. It is available to developers at no charge from the company's Web site.

General Magic has proposed a Mobile Agent Facility specification[14] to OMG as an extension to CORBA. Most products of General Magic have embedded Odyssey in applications supporting "the notification of priority messages or critical information according to preset rules based on user preferences."

8.2.6   Smart Bookmarks from FirstFloor

Smart Bookmarks[15] is a utility designed for individual users who want to manage personal Web content. Agents manage the delivery of Web content to the desktop, automatically monitor for new or changed content, and schedule updates to refresh content on the workstation. A sample screen shot is shown in Figure 8-3.

---

12. See http://www.genmagic.com/.
13. See http://www.genmagic.com/agents/.
14. See http://www.genmagic.com/agents/MAF/.
15. See http://www.firstfloor.com/.

8.2.7 WebCompass from Quarterdeck

WebCompass[16] is a search utility that can access a variety of Web resources, from normal Web sites, the Usenet, FTP, gopher sites, and intranet sites. It comes with the parameters for over 35 resources, along with the ability to add customized ones. Its features include the following:

- Ranks the results of searches for relevance on a 1-to-100 scale
- Builds comprehensive summaries of results gathered from searching
- Automatically organizes results by topic
- Automatically updates results
- Uses search results to fine-tune further searches
- Includes customizable relational database of search topics
- Includes thesaurus to assist in searching

8.2.8 WebWhacker from Blue Squirrel

WebWhacker[17] is a utility that can download entire Web sites, including text and images, for archiving and viewing offline. Unattended content delivery can be scheduled, and important sites monitored for updates.

> Download Web sites to your laptop and surf the Web anywhere. Sites "whacked" to your hard drive are a mirror image of the same information on the Internet.

Some features of WebWhacker are as follows:

- Shares entire Web sites with others via HTML or compressed WIF exports
- Saves Web sites to removable storage and with compressed content
- Filters by file size, MIME file type, file extension, and server directory location
- Downloads background sounds, dynamic images, Shockwave, and Java
- Retrieves automatic updates via the Internet using Blue Squirrel's InstantX Technology

A screen shot of WebWhacker "whacking" a Web site is shown in Figure 8-4.

---

16. See http://www.qdeck.com/ and http://arachnid.quarterdeck.com/qdeck/products/wc20/ for information on WebCompass.
17. See http://www.bluesquirrel.com/whacker/.

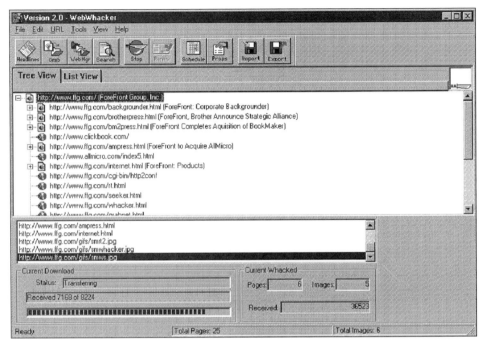

Figure 8-4   "Whacking" a Web Site

8.2.9   Who's Talking from Software Solutions

Who's Talking[18] is a specialized search agent whose purpose is tracking the use of your trademarks and copyright material by other parties, particularly competitors. This agent scans the hidden text of HTML pages, such as META tags.

> More than just a search engine spider, Who's Talking spiders the actual results and reports back to you exactly where the offending trademark, image file, or URL appears on the site. Who's Talking conducts a complete keyword, key phrase or file name search of the major search engines, compiles and parses the results and then scans every line of code on every suspect page and reports the exact location of each occurrence. This includes all hidden text and tags. The results are placed in a database and future searches indicate new, removed and returned pages allowing you to track new and recurring violations.

This product is a good example of an embedded search procedure specialized for a specific type of search.

---

18. See http://softwaresolutions.net/whostalking/.

8.3 Hypertext Analysis and Transformation

This section describes tools that analyze and transform hypertext data (e.g., Web pages). These tools are distinct from data analysis tools, such as OLAP and data mining.[19]

Historical Note

One of the first tools in this category actually predates the Web. The Wide Area Information Server (WAIS) was the information search resource long before the Web achieved its present global popularity. Based on the ANSI/NISO Z39.50 standard for information retrieval, WAIS systems have indexed a variety of traditional library materials.[20]

A summary of the hypertext analysis tools is given in Table 8-3.

Table 8-3 Tools for Hypertext Analysis and Transformation

Tool	Vendor/Developer	Description
Hypertext Analysis and Transformation		
AltaVista Search	Compaq Computer	Index server with personalization
Cambio	Data Junction	Data extraction and transformation
Compass Server	Netscape	Index server
Dynamic Reasoning Engine	Neurodynamics	Index server based on neural nets
EXTRACT Tool Suite	Evolutionary Technologies	Data extraction and transformation
Index Server	Microsoft	Index server
Integrity	Vality Technology Inc.	Data cleaning and transformation
Intelligent Miner for Text	IBM Corporation	Data mining extended for text
LinguistX	Inxight Software, Inc.	Linguistic analysis tools for OEM
NetOwl Intelligence Server	IsoQuest Inc.	Index server
RetrievalWare	Excalibur Technologies	Index server
Search'97	Verity Inc.	Index server
SearchServer	Fulcrum Technologies	Index server
SmartCrawl	Inktomi	Web crawler
Ultraseek	InfoSeek Corporation	Index server with crawler
Webinator	Thunderstone	Index server
ZyIndex	ZyLab International Inc.	Data indexing

19. A list of tools in this category can be found in the product directory of *DBMS* magazine at http://www.dbmsmag.com/pcquery.html.
20. See http://www.cni.org/pub/NISO/docs/Z39.50-1992/www/Z39.50.toc.html.

In general, this category contains the best products to support a production-level operation. SmartCrawl from Inktomi, AltaVista Search from Digital, and Search'97 from Verity are some examples of robust products.

The commercial products for Web crawling and indexing are starting to have the proper functions for Web farming. The important issue is the customization of the discovery and acquisition process for a selective list of topics. Most are directed toward organizing intranet pages, as opposed to finding relevant external pages (which are more complex). The process should be highly selective, dealing with the complexity of frames, security with user name and password, and parameters for Web-enabled databases. In addition, the capabilities for periodic probes to previous targets and for smart archiving of incremental images are needed.

8.3.1   AltaVista Search from Compaq Computer

The AltaVista Search[21] product family commercializes the software base of the AltaVista service and, for Digital (now Compaq), highlights the capacities of its Alpha hardware platform. The search coverage is quite broad, from all types of Web servers to over 200 different file formats, including the Microsoft Office 97 family, Adobe Acrobat PDF, PostScript, and relational databases. Some notable features are as follows:

- Indexes full directory structures on Web servers
- Indexes frames
- Provides full customization capabilities for query and results pages
- Includes standard user interfaces in 23 languages
- Includes improved Scooter (i.e., Web crawler) performance and quality
- Enables the crawler operations to be scheduled

8.3.2   Cambio from Data Junction

Cambio[22] is a utility for extraction and transformation of both unstructured and structured data. With a 10-year history behind it, this product has encountered (and converted) most file formats known to mankind.

The following passage illustrates that the Cambio product has an acceptance of Web farming.

> For the moment, everyone is looking at the WWW as a target for data (and throwing every conceivable jumble of data up there). An exciting dimension that is often overlooked is exploiting the WWW as a *Source* of database data. Who wouldn't want to be able to siphon off just the

21. See http://www.altavista.software.digital.com/search/index.htm.
22. See http://www.datajunction.com/.

data fields they need, and drop them right into their database of choice? Of course, a huge roadblock stands in the way—this massive hodgepodge of WWW data is stored in millions of different and loosely structured text files—making the data until now unreachable. To overcome this obstacle, and tap into the goldmine of WWW data Cambio32 is the answer![23]

8.3.3 Compass Server from Netscape

Netscape Compass Server[24] provides a broad set of functions (search, index, browse, and personalize) for managing content across the Internet, intranets, and databases. Based on the Verity SEARCH '97 indexing engine, Compass Server provides an advanced query interface that enables users to construct multipart queries, combining keywords, phrases, and attribute search items, thus creating highly targeted queries.

Some notable features are as follows:

- Delivers customized daily newsletters based on user preferences via email, a Webcasting channel, or a personal Web page
- Scales to support document indexing across thousands of servers
- Indexes any brand of Web or FTP server
- Indexes multiple document formats, including HTML, PDF, Microsoft Office, and WordPerfect
- Distributes the Web crawling processing for round-the-clock robot operation to increase the scale of deployment and minimize resource requirements, using multiple Web crawlers

Another notable feature is a category tree to organize content. Administrators have the ability to construct the category tree with a graphical view of the hierarchy and a set of rules that Web crawlers use to categorize documents. These categorization rules take advantage of HTTP header information for documents that are retrieved by the robot, enabling categorization based on URL, protocol, and HTML META tag data.

Users can subscribe to the categories for their personalized profiles. At any time, users can extend their profiles by refining categories to include or exclude such things as author or specific text. The personalized profile also includes social filtering, the process whereby the members of a workgroup support one another through ranking documents they read for value and significance to the business. Members may add their ranking to an item using a five-level scale. The profile manager automatically calculates a revised overall importance for the item as new readers continue to select importance levels.

---

23. See http://www.datajunction.com/products/prod_idx.htm.
24. See http://home.netscape.com/comprod/server_central/index.html.

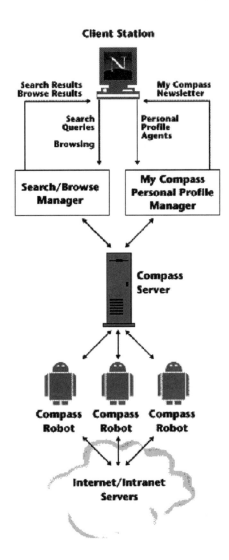

Figure 8-5
Architecture of
Compass Server

The overall architecture of Compass Server is shown in Figure 8-5. Note the personalization facility on the top right and the distributed Web crawling on the bottom.

8.3.4 Dynamic Reasoning Engine from Neurodynamics

Dynamic Reasoning Engine (DRE)[25] from Neurodynamics is a neural-net text analysis and data mining system with the unique ability to search vast quantities of data from numerous sources. The unique feature of DRE is that it can automatically suggest to the user links to potentially relevant documents.

---

25. See http://www.camneuro.stjohns.co.uk/frameadt.htm.

Getting Smart by Integrating the Data

After six months of operation, the data collection was getting unwieldly at 2.8 GB in the \DATA directory. The problem was not disk space, since the system had more than 10 GB of free space. Alice summarized the problem: "We just get lost in the stuff. There are 83 directories with 23,529 files in nine different format types. It's all indexed, but it's still a mess."

The group explored several knowledge management systems and decided on one that integrated all the files into a single logical object-oriented database. After a few months of difficult transition, Alice judged the effort approvingly: "At least now we can track each item with its creation date, authorship, copyright restrictions, and derived transformations. It isn't pretty, but it works!"

Next installment is on page 251.

Some notable features are

- Natural language queries
- Fuzzy matching for inaccurate data searching
- Indexing that allows direct real-time input, such as from live news wires

8.3.5 EXTRACT Tool Suite from Evolutionary Technologies

The ETI•EXTRACT Tool Suite[26] is a set of data extraction and transformation tools for "automating enterprise-wide data integration." With a simple point-and-click interface, users specify what data to select from legacy and operational files, what transformations and conversions to perform on the data, and how to move the converted data to the appropriate target files. ETI•EXTRACT Tool Suite then generates the source code and executes the programs needed to collect and move existing data into new applications or database systems. The tool suite can generate programs in virtually any programming language (including C, COBOL, RPG, Natural, and SAP's ABAP/4) to support native access for common databases (such as DB2, IMS, Oracle, Informix, Sybase, Teradata, IDMS, and ADABAS), as well as files from COBOL, C, and SAP R/3. ETI•EXTRACT also captures extensive metadata and provides flexible metadata management, which is critical for audit trails and for data warehousing design.

---

26. See http://www.evtech.com/.

8.3.6   Index Server from Microsoft

The Microsoft Index Server can index documents written in seven languages and in most formats. It supports full-text searches from any Web browser.

The Index Server uses content filters to extract the textual information contained within a formatted file. Content filters are associated with particular document formats and are written to the IFilter ActiveX programmatic interface. By writing an ActiveX content filter, software authors can expose their contents to Index Server for indexing and retrieval by end users.

8.3.7   INTEGRITY from Vality Technology Inc.

The INTEGRITY Data Re-engineering Environment[27] is a data cleaning and transformation tool that re-engineers source data into a consolidated view of business entities. To build the complex relations as buried in legacy data, INTEGRITY's process is fourfold: data investigation and metadata mining, data standardization, data integration, and data survivorship and formatting. The sense of these phases is captured in the following passage:

> Analysts say that Vality Technology may be the only vendor "down in the trenches" at the data-value level, solving complex data-transformation problems that cannot be solved any other way—data value by data value, character by character.... Working at the record-occurrence level, INTEGRITY detects, classifies, and specifies data from any source for proper mapping to any target. In contrast, metadata propagation tools cannot ensure data quality because they map at the meta level, not the record-occurrence level.

8.3.8   Intelligent Miner for Text from IBM Corporation

Intelligent Miner for Text[28] is a data analysis system extended for textual data. The product identifies "hidden correlation in data by performing predictive modeling, database segmentation, link analysis and deviation detection using a variety of data-mining techniques."

The rationale behind the text analysis is stated in the following passage:

> About 80% of the world's stored data is in the form of text documents and, at best, we have the time to read only a fraction of it. Innovative tools are needed to navigate through this mass of documents, like

---

27. See http://www.vality.com/.
28. See http://direct.boulder.ibm.com/bi/tech/mining/textmine.htm.

newspaper articles, and pull out the pieces of most interest to us in a quickly readable and accessible format.

IBM's text mining solutions are designed to cut through mountains of text-based data and discover the hidden nuggets of information that you need to know. Applying text mining techniques to customer complaint letters, for example, can discover the major reasons for customer complaints and present them to you in a quick, intelligible manner. By searching and mining business news wire documents that mention your company, text mining can reveal a corporate image of your company in vivid detail.

IBM's text mining solutions include the following components:

- InfoDetector: Mine text-based documents to find out what kind of customers you have and what they're buying. The main functions provided by InfoDetector are automatic data segmentation (clustering), comparison of two segmentations, interactive visualization of results, generation of reports, and data export. InfoDetector is based on an innovative analysis method, called Relational Analysis, which includes factorial analysis, hierarchical methods, or non-H methods (inertial methods like K-means).

- Technology Watch: Spot technology trends, identify the important players in technology areas and watch your competition. Technology Watch uses a keyword-mapping scheme in which all documents are represented by rows in a two-dimensional table. Each row has one binary column indicating the presence of each keyword or descriptor found in any document. Based on a clustering of these binary columns, Technology Watch automatically classifies the documents by content into a number of groups.

- Text Navigator: Sift through large numbers of documents and separate the wheat from the chaff in meaningful clusters. Text Navigator analyzes the content of several thousand documents, clusters similar items together, and displays the large collection in an organized fashion.

- FLASH (Fast Look-up Algorithm for Structural Homology):[29] An offshoot of research on computer vision to efficiently detect similarities. FLASH uses a "probabilistic indexed algorithm," which looks for matches only where it is likely to find them in the database. FLASH has been applied to a fingerprint identification program that examines the ridges and valleys that make up human fingerprints. It is also being used to rapidly identify potential DNA and protein sequence matches in the Human Genome Project, which is producing sequences of DNA represented by strings of letters that designate the nucleotides in DNA.

---

29. See http://www.research.ibm.com/topics/popups/deep/math/html/flash.html.

8.3.9 LinguistX from Inxight Software, Inc.

LinguistX is a set of "linguistic transducers" that "enable highly accurate document analysis and word morphology" in eight languages.[30] Xerox research linguist Lauri Karttunen pioneered the linguistic techniques on which this product is based.

The specific functions performed with LinguistX are (as quoted from product specs)

- Tokenizing: separates a document into sentences and individual words. While English punctuation and spacing often provide a good indication of word and sentence boundaries, special cases such as contractions *(isn't* or *y'all)*, possessives *(Bart's)*, and abbreviations *(Inc.)* can make accurate tokenization a non-trivial task. Additionally, documents in languages that do not place spaces between words, such as Japanese, require very sophisticated analysis for correct tokenization.

- Stemming: identifies all possible root forms of a word. Unlike pattern-matching methods (such as wildcarding or tail-chopping) that degrade the accuracy, LinguistX generates only linguistically correct stems.

- Morphological analysis: a more advanced form of stemming that identifies the grammatical features of a word in addition to its root forms. Morphological analysis will show, for example, that the root word *ground* can be considered as a noun, an adjective, or a verb. Morphological analysis provides value to applications where the grammatical features of a word are important.

- Tagging: builds on morphological analysis by choosing the part-of-speech category for a group of words by examining them in the context of a sentence. Tagging is especially important for applications, such as language translation, where proper grammatical understanding is critical, and in situations where searches based on a grammatical aspect of a sentence are desired (such as noun phrase identification searches).

- Morphological inflection: the inverse process from stemming and analysis, in which root forms are converted into inflected forms, such as turning *can* into *could*.

- Summarization: examination of content in real time to identify the key phrases and extract sentences to form an indicative summary, either by highlighting excerpts within a document or creating a bulleted list of the document's key phrases.

- Language identification: determination of a document's language and character set encoding, which is an essential step when sorting documents for automated processing.

---

30. See http://www.inxight.com/content/75.html.

An efficient compression algorithm enables LinguistX to store text in less storage than the original source. For instance, a half million English words are stored in under 250 KB of storage (or two words per byte), and more than 5.7 million French words are stored in under 250 KB (or 20 words per byte).

8.3.10 NetOwl Intelligence Server from IsoQuest Inc.

NetOwl Intelligence Server[31] is a text analysis server developed by IsoQuest and built on the NetOwl Extractor core engine. It uses sophisticated pattern-matching techniques to build an index of personal names, corporate names, place names, locations, dates, monetary amounts, and other key phrases. This enhanced index targets exactly the key documents sought and presents them to users in summarized form.

A white paper is available (in Acrobat PDF) that explains the pattern-matching techniques.[32] Several common problems with indexing text were described, as shown in Table 8-4.

Table 8-4   Examples of Pattern-Matching by NetOwl

Description	Examples
Names overlapping other names	Murphy Oil *vs.* Murphy Department Stores
Names overlapping words	Prime Computer *vs.* prime beef
Organization / place ambiguity	State College, PA *vs.* Imperial College, London
Corporations containing person names	J. C. Penney Co.
Corporations containing place names	Sante Fe Southern Pacific Corp.
Names containing AND	Atlantis Mill and Lumber Co.

The screen shot in Figure 8-6 shows the most relevant items indexed within a sample set of news items. Under Person, the name *Bill Gates* appears in three documents, along with its associations with other persons and phrases.

The NetOwl Intelligence Server runs on Unix and Windows NT platforms.

---

31. See http://www.isoquest.com/.
32. See http://www.isoquest.com/DownLoad/NOWexWP.pdf.

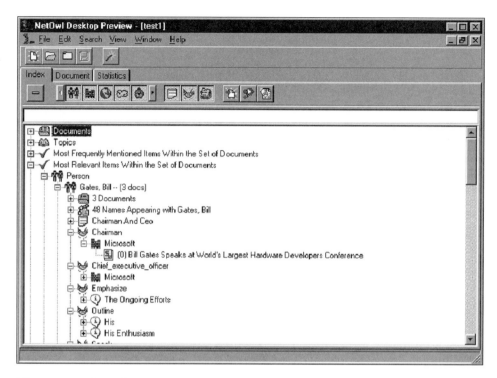

Figure 8-6   Screen Shot of NetOwl Desktop Showing a Person Breakdown

8.3.11   RetrievalWare from Excalibur Technologies

RetrievalWare is an index server with special capabilities with image and video objects.[33] As a family of products, RetrievalWare is scalable from workgroups to the enterprise. Its indexing is driven by a sophisticated semantic dictionary and pattern-matching algorithm:

> RetrievalWare's powerful, embedded, full semantic dictionary of more than 400,000 word meanings, 50,000 language idioms, and 1.6 million word associations, expands queries and yields results based on word meanings, related words, and true concept analysis. APRP [Adaptive Pattern Recognition Processing] technology recognizes patterns in digital code to "fuzzy" search damaged, misspelled or poorly scanned data with extremely accurate results.

---

33. See http://www.excalib.com/.

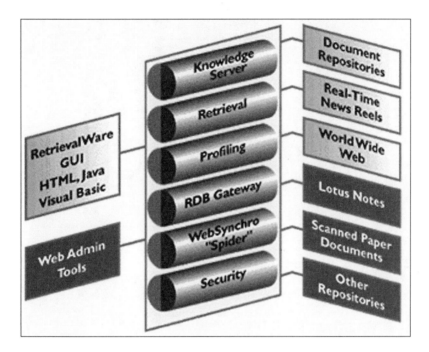

Figure 8-7   Architecture for Excalibur RetrievalWare

Internet Spider is described as the industry's first "multimedia" Web crawler. It has flexibility in directing its exploring behavior:

> Excalibur Internet Spider navigates the Web based on instructions you provide. Using specifications such as document type, hostname, directory, domain, and crawling depth and width, Excalibur Internet Spider can crawl as deeply, broadly, and as often you want it to explore. While crawling, Excalibur Internet Spider builds and maintains a searchable database of information about each location visited. . . . Businesses and application developers can access, develop, and leverage knowledge collected from all documents and information published on the Web. Highly configurable and multi-threaded, Excalibur Internet Spider allows you to closely monitor topics of interest on your intranets and the Web, based on knowledge profiles.

RetrievalWare also includes application development tools ranging from MS Visual Basic to C-callable libraries.

The RetrievalWare product family has the architecture shown in Figure 8-7. It runs on UNIX and Windows 95/NT platforms.

Figure 8-8 Architecture for Verity Search '97

8.3.12 Search '97 from Verity Inc.

The Search '97 application suite, from Verity,[34] includes Search '97 Personal, Information Server, and Agent Server, as well as a number of intelligent search components, shown in Figure 8-8.

Search '97 integrates a full-text indexing search engine with intelligent search components and supports dynamic personalization and delivery of information across the enterprise. It also features an intuitive search interface that guides users to quickly locate the exact information they need and create their own custom profile of interest.

8.3.13 SearchServer from Fulcrum Technologies

SearchServer,[35] from Fulcrum Technologies, is a multi-platform indexing and retrieval server engine for full-text retrieval applications. It operates on Windows 95, Windows NT, OS/2, Macintosh, and Unix (SVR4, OSF/1, HP-UX, AIX, Solaris, Novell UnixWare, SINIX, IRIX, and SunOS) platforms. Strong features of SearchServer are its close integration with SQL and its compliance with ODBC.

SearchBuilder toolkits integrate with graphical development tools so that MIS professionals and third-party developers can build client/server text-retrieval applications that access Fulcrum SearchServer.

PC DOCS Group International has acquired Fulcrum Technologies in a stock trade.

---

34. See http://www.verity.com/.
35. See http://www.fulcrum.com/.

8.3.14 SmartCrawl from Inktomi

The SmartCrawl system[36] is described as the world's fastest Web crawler, with an indexing capacity of over 10 million documents per day. The system runs on a coupled cluster of inexpensive workstations that can be expanded to accommodate increases in database size or number of users. High performance is achieved through sophisticated parallel processing that executes over a thousand simultaneous network operations (threads) per CPU. This level of performance is critical for providing fresh and accurate searching, especially as the Web continues to grow. This technology powers some of the world's largest Internet search engines, such as HotBot.[37]

Slurp is the Web-indexing robot that collects documents from the Web to build a searchable index for the HotBot search engine. Slurp adheres to the 1994 Robots Exclusion Standard (RES) and is "somewhat more forgiving."

8.3.15 Ultraseek from InfoSeek Corporation

The Ultraseek Server[38] from InfoSeek Corporation is another mature Web indexing and crawling product. This product is used as the base for the InfoSeek[39] discovery service, along with various other companies (e.g., Auto-By-Tel, Borders Group, CMP Media, Datek Online, DLJ/Direct, Microsoft, PeopleLink, Bell Atlantic, CSX, UPS, Sun Microsystems, 3Com, Boeing, Sony Online, IDG, NASA, and Reuters).

Ultraseek can index up to 15,000 documents per hour and has an interface to advanced search features, a "find similar" feature, the ability to search newsgroups, and support for six European languages (French, German, Spanish, Dutch, Italian, and Portuguese).

A trial version is available for a free download from InfoSeek's Web site.

8.3.16 Webinator from Thunderstone

Webinator[40] is one of three products from Thunderstone, a pioneer in document retrieval systems. Webinator creates a retrieval interface for collections of Web documents by indexing multiple sites into one common index. It provides an SQL query interface to the database (Texis) for maintenance and reporting. Multiple index engines (Metamorph) can run concurrently against a common database.

Texis is a fully integrated SQL relational database that queries and manages natural language text, standard data types, images, video, audio, and other payload data. Texis is used in many Web applications such as message profiling and handling,

---

36. See http://www.inktomi.com/.
37. See http://www.hotbot.com/.
38. See http://software.infoseek.com/.
39. See http://www.infoseek.com/.
40. See http://www.thunderstone.com/.

image library management, help-desk support, online news retrieval, business intelligence, research libraries, litigation support, and Internet retail operations.

Metamorph is a real-time concept-based search package. It will search through anything without any preprocessing steps. Typically, it is used any time preindexing is either inconvenient or impossible. Metamorph has an English-language vocabulary of 250,000 word and phrase concept associations for natural language queries. It also provides excellent proximity control, fuzzy searches, true regular expression matching, and numerical value searches.

8.3.17   ZyIndex from ZyLab International Inc.

ZyIndex[41] is a text-file indexing program that makes large amounts of structured and unstructured documents accessible by building an index of content words. ZyIndex locates documents based on their content. Through the ZyImage product, it is integrated with the optical character recognition (OCR) technology from Calera WordScan to convert paper documents into electronic archives.

8.4   Information Visualization

This section describes a sampling of tools for information visualization (IV). This area has the greatest potential for advancing Web farming. The challenge is more than allowing people to "see" massive and complex amounts of Web content. The challenge is actually enabling people to identify the relevant information and to reorganize it to create new information.

The marketplace for IV tools is still embryonic. There is an exploding market for OLAP and data mining, but these IV tools assume that the data is structured in a star schema (or equivalent) to allow the usual drill-down, roll-up, and pivoting operations on additive attributes. There is an exploding market for computer-aided design and scientific visualization, but these IV tools assume that the data is primarily arranged in a physical three-dimensional space.

For Further Information

An excellent resource center for information visualization tools is the Cyber-Geography Research,[42] which is an initiative by Martin Dodge at the Centre for Advanced Spatial Analysis, University College, London. Scan the Atlas of Cyberspaces, especially under the topics of information maps, information landscapes, and information spaces.

---

41. See http://www.zylab.com/.
42. See http://www.cybergeography.org/.

Table 8-5 Tools for Information Visualization

Tool	Vendor/Developer	Description
Information Visualization		
Discovery for Developers	Visible Decisions Inc.	Developer toolkit
SemioMap	Semio Corporation	Info-space navigator
SmartContent System	Perspecta	Info-space navigator
Spotfire Pro	IVEE Development	Multi-dimensional data visualizer
UMAP	TriVium	Info-space navigator
Visual Insights	Lucent Technologies	Multi-dimensional data visualizer
VizControls	InXight Software, Inc.	Toolkit of visualization techniques
WEBSOM	Helsinki University	Info-space navigator

A summary of the information visualization tools is given in Table 8-5. Not available in the marketplace are IV tools that have a flexible interface driven by a semantically rich database. The IV interface should invoke the analysis routines, all of which should feed on the same database. The visual representation should be highly flexible, offering many alternatives for mapping a database instance to one or more visual instances.

A frequent misconception is that visualization is the final stage of analysis. In other words, an IV tool presents the results after the real analysis processing has occurred. In contrast, an IV tool should be the focus for analysis. Starting with raw data, an IV representation should drive both the discovery and the analysis through successive stages of refinement, resulting in *actionable intelligence* (as it might be labeled by our business intelligence colleagues).

8.4.1 Discovery for Developers from Visible Decisions Inc.

Discovery for Developers[43] (plus various toolkits) is a framework for programmers to construct "interactive, information-rich, true 3D-information visualizations of both dynamic and static data." It supports data connectivity to these visualizations and is available for Windows 95, Windows NT, Silicon Graphics, Sun, Digital, HP, and IBM workstations.

---

43. See http://www.vdi.com/.

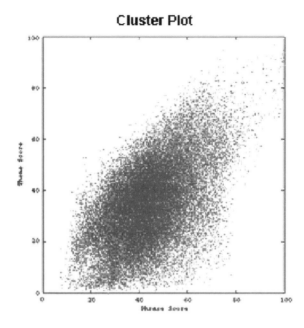

Figure 8-9
Cluster Plot of
Similarity

8.4.2 MAPit from Manning & Napier Information Services

The MAPit product,[44] from Manning & Napier Information Services (MNIS), is a visualization tool that plots the similarity of documents on several dimensions. Figure 8-9 is an analysis of patent information for competitive assessment. This cluster plot shows approximately 85,000 dots representing patent claims. The positions of the dots on the graph indicate how similar the corresponding claims are in terms of subjects and phrases. The vertical dimension analyzes similarity from a subject perspective, and the horizontal dimension analyzes similarity based on terminology and phrases.

> A useful analogy is to think of the vertical axis as showing similarity at the level of a table of contents at the front of a book, and the horizontal axis representing similarity at the level of an index in the back of a book. In the upper right corner, both metrics agree that it's a very close match.

---

44. See http://www.mnis.net/mapitdemo/.

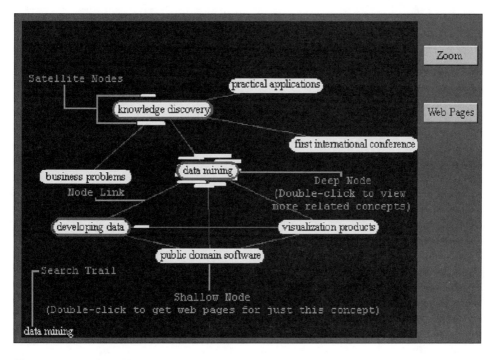

Figure 8-10   SemioMap

8.4.3 SemioMap from Semio Corporation

The SemioMap is the visualization of a lexical structure generated from semiotic analysis (the study of signs and their usage within a culture).[45] The objective is to navigate through a complex subject structure until you find the proper topic. An example of this navigation is shown in Figure 8-10. The ovals are nodes, each representing a collection of documents for a specific subject. A node with boxes behind it is a deep node that, when you double-click on it, will expand to show more detail. A node without boxes is a shallow node that, when you double-click on it, will list Web pages containing data about its subject. A search trail is maintained in the lower left.

Try the SemioMap demonstration[46] with a subject of your choice. Semio has collected only about a million Web pages, so the subject coverage may be limited. A version for Windows NT is available for download and installation on a Web server.

---

45. Daniel Chandler, "Semiotics for Beginners," http://www.aber.ac.uk/~dgc/semiotic.html.
46. See http://www.semio.com/demo/demo3.html.

8.4.4   SmartContent System from Perspecta

SmartContent[47] is a meta-information visualization and index server from Perspecta, which was founded in January 1996 by alumni of the MIT Media Lab along with Nicholas Negroponte. They have a "vision of dramatically enhancing the way people experience and understand information."

The SmartContent Server discovers relationships between documents and creates visualizations (which are called SmartContent Spaces) based on these relationships. The meta-information of these relationships includes a standardized dictionary of terms and relationships, as well as document attributes such as source, author, and date.

An Information Space Markup Language (ISML) is used to represent these visualizations. This language is similar to XML:

> While XML is rapidly gaining broad industry support as the way to create intelligent, structured information, most of the applications for XML have been oriented to the routing and exchange of information. In contrast, Perspecta's SmartContent System leverages XML and its meta-data as the basis for organizing complex data types such as text, graphics, video or audio, to identify connections between pieces of information, and to build information structures that highlight those connections for users who need to navigate and access the information.[48]

The SmartContent system uses a dynamic, "just-in-time" protocol called Information Streaming Transport Protocol (ISTP) to communicate a SmartContent Space that can consist of tens of thousands of documents about hundreds of topics and thousands of subtopics and related topics. ISTP offers higher interaction with a client, such as that of RealAudio data stream:

> Instead of downloading the entire space, ISTP allows the user to "fly" through the space, progressively downloading only the regions of the space which are required to support the user's exploration. The result is a fluid, immersive environment in which the user can focus on the information itself—rather than the process of looking for information.

SmartContent includes an embedded version of Informix Universal Server.

---

47. See http://www.perspecta.com/.
48. See http://www.perspecta.com/whatsnew/releases/pr_xml_12_8_97.html.

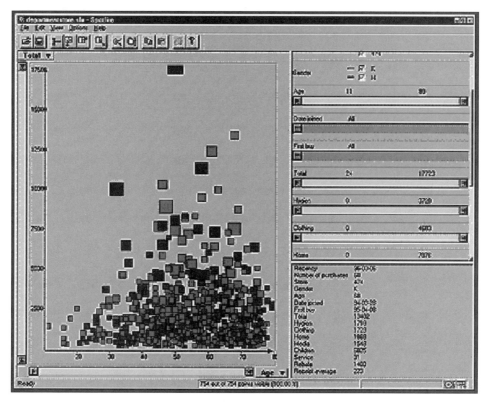

Figure 8-11   IVEE Spotfire Analysis of Department Store Sales

8.4.5 Spotfire Pro from IVEE Development

Spotfire Pro[49] is a visual data mining tool used by high-profile customers in market-ing, finance, manufacturing, and R&D applications.

IVEE Development AB develops and markets visual data mining tools allowing the intuitive exploration of data warehouses and databases. IVEE is a small company headquartered in Göteborg, Sweden, with an office in Boston.

In Figure 8-11, a customer database of a department store is shown.[50] Each colored marker represents a customer, colored by gender, with marker size indicating the amount of money spent on clothing. You can select details of particular customers by clicking on the marker. To filter only those customers who have purchased clothing for at least $500, for example, you simply move the appropriate slider to the right.

49. See http://www.ivee.com/.
50. Visual Data Mining, *BYTE,* July 1997.

Spotfire Pro is available for the Windows 3.x, Windows 95, and Windows NT platforms and imports data from databases, spreadsheets, and text files.

8.4.6   UMAP from TriVium

UMAP, from TriVium[51] (an innovative French company), is a visualization tool that is intriguing in its spatial arrangement. The tool focuses on discovering relevant information that is buried in other information. Initially, UMAP uses other search services (e.g., AltaVista and Yahoo) to collect Web pages. It compiles an index of terms and analyzes the distances between terms. UMAP then displays a space of terms in proper relationship to each other. The tool requires patience to tune parameters for a meaningful display.

Figure 8-12 shows the demo version searching for information on the "electric industry" topic. The frequency of occurrence of terms is shown by the red-to-blue spectrum (red is highest). The terms are shown on the left in frequency order (the term "electric" is the most frequently occurring term). The URL list on the right shows the specific URLs related to either terms or areas in the display.

8.4.7   Visual Insights from Lucent Technologies

Visual Insights[52] is an interactive data analysis package that integrates over 30 data visualizations, each performing a specific function or applying statistical analysis techniques to data. The visualization is "designed to uncover critical trends and patterns hidden in large volumes of data, enabling managers to make more timely and informed business decisions."

8.4.8   VizControls from Inxight Software, Inc.

VizControls, from Inxight,[53] is the commercialized version of several visualizations based on research at Xerox PARC. The VizControls technology is available through OEM agreements with other software vendors (such as Microsoft, Oracle, Verity, InfoSeek, and Comshare).

The VizControls technology includes four distinct visualizations:

- Hyperbolic Tree
- Table Lens
- Cone Tree
- Perspective Wall

51. See http://www.umap.com/.
52. See http://www.visualinsights.com/.
53. See http://www.inxight.com/.

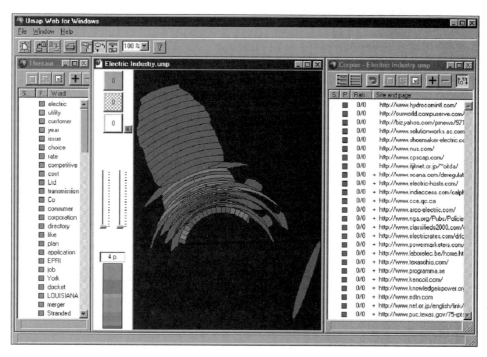

Figure 8-12   UMAP of Web Sites for the Electric Industry

The hyperbolic tree is good for navigating around a massive hierarchy many times larger than can be displayed at any one time, such as large Web sites, subject directories, and parts assemblies. When you click on a region of the tree, the figure warps to highlight that portion of the hierarchy. An example of the hyperbolic tree is shown in Figure 8-13, using the Xerox Web site as its target.

To better understand its dynamics, see the animated version of this figure.[54] Better yet, browse a Web site of your choice using the Java applet version. Try the Library of Congress. The input data to the applet is a simple hierarchical list of URLs and titles, as shown here:

```
http://lcweb.loc.gov/;Library of Congress Home Page
  http://lcweb.loc.gov/harvest/query-lc.html;Keyword Search of Library of Congress ...
    http://lcweb2.loc.gov/ammem/ammemhome.html;Digital Collections (American Memory)
    http://lcweb2.loc.gov/glin/glinhome.html;Global Legal Information (GLIN)
    http://lcweb2.loc.gov/frd/cs/cshome.html;Country Studies
    http://lcweb2.loc.gov/hlas/;HLAS Online
    http://lcweb2.loc.gov/pow/powhome.html;POW/MIA Database
    http://lcweb.loc.gov/global/search.html;Internet Search Tools (Library of ...
      http://www.albany.net/allinone/;All-In-One Search Page
      http://www.clearinghouse.net/;The Argus Clearinghouse
      http://www.ncsa.uiuc.edu/SDG/Software/Mosaic/MetaIndex.html;Internet ...
      http://www.w3.org/hypertext/DataSources/ByAccess.html;Global List of Servers
```

54. See http://www.inxight.com/inprodvz.htm.

Figure 8-13
Inxight Hyperbolic Tree

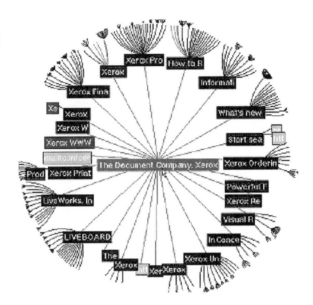

The Inxight technology from Xerox PARC is certainly innovative but in its early stages of commercialization. The table lens is good for viewing large spreadsheet-like tables with numeric data. The cone tree is good for viewing and editing massive hierarchical structures, like file directories or organizational charts. Finally, the perspective wall is good for arranging a large set of discrete objects, like documents or Web pages, along a linear dimension, like time. However, these visualizations are not yet available from Inxight.

8.4.9   WEBSOM from Helsinki University

The Web Self-Organizing Map,[55] or WEBSOM, is a research project at the Neural Networks Research Centre of the Helsinki University of Technology. WEBSOM is a means for organizing text documents into a meaningful map for exploration and search. Related documents appear close to each other on a two-dimensional density grid.

A sample of a WEBSOM visualization is shown in Figure 8-14.

One advantage of WEBSOM is an algorithm to arrange massive information into a meaningful two-dimensional space based on traditional keyword associations. A disadvantage is that WEBSOM is not available as a commercial product.

---

55. See http://websom.hut.fi/websom/ and Section 7.8 of T. Kohonen, *Self-Organizing Maps,* second edition, Springer, 1997 (3-540-62017-6).

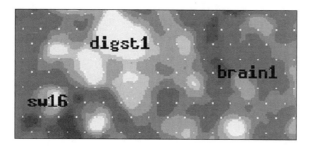

Figure 8-14
WEBSOM
Density Grid

8.5 **Extended Relational Databases**

This section introduces the major relational database products that have extended their functionality toward object-oriented, and particularly intelligent, text and image processing.

Table 8-6 simply lists the extended relational databases, since abundant information is available from many sources on each of these products.

In general, the products in this category are excellent for maintaining large data stores of hypertext within a production environment; however, these products are usually weak in their discovery and acquisition functions.

Table 8-6 Tools for Extended Relational Databases

Tool	Vendor/Developer
Extended Relational Databases	
Standard Full-Text Search	Sybase, Inc.
DataBlades	Informix Corporation
MS SQL Server	Microsoft Corporation
Universal DB2	IBM Corporation
ConText	Oracle

8.6 Data Marts

This section covers the data marts—data warehousing systems that focus on a single subject area and are usually employed at the workgroup level within an enterprise. The advantage of data marts is that they integrate a variety of components from extraction, transformation, database loading, metadata management, and query processing. The disadvantage is that they are usually not scalable to the enterprise level, leading to a proliferation of independent data marts that fragment information across the enterprise.

Data marts are usually weak in Web crawling and hypertext analysis functions, so that they need to be combined with other products for Web farming. A summary of the data mart tools is given in Table 8-7.

Other data mart products that are not described below are SmartMart,[56] from Information Builders; Broadbase Server,[57] from Broadbase; and Warehouse Executive,[58] from Prism Solutions.

8.6.1 Data Mart Solution from Sagent Technology

Data Mart Solution, from Sagent Technology,[59] is an integrated set of data warehousing tools for populating the data mart and creating metadata to enable end users to access, distribute, and collaborate on the data. The Data Mart Solution runs on a Windows NT platform.

Table 8-7   Tools for Data Marts

Tool	*Vendor/Developer*
Data Marts	
Data Mart Solution	Sagent Technology
Intelligent Warehouse	Platinum Technology
PowerMart Suite	Informatica Corp.
Tapestry	D2K Inc.
Visual Warehouse	IBM Corporation

---

56. See http://www.ibi.com/.
57. See http://www.broadbase.com/.
58. See http://www.prismsolutions.com/.
59. See http://www.sagenttech.com/.

8.6.2 Intelligent Warehouse from Platinum Technology

The Intelligent Warehouse,[60] from Platinum Technology, was formerly owned by Hewlett-Packard, Inc. It is a middleware management layer that creates a single virtual warehouse from multiple independent databases. Intelligent Warehouse runs on HP-UX, but the other databases may run on separate HP or non-HP server platforms. Intelligent Warehouse also supports most popular data access, reporting, and OLAP tools running on Windows NT, Macintosh, OS/2, and Unix platforms, as well as those running through Web browsers.

8.6.3 PowerMart Suite from Informatica Corp.

The PowerMart suite[61] is an integrated set of data warehousing tools for building, deploying, and managing data warehouses. PowerMart propagates data from operational transaction databases using a "real-time extract/transform/load engine."

8.6.4 Tapestry from D2K Inc.

Tapestry[62] is a set of data warehousing tools that "helps corporations build a comprehensive, scaleable, information framework to enable knowledge collaboration within and between work groups." One component, the Tapestry Server, performs data movement, transformation, scheduling, documentation, and monitoring. Another component, the Tapestry Catalog, is a metadata repository that tracks the activities and processes of the other components. Tapestry works with the Oracle, Sybase, Informix, and Microsoft SQL Server databases.

8.6.5 Visual Warehouse from IBM Corporation

Visual Warehouse[63] is a set of data warehousing tools that "replicate data from a variety of operational data sources; aggregate, summarize, cleanse, or enhance the data; and make it available to end users through their favorite decision-support tools."

---

60. See http://www.hp.com/go/datawarehouse.
61. See http://www.informatica.com/.
62. See http://www.d2k.com/.
63. See http://www.ibm.com/.

Table 8-8   Tools for Knowledge Management

Tool	Vendor/Developer	Description
Knowledge Management Systems		
Agentware i3	Autonomy, Inc.	Preference profiling
Dataware II KMS	Dataware, Inc.	Electronic publishing
deliveryMANAGER	VIT	Information delivery with P&S
FireFly Passport Office	Microsoft	Preference profiling
Folio Suite	Open Markets, Inc.	Electronic publishing with Folio InfoBase
InfoMagnet	CompassWare Devel	Preference profiling
Knowledge Server	Intraspect	Collaborative groupware with Verity
KnowledgeX	KnowledgeX, Inc.	Semantic net visualization
Livelink Intranet	Open Text, Inc.	Balanced KMS with strong crawler
WisdomBuilder	WisdomBuilder, LLC	Lightweight KMS with intelligence flavor
WiseWire	Lycos Corporation	Collaborative and content filtering

8.7   Knowledge Management Systems

This section covers products that identify themselves as "knowledge management systems" (KMS). It is often difficult to confirm this assertion, since the definition of such a system is highly debatable. This is a rapidly growing product category and has significant overlapping of functionality with other categories we have explored.

A summary of the knowledge management systems is given in Table 8-8.

This is a fascinating collection of products, all of which position themselves as high-end knowledge managers. Some come from a long tradition, such as Dataware and Folio (now part of Open Markets). Most are bold startups with a track record of only a few years. Collaborative filtering and preference profiling are major themes; WiseWire owns the technological high ground. The most balanced (and full-function in terms of Web farming) systems are Livelink, from Open Text, and Knowledge Server, from Intraspect.

8.7.1   Agentware i3 from Autonomy, Inc.

Agentware i3, from Autonomy,[64] is a KMS that has "a personalization infrastructure for online information providers who need to automatically understand their customers' unique interests." The term *i3* stands for *intelligent information infrastructure.*

---

64. See http://www.agentware.com/.

Agentware i3 uses Concept Agents, based on neural nets, to understand the interests of site visitors and dynamically deliver relevant content. As content changes, the Content Server dynamically links content and suggests other topics that may be of interest to the user.

> Autonomy's Adaptive Probabilistic Concept Modeling (APCM) technology enables our Agentware software to efficiently identify and encode the unique "signature" of the key concepts within text documents. APCM then uses this signature to seek out and uncover the presence of similar concepts in volumes of content such as a set of websites, a news feed or an email archive.

8.7.2 Dataware II Knowledge Management Suite from Dataware, Inc.

Dataware II[65] is a KMS that is "a complete system for enterprise information access and professional electronic publishing." It can be used alone or in conjunction with other components that provide enhanced functionality.

The components of Dataware are as follows:

- Source Cartridges are available to input formats such as those of Lotus Notes, Adobe Acrobat, document management servers, and others.
- The Query Server unites all available information into a single, searchable database. For organizations with information stored on multiple servers, even in different geographical locations.
- The Publisher makes possible custom styling of all stored information and enables users to publish material to CD-ROM and other media in a consistent format.
- The Agent Server monitors for updated information on specific topics and notifies users when the information becomes available.
- The Web Interface provides information access through standard Web browsers. The interface can be fully customized, and template Web pages are also provided.
- Toolkits are available to provide programmers with an extensive range of customization options.

---

65. See http://www.dataware.com/.

Dataware has licensed its products to the U.S. Patent and Trademark Office (PTO) to enable trademark examiners to

> search a multi-gigabyte database for registered trademark words and phrases, helping to support the PTO's goals of providing the fastest, most accurate service possible to customers and increasing awareness of intellectual property protection.[66]

8.7.3 deliveryMANAGER from VIT

The deliveryMANAGER system[67] is a KMS that claims to be

> the industry's first information delivery system that allows users to *subscribe* and *publish* information in a data warehouse, data mart, desktop or the Internet, in a single information catalog.

The deliveryMANAGER system has three components:

- The deliveryAGENT is the Web browser, or Windows user interface to the information catalog, enabling users to shop for structured data (tables, views) and unstructured data (text documents, spreadsheets, OLAP cubes, URLs, audio/video, executables, etc.). Information can be delivered in familiar desktop formats (such as that of Microsoft Office) directly to the desktop, email address, file server, or Web server.
- The metaWAREHOUSE is an information catalog built on an open relational database design. The catalog integrates business and technical metadata and includes source, target, logical, and physical definitions and their mappings, as well as calculated, derived, and transformed field definitions.
- The deliveryADMIN is an administrative tool used to register and manage information in the structured hierarchy of the catalog, determine what information should be accessible to whom, and analyze how information is used across the enterprise.

---

66. PR Newswire, December 2, 1997.
67. See http://www.vit.com/.

8.7.4 Firefly Passport Office from Microsoft Corporation

Firefly Passport Office[68] from Microsoft (which has acquired Firefly Network, Inc.), is a KMS that manages relationships with customers, affiliates, partners, suppliers, distributors, and so on through highly personalized interactions while protecting the individual's privacy. A Firefly Passport is a custom profile of each person, which captures information about preferences and interest levels regarding your business and your products.

> Businesses may leverage the valuable knowledge stored within these customer profiles to serve each person in a highly personalized manner, greatly increasing the effectiveness of every interaction. By better understanding the needs and interests of each individual, businesses
>
> have the ability to establish and grow profitable, long-term relationships with their customers. . . . As a result, you can provide an exceptional service that is personalized for every customer based on each person's interest in, opinion of, and association with your company, products, and services.

8.7.5 Folio Suite from Open Market, Inc.

The Folio Suite, from Open Market,[69] is a KMS that is "the industry standard for the production, management, and delivery of professional information." Content publishers can import HTML, SGML, XML, and documents in popular word processing formats into an indexed Folio *infobase* (using Folio's Flat File markup language) and deliver that content over an intranet, or the Internet, or on CD-ROM. With support of XML, the Folio infobase will be compatible with other open, standards-based solutions that author, parse, distribute, and render XML documents.

---

68. See http://www.firefly.com/.
69. See http://www.openmarket.com/products/folio/.

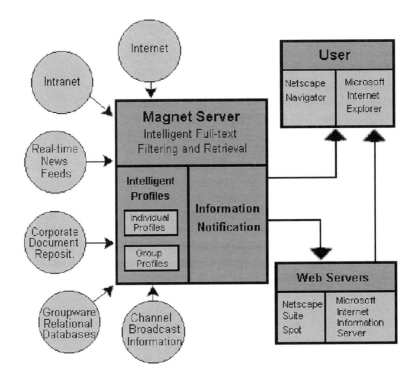

Figure 8-15 Architecture of InfoMagnet

8.7.6 InfoMagnet from CompassWare Development, Inc.

InfoMagnet[70] is a KMS that "leverages all information resources available to enterprise users" through "intelligent up-to-the-second filtering and retrieval of relevant information." Users can easily "teach" InfoMagnet their interests using Relevance Feedback technology to profile their preferences. InfoMagnet provides the user with a consolidated personal view of the current relevant information.

The architecture of InfoMagnet is shown in Figure 8-15. A screen shot of Info-Magnet using the Netscape browser is shown in Figure 8-16. Note the three-panel design, which gives the user the context for the document being studied.

---

70. See http://www.compassware.com/.

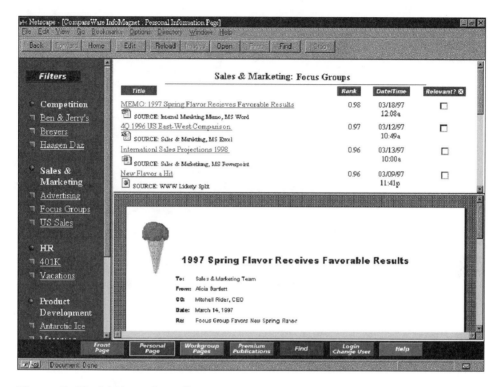

Figure 8-16   InfoMagnet Screen Shot

8.7.7   Knowledge Server from Intraspect

The Knowledge Server, from Intraspect,[71] is a KMS that "integrates the best features of collaboration, information retrieval/search, database and groupware software to create the first environment where people can easily share, discover and reapply each other's work."

The architecture of the Knowledge Server is shown in Figure 8-17. The Knowledge Server system consists of four main components: Knowledge Services, Discovery Services, Collaboration Services, and Distribution Services.

The repository is stored in a object-oriented database from Objectivity. The search engine (from Verity) creates full-text indexes, not only of documents, but also of the metadata, thus presenting a complete picture of all information. The server is written completely in the Java language; the entire product uses standard communications protocols.

---

71. See http://www.intraspect.com/.

Figure 8-17
Architecture of
Intraspect

A screen shot of the main window is shown in Figure 8-18. The screen design provides superior descriptions of the information's context—the what (title and type of information), who (author), when (time), and why (folder name, description, attached comments and discussions)—thus facilitating information discovery and retrieval. When information appears in more than one context, users have the ability to navigate to any of them, discovering new and varied uses of the same information.

8.7.8 KnowledgeX from KnowledgeX, Inc.

The KnowledgeX system[72] is a KMS that "provides solutions to organizations seeking to manage their intellectual assets and collective knowledge for competitive advantage" by "graphically revealing relationships from different information sources." KnowledgeX develops and markets software products for "acquiring, mapping, discovering, and sharing the knowledge that has a direct impact on your

---

72. See http://www.knowledgex.com/.

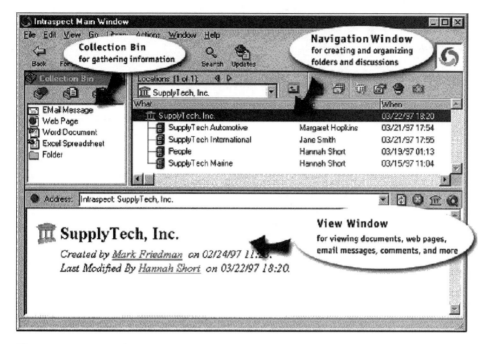

Figure 8-18   Main Client Window for Intraspect

business," thus helping firms "leverage their intelligence assets through intelligent knowledge management."

KnowledgeX uses the SmartParse component to apply lexical parsing and business rules to evaluate documents and identify individuals, organizations, postal addresses, Web sites, phones numbers, and interesting phrases, as well as items corresponding to a personal "hot list." A direct link to the source document is automatically recorded for items derived from documents so that checking the source document is simple.

A screen shot in Figure 8-19 shows an investigation of FedEx and its relationship to other concepts.

KnowledgeX implemented the KORE visualization, which is based on a cognitive mapping of objects (i.e., a category or collection) with relationships (i.e., nodes of two or more objects). Nodes of a relationship have a role (e.g., property or attribute) and a strength (i.e., the influence of that object in the relationship). For example, here is a simple relationship in KORE:

```
INDIVIDUAL: "John Doe" has IDENTIFIER: "123-45-6789" with ROLE: "Social Security Number"
```

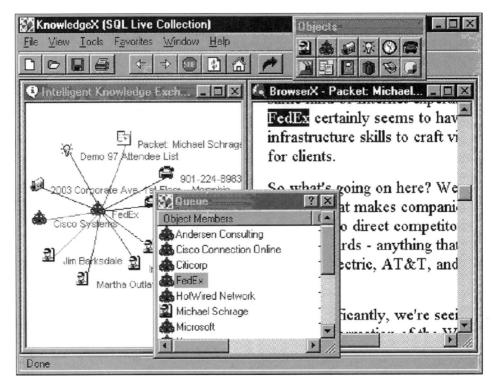

Figure 8-19 KnowledgeX Screen Shot

The visualization of KORE is shown in Figure 8-20 as a ball-stick image linked to text. The advantage of the KORE visualization is its rich semantic modeling linked to specific keywords within the textual data.

8.7.9 Livelink Intranet from Open Text, Inc.

Livelink Intranet, from Open Text Corporation,[73] is "a highly scalable, collaborative knowledge management application for intranets" supporting a tight integration of "enterprise document management, workflow, project collaboration and search engines."

Livelink consists of three basic components:

- A knowledge gathering system
- A knowledge distribution system
- A collaborative knowledge use system

---

73. See http://www.opentext.com/.

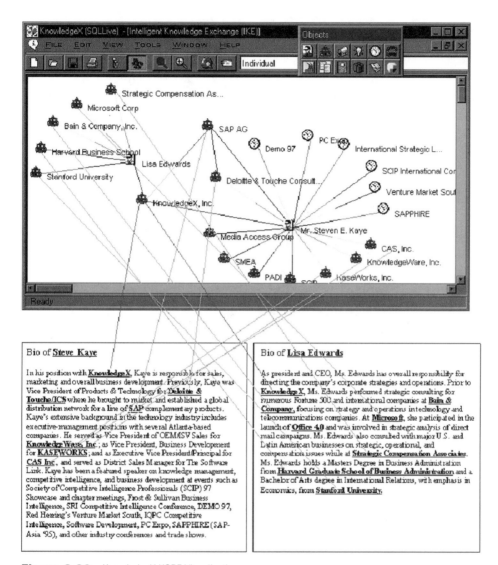

Figure 8-20 KnowledgeX KORE Visualization

Open Text makes the point that without the collaborate component, a KMS is "nothing but a large repository." With the collaborate component, workgroups are enabled "to put knowledge to work." Livelink is also fully Web-based and has an open architecture to ensure very rapid deployment, requiring only a Web browser on the user's desktop to access its full functionality.

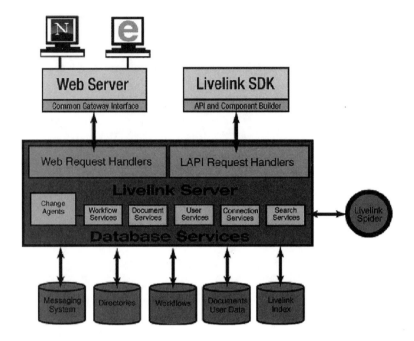

Figure 8-21 Architecture of Livelink

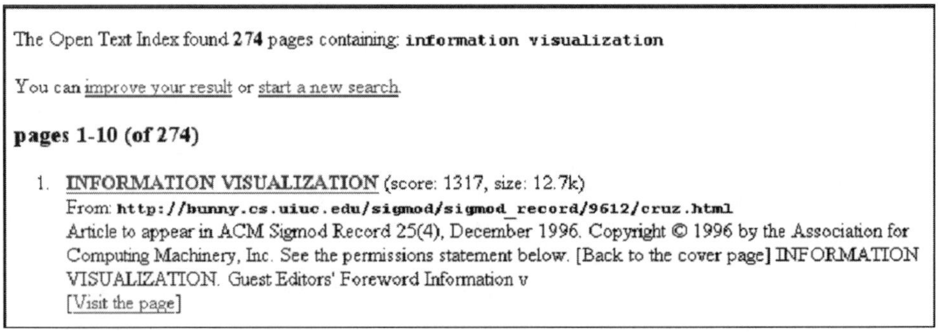

The Open Text Index found 274 pages containing: **information visualization**

You can improve your result or start a new search.

pages 1-10 (of 274)

1. **INFORMATION VISUALIZATION** (score: 1317, size: 12.7k)
    From: `http://bunny.cs.uiuc.edu/sigmod/sigmod_record/9612/cruz.html`
    Article to appear in ACM Sigmod Record 25(4), December 1996. Copyright © 1996 by the Association for
    Computing Machinery, Inc. See the permissions statement below. [Back to the cover page] INFORMATION
    VISUALIZATION. Guest Editors' Foreword Information v
    [Visit the page]

Figure 8-22 Sample Index Generated by Livelink

Figure 8-21 shows the architecture of Livelink.

Livelink Spider crawls your network and the Web, fetching information to be indexed and cataloged. Open Text's Livelink Spider is based on the same technology that drives the Open Text Index (a free Internet search service).[74] Figure 8-22 shows the results of searching on the phrase *Information Visualization* at the Open Text Index.

74. See http://index.opentext.net/.

Livelink runs on Microsoft Windows NT and popular UNIX platforms and supports most relational database management systems.

8.7.10 WisdomBuilder from WisdomBuilder, LLC

WisdomBuilder[75] is a KMS that "provides a solution to the problem of how to effectively analyze, manage, and mine the glut of raw data." The product is based on "25 years of experience in designing and developing intelligence processing solutions," applied by Kenneth W. Kisiel, for the U.S. intelligence agencies.

The notable features of WisdomBuilder are as follows:

- Supports direct import from HTML, SQL databases, and most document formats
- Allows the partitioning of research requirements into separate research sets
- Creates and tracks relationships among any object types
- Automatically analyzes message content using a user-generated data dictionary
- Navigates graphically through data relationships
- Supports multimedia file formats (BMP, JPG, GIF, PCX, TIF, WAV)
- Includes a standard set of list, profile, and relationship reports
- Disseminates reports in hard copy, HTML, popular file formats, and email
- Provides security through password protection and separate user accounts

WisdomBuilder requires a 486-compatible computer system or better and Microsoft Windows 3.1, 95, or NT.

8.7.11 WiseWire from Lycos Corporation

WiseWire, from Lycos (which has acquired WiseWire Corporation) is a KMS that uses "neural network technology combining collaborative filtering with content-based filtering."[76] Based on research at Carnegie Mellon University, WiseWire learns from people's preferences.

> WiseWire can adapt to any topic and can filter a variety of digital content. WiseWire's patent-pending technology delivers information in real time and personalizes automatically, with less of a "learning curve" than purely collaborative approaches.

---

75. See http://www.wisdombuilder.com/.
76. See http://www.wisewire-corp.com/.

Figure 8-23
WiseWire
Collaborative
Filtering

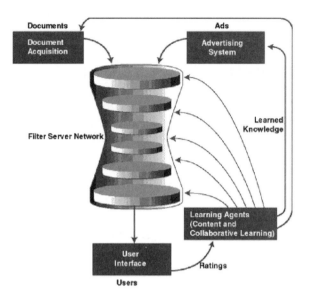

WiseWire can be integrated into an existing Web site, offering direct links to continuously updated, real-time information. It provides a "collective intelligence" that can follow popular trends very quickly, vary levels of personalization, and create "communities of interest" around any topic.

Figure 8-23 illustrates the architecture of LiveWire. From document acquisition or advertising selections, the Filter Server Network distills the personal rating of content, which then directs subsequent use. An interesting passage describes WiseWire as the opposite of a library:

> In fact, one could look at WiseWire as a library in reverse. In an actual library, people search for interesting documents; in contrast, WiseWire is a virtual library where documents search for and find interested people.

WiseWire Corporation offers a free consumer service, with personalized Wires, which is an excellent way of learning about this technology.[77]

---

77. See http://www.wisewire.com/tpl_home.emc.

8.8 Suitability for Web Farming

This section summarizes the tools described above and gives a rough rating as to their suitability for Web farming. The rating is based on how suitable a specific tool is for each of the four phases of information refinement—discovery, acquisition, structuring, and dissemination.

As given in Table 8-9, the ratings for the various tools range from zero to three stars. No stars imply that features that support the specified information activity are not present. One star implies limited or partial features (usually for a single-person context), requiring additional tools or extensive programming. Two stars imply adequate features and/or operation within a multiple-person context and a common database, but the product still requires some programming and extension. Three stars imply complete features for production-level operation with a common database, requiring only installation and configuration. These ratings are rough estimates based on a subjective review of available literature.

8.8.1 General Synopsis

Here is a brief summary of Web farming tools. The generic Web browser is a ubiquitous tool but has very limited functionality. Web agent tools are quite popular, but only for personal productivity. Hypertext analysis tools are rapidly maturing, but are still limited to querying document collections on discrete keywords. Information visualization tools have tremendous potential for discovery, but are limited to point solutions. Extended relational databases are mature server platforms, but have only recently understood hypertext processing. Data marts provide useful integration of components for data warehousing, but are clueless in unstructured data environments. Finally, knowledge management systems are solutions that are trying to find themselves.

No category (and no specific tool) adequately covers all the activities of Web farming. In other words, Web farming systems *per se* do not yet exist. There is little integration among some tools and there are wide gaps among others. Further, most tools focus on personal productivity for casual users, rather than on intelligence analysis by full-time professionals.

Over time, Web farming systems will emerge, but only if a clear architecture and motivation for such systems are defined. Meanwhile, Web farming will require an ongoing effort of integrating and extending available tools. (Where are the chewing gum and baling wire?)

An important requirement for a Web farming tool set is the close interaction of multiple client platforms with a common database server to support both the discovery and acquisition activities. Chapter 5, Architecture, emphasizes that the server should host background processes and the client platforms should perform analysis. Most of the tools described below reside only on a single platform and allow little cooperation with other platforms.

Table 8-9　Suitability Ratings of Tools for Web Farming

Tool	Vendor/Developer	D	A	S	D
Web Agents					
Alexa	Alexa Internet	◆◆			
Copernic	Agents Technologies Corp.	◆	◆		
LiveAgent Pro	AgentSoft Ltd.	◆	◆◆	◆	◆
NetGetIt	Crossproduct Solutions	◆	◆◆	◆	
Odyssey	General Magic	◆	◆◆		
Smart Bookmarks	FirstFloor	◆	◆		
WebCompass	Quarterdeck	◆◆	◆		
WebWhacker	Blue Squirrel	◆	◆◆		
Who's Talking	Software Solutions	◆	◆		
Hypertext Analysis and Transformation					
AltaVista Search	Digital Equipment Corp.	◆◆◆	◆◆	◆	◆
Cambio	Data Junction		◆◆	◆	
Compass Server	Netscape	◆◆	◆◆	◆◆	◆◆
Dynamic Reasoning Engine	Neurodynamics	◆	◆	◆◆◆	
EXTRACT Tool Suite	Evolutionary Technologies		◆	◆◆◆	
Index Server	Microsoft		◆◆	◆◆	
Integrity	Vality Technology Inc.			◆◆	
Intelligent Miner for Text	IBM Corporation	◆◆		◆◆	
LinguistX	Inxight Software, Inc.		◆◆	◆◆	
NetOwl Intelligence Server	IsoQuest Inc.	◆◆	◆	◆◆	◆◆
RetrievalWare	Excalibur Technologies		◆◆	◆◆	
Search'97	Verity Inc.	◆◆	◆◆	◆◆◆	◆
SearchServer	Fulcrum Technologies	◆◆	◆◆	◆◆	◆
SmartCrawl	Inktomi		◆◆◆		
Utraseek	InfoSeek Corporation	◆◆	◆◆	◆◆	◆
Webinator	Thurderstone		◆◆	◆◆	
ZyIndex	ZyLab International Inc.			◆	
Information Visualization					
Discovery for Developers	Visible Decisions Inc.				◆
SemioMap	Semio Corporation	◆◆		◆	
SmartContent System	Perspecta	◆◆		◆	◆
UMAP	TriVium	◆◆		◆◆	

Table 8-9   *(Continued)*

Tool	Vendor/Developer	D	A	S	D
Information Visualization (continued)					
Spotfire Pro	IVEE Development	♦			♦♦
Visual Insights	Lucent Technologies	♦♦			♦
VizControls	Inxight Software, Inc.	♦♦			♦♦
WEBSOM	Helsinki University	♦		♦♦	
Extended Relational Databases					
Standard Full-Text Search	Sybase, Inc.			♦♦	♦
DataBlades	Informix Corporation			♦♦	♦
Universal DB2	IBM Corporation			♦♦	♦
ConText	Oracle Corporation			♦♦	♦
Data Marts					
Data Mart Solution	Sagent Technology		♦	♦	♦♦
Intelligent Warehouse	Platinum Technology		♦	♦	♦♦
PowerMart Suite	Informatica Corp.		♦	♦	♦♦
Tapestry	D2K Inc.		♦	♦	♦♦
Visual Warehouse	IBM Corporation		♦	♦	♦♦
Knowledge Management Systems					
Agentware i3	Autonomy, Inc.		♦♦	♦♦	♦
Dataware II KMS	Dataware, Inc.		♦	♦♦♦	♦
deliveryMANAGER	VIT		♦♦	♦	♦♦♦
Firefly Passport Office	Microsoft		♦♦		♦♦
Folio Suite	Open Markets, Inc.		♦	♦♦	♦♦♦
InfoMagnet	CompassWare Development			♦♦	
Knowledge Server	Intraspect	♦		♦♦♦	♦
KnowledgeX	KnowledgeX, Inc.			♦♦	
Livelink Intranet	Open Text, Inc.		♦♦	♦♦♦	♦♦
WisdomBuilder	WisdomBuilder, LLC			♦	
WiseWire	Lycos Corporation				♦♦

*This table summarizes the tools described in this chapter. The right columns indicate a rough rating of suitability for the activities of D-A-S-D (i.e., discovery, acquisition, structuring, and dissemination).

A final comment about tools for Web farming: The boundary between a tool and a service is rapidly blurring. Some tools interact invisibly with a Web site for background data and parameters. Likewise, some services download huge Java applets that change the entire style of the user interface within the browser context. In the material below, we will provide several examples of this tool/service integration.

8.8.2   Production Database

The following criteria were given special importance in the ratings:

- Production-level operation
- Common database

A production-level operation implies that there is a secure server platform supporting multiple client platforms. It also implies that there is a high level of system availability (24×7) and reliability (99+% uptime).[78] A production-level operation should be remotely administered and have an automatic recovery mechanism so that any interrupted process is restarted at the point of the interruption. Finally, a production-level operation should be easily scaled upward so that increased service demand can be met through incremental additions to the system.

A common database implies that content is shared among analysts and users. There should be a close integration with the data warehouse, so that duplicate and inconsistent data is minimized between the database supporting Web farming and the database supporting the warehouse. In addition, the database is the single point of control for coordinating all Web farming activities. Finally, collaboration among all persons should be encouraged so that there is a pooling of common knowledge and an avoidance of common mistakes.

8.8.3   Discovery

The tools that best support discovery for Web farming are concentrated in the categories of Web agents, hypertext analysis, and information visualization. The Web agents have the advantage of a mass market for browser-related utilities, stimulating production of many innovative products. However, Web agents tend not to have the robustness for group discovery activities. The hypertext analysis tools definitely have the strength for group and enterprise operations, but they tend to be behind the technology curve.

---

78. A new slogan for high reliability, from Hewlett-Packard, is "5nines:5minutes," implying 99.999% annual end-to-end availability and only five minutes of downtime per year.

8.8.4   Acquisition

The tools that best support acquisition for Web farming are spread across the categories of Web agents, hypertext analysis, and knowledge management systems. The Web agents are excellent, but only in the context of a single workstation. There is "industrial strength" in some of the hypertext tools, such as Search '97, from Verity; RetrievalWare, from Excalibur Technologies; AltaVista Search, from Digital; and SmartCrawl, from Inktomi.

The KMS products are usually spotty in their handling of Web content, since they assume internal documents and email are their primary content.

The data marts also have excellent abilities to acquire structured data from operational systems, but they lack any real abilities for handling Web content.

8.8.5   Structuring

The tools that best support structuring for Web farming are concentrated among tools for hypertext transformation and knowledge management. The hypertext tools are excellent for generating lists of items according to some relevance criteria, but they often lack the ability to generate a tabular data stream suitable for loading into a relational database. The knowledge management systems are strong in hierarchical structuring across a variety of data formats, but have similar weaknesses in database loading.

The data marts and extended relational databases certainly perform wonders with numeric data but lack strength with text or images.

8.8.6   Dissemination

The tools that best support dissemination for Web farming are concentrated among data marts and knowledge management systems. The data marts have their traditional strength in information delivery, and the KMS products have added some innovative twists. The real solution at the enterprise scale is those products that implement a robust publish-and-subscribe mechanism, fostering a dynamic information marketplace throughout the enterprise.

The bottom line is that a single complete Web farming tool does not exist commercially. There must be considerable integration among the tools before a single product will constitute a suitable system.

As with the evolution of data warehousing systems, integrated Web farming systems will emerge over time, but only after a clear definition of such tools and the market motivation for them are established.

Meanwhile, Web farming will require an ongoing effort of integrating and extending commercially available products with home-grown development—a little chewing gum here and a bit of baling wire there.

Chapter Nine

Resources

The farmer is completely dependent on the basic resources of sun, rain, seed, and fertilizer. Without any one of those resources, his crop would not grow. Likewise, Web farming requires some basic resources—information content about the topics of interest.

This chapter is meant to be an overview rather than an inclusive listing. The resources described are a small sampling of those available on the Web, and more are added each day. We hope this chapter will inspire a continuing refinement of the latest and greatest in Web resources. Suggestions are included for making this refinement both productive and enjoyable.

The Web resources described in this chapter were compiled in early 1998. It is likely that many of these URL links will become invalid over time. The Web site for this book (http://webfarming.com/) contains an up-to-date listing of these resources. In addition, a search using a major discovery service with the key phrases of any description will likely uncover the revised links.

There is a diverse array of content providers on the web, and this diversity will explode over the coming years. For a new content provider, there is a low barrier to entry and a low recurring cost. The economics that motivate a content provider to provide content are varied and sometimes irrational. The economic calculations are often based on advertising revenue, whose ability to provide profits is doubtful for a user who is seriously Web farming.

In Chapter 1, Motivation, the relationship of quality to coverage of Web content was introduced. The point is that the *"flaky-free"* content should be a continuing source for Web farming, although the bulk of information may be supplied by commercial concerns and governmental institutions. The quality of Web content from commercial providers and government agencies is higher than that obtained freely from open Web sites. However, the "flaky-free" content covers a vastly broader spectrum of topics—a spectrum that is changing and expanding every day.

The challenge for the Web farming function is to find, over time, a balance among a variety of Web resources. This balance should maximize the business value of the content while minimizing the expense of its discovery and acquisition.

This chapter is organized into a number of sections, shown below.

- General Discovery Services: search for general Web content
- Meta–Discovery Services: adding value to the various discovery services
- Specialized Directory Centers: resource centers that specialize in specific topics
- General Content Providers: large content providers with a variety of databases
- Industry-Specific Content Providers: specializing in a vertical industry
- Market Research Firms: providers specializing in the nature and trends of markets
- Library Services: providing resources from major research libraries
- General News Agencies: covering global events and topics
- IT Trade Publications: news agencies specializing in the IT industry
- Investment Services: providing data about investment (usually stock) performance
- Related Publications: covering topics of interest to Web farming

- Professional Societies: associations related to Web farming
- Book Distributors: for cross-indexing of books in print and associations among books
- Intelligence and Investigative Resources: the old-timers in the business
- U.S. Government Agencies: cornucopias of free data

This chapter explores a wide variety of Web resources. Browse through this material quickly, and note those resources that have the highest potential for meeting your needs. Investigate those resources further by exploring their Web sites and by communicating directly with the providers.

9.1 General Discovery Services

The topic of discovery services is a complex and ever-changing one. There is one important distinction—search versus directory. The search (or crawl) services systematically explore links from one page to the next, accumulating an index to each specific Web page based on its title, keywords, author, and body text. The directory (index, switchboard, or clearinghouse) services also scan the Web for useful and interesting Web pages, but organize references into hierarchical directories on similar topics.

The specific services covered in this section are

Search

- AltaVista: the grand web searcher of them all
- Excite: a growing influence
- HotBot: a runner-up to Alta Vista
- InfoSeek: stable and competent
- Lycos: good basic search that includes sounds and images
- Northern Light: new, with unique folder organization
- Web Crawler: small and quick

Directory

- Argus Clearinghouse: a site to scan periodically
- Inter-Links: small and unique
- Librarians' Index: unique and highly professional
- Magellan: lots of rated sites
- Mining Company: new and a runner-up to Yahoo!
- Yahoo!: the grand directory of them all

9.1.1   For Current Information

For current information, check the Yahoo! directory for "Search and Navigation."[1]

Also, the Search Engine Watch maintains a continuous analysis of the various discovery services.[2] It offers a free monthly e-magazine giving the latest in search services.

Web Farmers

Subscribe to the free monthly e-newsletter from SE Watch.

Finally, visit periodically the InfoPeople site maintained by Carole Leita. The main page,[3] shown in Figure 9-1, is excellent. Note especially the two indexes to discovery services—Best Search Engines and Best Indexes—on this main page.

The specific discovery services are listed below, with a brief description for each.

9.1.2   AltaVista

One of the more popular search engines is AltaVista,[4] which is managed by Digital Equipment Corporation. It has an extensive database of Web pages (over 100 million) and newsgroups (over 14,000), along with an efficient query capability. It has extensive advanced query features. AltaVista is the best search server, but it returns lots of results that must be refined.

Web Farmers

Get to know the advanced query features of AltaVista.

9.1.3   Argus Clearinghouse

The Argus Clearinghouse[5] is an excellent index of indexes; it contains a well-organized topical guide to various sites created by individuals who specialize in specific topics. Use when you need further depth in a subject.

---

1. See http://www.yahoo.com/Business_and_Economy/Companies/Internet_Services /Search_and_Navigation/.
2. See http://www.searchenginewatch.com/.
3. See http://sunsite.berkeley.edu/InternetIndex/.
4. See http://www.altavista.digital.com/.
5. See http://www.clearinghouse.net/.

9.1.4 Excite

The strong features of Excite[6] are product reviews, Usenet news and classifieds, and current headlines (from over 300 news sources), along with a keyword and concept search engine. Results can be grouped by sites.

9.1.5 HotBot

HotBot[7] is an excellent feature-packed search service based on the Inktomi engine.[8] Good for searching for people, it allows field searching by URL, date, location, and media type. HotBot has a database close to AltaVista's in page counts. This site and AltaVista are the best for deep searching.

9.1.6 InfoSeek

Infoseek[9] has indexed the full text of over 50 million pages. It is unique in automatically recognizing names, capitalized word phrases, and word variants (e.g., man = men). Infoseek has advanced searching on fields, such as links, URLs, and titles).

9.1.7 Inter-Links

Inter-Links[10] is a directory offering "Internet navigator, resource locator, and tutorial." This site is unique in that it is "the product of a single individual, working without remuneration, after office hours, and as a public service."

9.1.8 InterNIC WhoIs Search

The InterNIC WhoIs Search[11] is the best place to find information about domain names, especially COM and ORG top levels.

---

6. See http://www.excite.com/.
7. See http://www.hotbot.com/.
8. See http://www.inktomi.com/.
9. See http://www.infoseek.com/.
10. See http://alabanza.com/kabacoff/Inter-Links/.
11. See http://rs.internic.net/cgi-bin/whois/.

Figure 9-1   Librarians' Index

9.1.9   Librarians' Index

Hosted by the Digital Library SunSITE,[12] one of the more thoughtful directories with an emphasis toward academics and research is created by Carole Leita.[13] Recently retired from the Berkeley Public Library, she is devoting her time to teaching librarians about the Internet and supporting the InFoPeople project[14] in Berkeley.

9.1.10   Lycos

Lycos[15] supports the basic set of search operators along with searching for sounds and images.

---

12. See http://sunsite.berkeley.edu/InternetIndex/.
13. See http://www.austinfree.net/leita/.
14. See http://infopeople.berkeley.edu:8000/.
15. See http://www.lycos.com/.

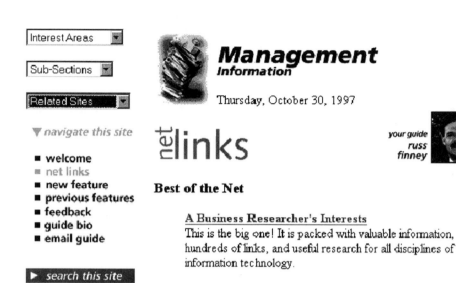

Figure 9-2 "Your Guide" to Management at the Mining Company

9.1.11 Magellan

Magellan[16] maintains an extensive subject tree of 60,000 reviewed pages with a rating scheme, along with over 50 million pages that are unrated. Magellan is owned by Excite.

9.1.12 Mining Company

The Mining Company[17] specializes in well-constructed guides to specific subject areas and is a major challenger to Yahoo. Experts in a subject area (called guides) maintain several hundred annotated guides. It is nice to put a face to the subject organization, as shown in Figure 9-2.

---

16. See http://www.mckinley.com/.
17. See http://home.miningco.com/.

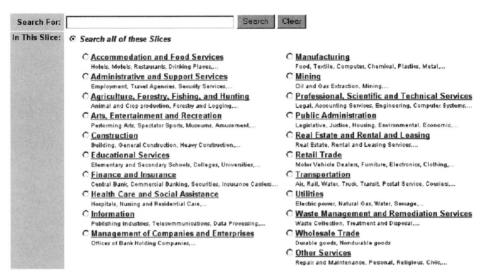

Figure 9-3 Main Menu for Pinstripe

9.1.13   Northern Light

Northern Light[18] is a new search service that combines Web content with a special collection of articles from more than 1,800 magazines, journals, books, and newspapers. Summaries from this special collection are free, but full-text retrieval is fee-based. Northern Light uses a "folder" approach to refining queries, as described in the section "Refining the Search" in Chapter 10, Techniques.

9.1.14   Open Text Pinstripe

Open Text Pinstripe[19] is a Web site designed for business users. Figure 9-3 shows the top-level categorization, based on a general industry classification.

9.1.15   WebCrawler

WebCrawler[20] is a small database but has a good relevancy ranking. It is good for quick searches. WebCrawler is owned by Excite.

18. See http://www.nlsearch.com/.
19. See http://pinstripe.opentext.com/.
20. See http://webcrawler.com/.

Figure 9-4   Yahoo! Main Page (the entry point to over 50,000 directory pages)

9.1.16   Yahoo!

Yahoo![21] is the oldest discovery service and still the best for directory-oriented searching. Yahoo! has over 50,000 directory pages, all starting from its main page, shown in Figure 9-4. Yahoo! is branching out into a variety of other services (e.g., stock quotes) as its business matures. See the Yahoo-How-To tutorial.[22]

---

21. See http://www.yahoo.com/.
22. See http://howto.yahoo.com/.

Web Farmers

Get to know the Yahoo! directory structure.

9.2 Meta–Discovery Services

Another strategy for the initial phase of discovery is to use a meta–discovery service. This type of service sends your query to multiple discovery services and then integrates the results. This is an excellent way to survey the variety of sources and subtopics before refining your query. It is also an excellent way to generate tons of garbage.

For Current Information

See the Yahoo! site on "All-in-One Search Pages"[23] and the Librarians' Index[24] for "Meta Engines."

9.2.1 Daily Diffs (by InGenius Technologies, Inc.)

InGenius Technologies[25] (IGT) specializes in automated change monitoring and notification services. IGT offers a free service called Daily Diffs.[26] This service monitors several hundred Web pages of general interest. A complementary service called javElink[27] monitors a customized list of Web pages and reports any changes to your personal account, highlighting the location of each change.

An example of IGT's unique reporting of Web page changes is shown in Figure 9-5. The figure shows the Web page for the current press releases for Ericsson Inc. Ericsson posted a new release on April 17, 1988 that is highlighted in Figure 9-5.

---

23. See http://www.yahoo.com/Computers_and_Internet/Internet/World_Wide_Web
/Searching_the_Web/All_in_One_Search_Pages/.
24. See http://sunsite.berkeley.edu/InternetIndex/.
25. See http://www.ingetech.com/.
26. See http://www.dailydiffs.com/.
27. See http://www.javElink.com/.

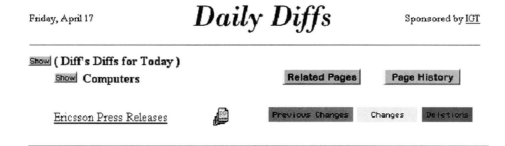

Friday, April 17   *Daily Diffs*   Sponsored by IGT

Show (Diff's Diffs for Today)
Show Computers

Related Pages   Page History

Ericsson Press Releases

Previous Changes   Changes   Deletions

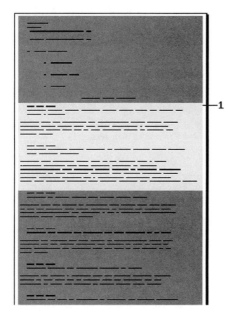

**Changes to "Ericsson Press Releases"
found on Apr 17:**

1. Apr 17, 1998 ERICSSON D-AMPS
    IS-136 WIRELESS OFFICE SYSTEM
    MAKES ONE PHONE, ONE...

    Ericsson Inc. has introduced its premise-
    based D-AMPS IS-136 (TDMA)
    Wireless...

    Apr 17, 1998 ERICSSON WIRELESS
    OFFICE SERVICES TO PROVIDE
    DIGITAL SYSTEM...

    Ericsson Inc. announced today that it has
    entered into a joint marketing...

Figure 9-5   Showing Changes to a Web Page

9.2.2 Mamma.Com

The "mother" of all metasearches, it's a fast one! Mamma uses up to seven search
engines at once, plus highly rated Web sites, lists of magazines (by category), and
lots of newspapers (by location).

9.2.3 MetaCrawler

MetaCrawler[28] allows you to search concurrently through multiple search crawlers,
including itself, Lycos, Excite, AltaVista, and Yahoo!

---

28. See http://www.metacrawler.com/.

9.2.4 MetaFind

Excellent! MetaFind[29] is a new service with broad coverage. Also known as Dogpile,[30] which is more descriptive of what you often get with metasearches.

9.2.5 SavvySearch

SavvySearch[31] is an experimental search engine that sends your query to many search engines at once. The results are displayed in any of several languages. Note the excellent documentation. It is operated by the computer science department at Colorado State University.

9.2.6 Search.Com

Effective use of hundreds of search engines from various content providers, all integrated into one site. (See Figure 9-6.) Note the selective use of search engines depending on the general subject area.

9.3 Specialized Resource Centers

This section covers several subject-oriented resource centers related to Web farming. Each of these centers is maintained by an author who is an expert on its subject. Hence, there is a deeper understanding of each topic, resulting in a well-organized directory linking to highly relevant sites. A specialized directory is similar to an annotated bibliography.

9.3.1 Business Researcher's Interests

Through the guidance of Yogesh Malhotra, *A Business Researcher's Interests,* or BRINT, has become an excellent site for research and academic material related to business.[32] Topics include business and technology, journals, magazines, international, news wire, reengineering (BPR), knowledge management, intranets, virtual organizations, complex systems, e-commerce, Web strategy, information policy, intellectual property, education and research, W(h)ither MIS?: trends and issues, and MIS research.

---

29. See http://www.metafind.com/.
30. See http://www.dogpile.com/.
31. See http://guaraldi.cs.colostate.edu:2000/form/.
32. See http://www.brint.com/.

Figure 9-6 Main Menu for Search.Com

Highly recommended is a subarea on knowledge management—the World Wide Web Virtual Library Knowledge Management, which contains a number of white papers along with an active discussion forum.[33]

9.3.2 Data Warehouse Center

This is an excellent site for Web content about data warehousing.[34] Maintained by Larry Greenfield of LGI Systems, it covers the topics of end-user tools, infrastructure technology, tool vendors, publications, and service providers. Larry has been very diligent in maintaining current information on this site!

9.3.3 Polson's Industry Research Desk

Industry Research Desk[35] is a family-run site by Gary Polson, provides "tools for researching specific companies, industries, and manufacturing processes." He has a good methodology for researching a company using Web resources.

---

33. See http://www.brint.com/km/.
34. See http://pwp.starnetinc.com/larryg/.
35. See http://www.virtualpet.com/industry/howto/search.htm.

9.4   General Content Providers

This section covers a small sampling of the general content providers. Some are established $100M+ vendors (e.g., DIALOG and NEXIS-LEXIS), and some have just begun an operation with some unique approach (e.g., Amlet, Electric Library, and KnowX).

Web Farmers

Note those providers that will customize to your specifications and provide structured data.

For current information, check the following Yahoo! directories related to content providers: online services,[36] databases,[37] publishers,[38] and information brokers.[39]

9.4.1   Acxiom

Acxiom[40] provides a spectrum of data products, data integration services, and mailing list services, as well as data warehousing and decision support services, to major firms in the U.S. and the U.K. Located in Conway, Arkansas, Acxiom was founded in 1969, went public in 1983, and currently has sales of $400+ million. It employs over 3,300 associates worldwide.

Acxiom is one of the few content providers that understand data warehousing. It provides services to combine multiple online files from different sources into a data warehouse. Acxiom enhances name and address information and eliminates duplicates.

9.4.2   American Business Information

Founded in 1972, American Business Information (ABI)[41] is a provider of business and consumer marketing information products and data processing services in the U.S. and Canada. ABI is a publicly held company with more than 1000 employees and revenues exceeding $150 million per year. More than 1 million customers use ABI to generate sales leads, find new customers, develop direct mail and telemarketing campaigns, and conduct market research.

---

36. See http://www.yahoo.com/Business_and_Economy/Companies/Computers/Networking /Online_Services/.
37. See http://www.yahoo.com/Business_and_Economy/Companies/Information/Databases/.
38. See http://www.yahoo.com/Business_and_Economy/Companies/Information/Databases /Publishers/.
39. See http://www.yahoo.com/Business_and_Economy/Companies/Information /Information_Brokers/.
40. See http://www.acxiom.com/.
41. See http://www.salesleadsusa.com/.

ABI's sources include

- 5200 Yellow Pages directories and hundreds of Business White Pages directories
- Annual reports, 10-Ks, and other SEC information
- Federal, state, and municipal government data
- Leading business magazines, newsletters, and major newspapers
- Postal Service information: NCOA, ZIP+4, and carrier route files

Note the following claim:

> We don't scan information; we go through a tedious process of manually inputting each piece of information. These sources help us identify virtually every business: U.S. and Canadian. Then we make 16 million phone calls to ensure the accuracy of our data, information does not go into our database until it's verified by our telephone research staff. By calling all 11 million businesses every year (and more often for larger companies), we keep up with the dynamic business environment. We confirm addresses and phone numbers, weed out companies who have gone out of business, and collect additional information: Name of the Owner or Key Executive, Number of Employees, Primary Line of Business, etc. Our telephone verification process is what sets our database apart from our competitors.

Some specific services are

1. Residential database for the U.S. and Canada, consisting of
   - 80 million U.S. households—nearly 100 million people
   - 14 million Canadian households—over 17 million people
2. Business Profiles and Credit Reports: "Need to know more about any particular business? We can help. Our Business Profiles and Credit Reports will give you in-depth information about specific companies, including
   - Company name, address, and phone number
   - Estimated annual sales
   - Name of the owner or top decision-maker
   - Credit rating code
   - Number of employees
   - Primary and secondary lines of business"
3. Customer Analyzer: "(New Service!) Simply give us your customers' phone numbers and we'll provide you with a Free Market Analysis. We'll tell you. . .
   - Who your customers are!
   - What they are like!
   - How to find more prospects like your best customers!"

9.4.3   Amulet

Amulet, Inc.[42] uses IsoQuest NetOwl Extractor software to gather, filter, and package information from over 1,600 sources. Amulet is located in Acton, MA.

9.4.4   Corporate Technology Information Services

Corporate Technology Information Services[43] (CorpTech) publishes high-quality data company information on 45,000+ U.S. high-tech manufacturing, development, and service firms. Both free and for-fee information. Demographics of industries by SIC. Privately held companies are emphasized.

9.4.5   Dialog Information Services

DialogWeb,[44] from Dialog Corporation, offers the following services: Custom DIALOG® is designed to fit your company and simplify the search process. DIALOG® and DataStar (SM) give you access to more than 600 online databases. With KR BusinessBase, you can acquire information on over 13 million public and private companies. The KR OnDisc (TM) collection includes nearly 80 files on CD-ROM, giving you direct local access to the information you want. KR ProBase (SM) is a Windows-based product that allows easy access to the DataStar (SM) database collection. KR ScienceBase (SM) is a World Wide Web application that furnishes scientists with easy access to published literature. KR SourceOne (SM), one of the world's largest document suppliers, offers two kinds of service: KR SourceOne, full-service document delivery, and UnCover, self-service document delivery. The K-R Info Training and Seminars section keeps you aware of upcoming seminars and also gives you specific solutions to common problems. Check out the Quantum program, which is "designed to help information specialists become *InfoStars*—proactive, visible, and adept at leading, managing and embracing change."

Dialog Information Services (formerly part of Knight-Ridder Information, Inc.)[45] has been acquired by M.A.I.D[46] for $420 million, and the combined company has been renamed the Dialog Corporation.

42. See http://www.amulet.com/.
43. See http://www.corptech.com/.
44. See http://www.dialogweb.com/.
45. See http://www.krinfo.com/.
46. See http://www.maid.com/.

Getting Smart by Visualizing Information

After the database integration, a similar problem arose. The material was all contained in the database, but its complexity was overwhelming. A single hierarchical outline had served well as a road map in the initial months. However, the outline grew to a complex maze that few could comprehend.

The CTO, Richard, attended a conference on knowledge engineering. The talks were intriguing but too blue-sky to be of practical value to ABC. Several new products in the information visualization (IV) area were exhibited; one of them had partnered with ABC's database vendor. Alice asked for an evaluation copy and tried it on ABC's data. The IV tool generated some strange figures, which took considerable time to interpret. After a series of telephone conferences and a visit by a vendor rep, Alice started to catch on to the figures. The freedom of moving through thousands of items, clustering some and decomposing others, gradually made it possible to clarify the essential structures within the data. For Alice, a stroll through business intelligence cyberspace was changed forever.

Next installment is on page 299.

9.4.6 Disclosure

Disclosure,[47] a subsidiary of Primark Corporation, is a provider of financial intelligence delivered via online and CD-ROM-based research tools. Databases include 5 million financial filings from SEC EDGAR, Canada, and WorldScope.[48]

9.4.7 Dow Jones Business Information Services

Dow Jones Business Information Services[49] is part of Dow Jones & Company, which publishes the *Wall Street Journal* and its international editions, the Wall Street Journal Interactive Edition, *Barron's* magazine, and other periodicals. It also offers the Dow Jones Global Indexes, electronic information services, the Ottaway group of community newspapers, and a custom clipping, tracking, and alert service. The WSJ Interactive Edition has over 150,000 paid subscribers.

---

47. See http://www.disclosure.com/.
48. See http://www.worldscope.com/.
49. See http://bis.dowjones.com/.

9.4.8 EBSCO Information Services

EBSCO Information Services[50] provides integrated and cost-effective access to information through three related divisions: EBSCO Subscription Services, EBSCO Publishing, and EBSCOdoc. It provides a one-stop online reference system with full-text access to 1,500 magazines, along with 30 proprietary databases.

9.4.9 EDGAR-Online

EDGAR-Online[51] provides subscribers with current SEC EDGAR data designed for popular Web browsers. EDGAR-Online is a private service of Cybernet Data Systems, Inc. of Norwalk, Connecticut. EDGAR-Online has partnering arrangements with PC Quote, Big Charts, Hoover's Inc., News Alert, Zacks Investment Research, Wall Street Research Net, and Company Link.

The various services to individuals are as follows:

- EDGAR-Online People: Allows users to search through SEC filings by an executive's name. A user can retrieve various details on corporate executives including company position, corporate board memberships, stock ownership, and executive compensation.
- EDGAR-Online Glimpse: Extracts the Management's Discussion and Analysis section of a 10-Q or 10-K at the touch of a button.
- EDGAR-Online Full Search: Packaged and advanced searching by filing type, industry, location, and other criteria.
- EDGAR-Online Watchlist Alerts: Instant email notification when SEC data is filed that meets the specific parameters defined by the user.

9.4.10 Electric Library

Electric Library,[52] by Infonautics,[53] provides a complete general-reference database consisting of full text from over 900 magazines, 150 newspapers, 2,000 books, and encyclopedias, as well as 20,000 photos and maps. Infonautics also provides digital publishing services to customize information for specific companies.

---

50. See http://www.ebsco.com/.
51. See http://www.edgar-online.com/.
52. See http://www.electriclibrary.com/.
53. See PR Newswire, July 2, 1997 and http://www.electriclibrary.com/.

9.4.11 Encyclopaedia Britannica

The goal of Encyclopaedia Britannica is to be "a leader in creating products that turn information into knowledge in the electronic age," by working "to make knowledge more accessible, more enjoyable and, consequently, more popular." Encyclopaedia Britannica focuses on its traditional strengths, such as arts, literature, history, geography, and science. The company also plans to extend its editorial and organizational expertise into areas such as music, computers, medicine, and sports—subjects that affect daily life and culture. It provides Britannica Online,[54] Britannica CD-ROM, and the famous (and heavy) 32-volume Encyclopaedia Britannica.

9.4.12 Fairfax RESEARCH (AgeSearch)

Fairfax RESEARCH provides AgeSearch[55] as a fee-based newspaper research and information service with offices in Sydney and Melbourne, providing access to the editorial facilities of The Age and other resources of the John Fairfax Publishing group.

9.4.13 FreeEDGAR

FreeEDGAR,[56] a service of Partes Corporation, is a free online service that provides analysts with the ability to pull EDGAR data directly into financial models by generating Microsoft Excel spreadsheets with the click of a button. With personalized "watch lists," FreeEDGAR can instantly notify users when companies submit new filings.

9.4.14 GaleNet

GaleNet,[57] part of International Thomson Publishing,[58] offers information about biography, literature, business bibliography, associations, multicultural studies, and all areas of educational curriculum. Beginning with the now-classic Encyclopedia of Associations, first published in 1954, Gale products have become essentials on the reference shelves of every major library worldwide. Founded in Detroit by Frederick Gale Ruffner, the company has established a reputation for producing comprehensive, easy-to-use, and accurate reference books.

54. See http://www.eb.com/.
55. See http://www.theage.com.au/agesearch/.
56. See http://www.freeedgar.com/.
57. See http://galenet.gale.com/.
58. See http://www.thomson.com/.

Yahoo! Inc.

Yahoo! has been swift to mine the Internet's rich potential. Santa Clara, California-based Yahoo! is the most popular directory for getting around the World Wide Web. Its free navigational guide is available on several online networks and browsers, including Netscape Navigator and the Microsoft Network. Each day Internet surfers call on Yahoo! to view over 20 million "pages" of electronic data. Yahoo! has more than 550 advertisers (paying 3-8 cents per "impression") that account for almost all of its sales.

As Stanford grad students, David Filo and Jerry Yang developed the Yahoo! search engine to compile a list of their favorite Internet sites. They set up their own Web index site in 1994, and it was soon accessed by thousands of Web surfers each day. Commercialization followed and high-tech executive Timothy Koogle came in as CEO. In 1995 Yahoo! and publisher Ziff-Davis began work on "Yahoo! Internet Life," an online and print magazine.

Despite its meager revenues, the company's estimated valuation at the time of its 1996 IPO was $300 million. Investors hollered "Yahoo!" as the stock price rose to $43 from $13 during its first day of trading. SOFTBANK (Ziff-Davis's owner) owns 35% of Yahoo!, investment firm Sequoia Capital 16%, and Filo and Yang each own about 14%.

Yahoo! has expanded through strategic partnerships. An agreement with rival AltaVista allows Yahoo! users to get results from AltaVista as well. Yahoo! has also dabbled in electronic commerce and teamed up with local content providers to create online regional guides such as Yahoo! Canada, Yahoo! France, and Yahoo! Japan. Other products include Yahooligans!, an Internet navigation guide for children. In 1997 Yahoo! and Netscape teamed up to develop a topic-based Internet navigation service for use on the Netscape Communicator browser. It also agreed to buy online White Pages provider Four11 for $95 million and began offering Four11's free RocketMail e-mail service.

Get the latest news on Yahoo! from News Alert

OFFICERS

President and CEO: Timothy Koogle, age 45, $150,000 pay
Chief Yahoo: David Filo
Chief Yahoo: Jerry Yang, age 28
SVP Finance and Administration and CFO: Gary Valenzuela, $123,750 pay
SVP Business Operations: Jeffrey Mallett, $125,000 pay

Figure 9-7   Sample Company Profile from Hoover's

9.4.15   Hoover's, Inc.

Hoover's, Inc.[59] is an Austin-based publisher of company information, covering more than 12,000 U.S. and foreign companies, both public and private. Hoover's distributes information through a variety of online media and on several Web sites (such as Hoover's Online, IPO Central, Cyberstocks, and StockScreener). Hoover's Marketplace also publishes business reference books and software products, along with more than 60 other business titles. The company profile of Yahoo! is given in Figure 9-7.

59. See http://www.hoovers.com/.

9.4.16 Infobase Publishers

Infobase Publishers[60] is a publisher of information for strategic planning and competitive intelligence in the defense, aerospace, and government markets.

9.4.17 Information Access Company

Information Access Company (IAC)[61] is a subscription-based service providing companies with access to business information databases. Founded in 1976 and headquartered in Foster City, California, IAC was acquired by the Thomson Corporation from Ziff Communications in December 1994. One of their databases is Company Intelligence, which includes over 200,000 companies worldwide and emphasizes privately held firms. Client interface is via InSite Pro. IAC currently offers a free 14-day trial.

9.4.18 Information America

Information America (IA),[62] located in Atlanta, Georgia, was founded in 1982 by an attorney and computer consultant who saw the need for providing the legal market with computerized public records. Information America provides a large online database with state-of-the-art document services to provide unparalleled information support to banks, financial services companies, corporations, law firms, and government agencies across the nation. Its unique blend of public records, investigative services, courthouse documents, and UCC filing services is used to obtain background data about businesses, locate assets and people, retrieve official public records, and secure financial interests. It is now part of the Thomson Corporation.

IA offers an impressive array of services, including Asset Locator, Bankruptcy Records, Business Finder, Corporate and Limited Partnership Records, County Records, Dun's Business Records Plus, Executive Affiliation, Lawsuits, Litigation Prep, Name Availability and Reservations, People Finder, Professional Licenses, Real Property, and Liens and Judgments.

9.4.19 Information Express

Information Express[63] offers customized document delivery systems for corporate, academic, and medical libraries.

---

60. See http://www.infobasepub.com/.
61. See http://www.informationaccess.com/.
62. See http://www.infoam.com/.
63. See http://www.express.com/.

9.4.20 Information Handling Services

Information Handling Services (IHS)[64] is a publisher of technical info products, covering the military, electronics, architecture, construction, aerospace, utilities, automotive, computers, petrochemical, and telecommunications areas. HIS was founded in 1959.

9.4.21 Information Quest

Information Quest[65] is a Dawson company offering Web-based information research, access and retrieval service, and timely email notices based on specific search criteria.

9.4.22 Institute for Scientific Information

The Institute for Scientific Information (ISI)[66] is the publisher of *Current Contents* and *Science Citation Index* and is offering a new service called CC Connect.

9.4.23 Investext Group

The Investext Group[67] provides general business analysis of companies, industries, products, and geographic regions. It offers a large electronic collection of investment research, market intelligence, and trade association information and has more than a million research reports from the most sought-after sources around the globe. The Investext Group is part of Thomson Corporation.

9.4.24 KnowX

KnowX[68] provides online public-record information via a search tool. Searches are free, but you pay for accessing the full detailed record. The primary source databases are from Information America. KnowX has added two real-property databases, allowing users to uncover "non-purchase deeded transactions such as refinances, construction loans, second mortgages and equity loans."

---

64. See http://www.ihs.com/.
65. See http://www.informationquest.com/.
66. See http://www.ininet.com/.
67. See http://www.investext.com/.
68. See http://www.knowx.com/.

9.4.25 LEXIS-NEXIS

The LEXIS-NEXIS services[69] contain more than 18,300 sources. More than 9.5 million documents are added each week to the more than 1 billion documents online. Mead Data Central provides LEXIS and NEXIS, the world's leading full-text online legal, news, and business information services. Mead Data Central is a division of the Mead Corporation, a leader in forest products and electronic publishing, headquartered in Dayton, Ohio.

9.4.26 M.A.I.D Profound

M.A.I.D Profound[70] offers a comprehensive online business intelligence service. Based in London, M.A.I.D (Market Analysis and Information Database) hosts information from over 4,000 of the world's most important business publishers, such as Associated Press, Disclosure, Dun and Bradstreet, the Economist Intelligence Unit, Extel, Frost & Sullivan, and Standard & Poor's. The information is stored electronically according to a common set of business criteria (market sector, company, brand, publisher, title) using a proprietary indexing system called Info-Sort, which places the information in logically connected categories. The result is a database that, while comprehensive, can be searched quickly and very precisely by clients to pinpoint the material exactly relevant to their needs.

M.A.I.D recently acquired Dialog Information Services from Knight-Ridder Information and combined their operations. The company was renamed the Dialog Corporation.

9.4.27 Manning & Napier Information Services

Manning & Napier Information Services (MNIS)[71] is a pioneer in text data mining, offering DR-LINK, an intelligent online service accessing more than 1,200 publications, and MNIS Profiler, a real-time alerting service delivered via protected Web account or email. Free evaluation is available.

Figure 9-8 shows an example of the Information Visualizer for DR-LINK.[72] Note its ability to filter on a variety of dimensions and observe the results at the bottom.

69. See http://www.lexis-nexis.com/.
70. See http://www.profound.com/.
71. See http://www.mnis.net/.
72. See http://www.mnis.net/press970911.shtml.

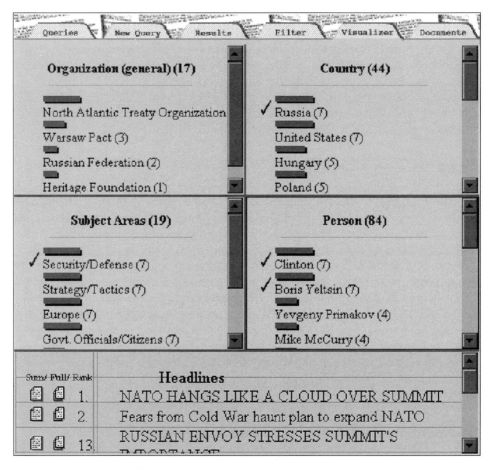

Figure 9-8 Information Visualizer for DR-LINK

9.4.28 MicroPatent

MicroPatent[73] specializes in patents from the U.S., European Patent Organization (EPO), and Patent Control Treaty (PCT) of the World Intellectual Property. The U.S. patents date back to 1974 for a full-text report, costing $3 per patent.

---

73. See http://www.micropat.com/.

9.4.29 Moody's Financial Information Services

Moody's Financial Information Services[74] covers over 10,000 U.S. corporations, 13,000+ non-U.S. companies, and over 10,000 municipal entities, along with real-time SEC EDGAR filings. Docutronics Information Services, a subsidiary of Moody's, provides global anonymous information and competitive intelligence gathering.

9.4.30 NewsNet

NewsNet[75] is a database of current full-text business and industry news from newsletters, newswires, and journals, and includes NewsFlash, a personal news-clipping service.

9.4.31 ProQuest Direct

ProQuest Direct,[76] a Bell & Howell Company, offers indexing and abstracts to over 5,000 periodicals, full-image coverage of nearly 1,400 periodicals, ASCII full text of another 1,000 periodicals, and citations of 1.4 million dissertations.

9.4.32 Questel-Orbit Online Services

Questel-Orbit Online Services,[77] a part of the France Telecom Group, is an international online information company specializing in intellectual property services (patent, trademark, scientific, chemical, business, and news information) with access to 250 databases in over 60 countries.

9.4.33 SilverPlatter Information, Inc.

SilverPlatter Information, Inc.[78] features extensive collections of premium knowledge-based electronic databases covering a broad range of disciplines. It uses a special Web front-end tool called WebSPIRS, a common gateway interface (CGI) application that provides access to ERL-compliant databases through any forms-capable browser. The underlying technology it uses to network with diverse databases is called Electronic Reference Library (ERL) technology.

---

74. See http://www.moodys.com/fis/.
75. See http://www.newsnet.com/.
76. See http://www.umi.com/.
77. See http://www.questelorbit.com/.
78. See http://www.silverplatter.com/.

9.4.34   TextWise

TextWise[79] is an R&D company based in the Computer Applications and Software Engineering Center at Syracuse University. TextWise specializes in the development of information retrieval technologies using natural language processing.

Elizabeth Liddy, an associate professor at Syracuse University's School of Information Studies, formed TextWise in 1993 to commercialize her natural language text retrieval technology.

TextWise research is being funded by Manning and Napier Information Services (MNIS) and several U.S. government research grants. The DR-LINK technology has been jointly developed by TextWise and Manning and Napier Information Services, based on original research conducted by Syracuse University in a DARPA TIPSTER research project.

9.4.35   Thomas Register

Thomas Register[80] on the Internet is the world's largest online industrial buying source. It makes the entire database of the Thomas Register of American Manufacturers available for your use online. Its proprietary search engine allows you to search the 155,000 companies in its database, classified under more than 57,000 product and service headings. More than 3,100 online supplier catalogs give you 44,000 pages of detailed buying and specifying information.

9.4.36   Thomson & Thomson

Thomson & Thomson[81] offers a trademark and copyright service. It recently added TRADE-MASKSCAN for trademark images and designs.

9.4.37   WESTLAW

WESTLAW[82] is the computer-assisted legal research (CALR) service of the West Group. It contains over 9,000 databases, including federal and state court cases, the United States Code Annotated and state statutes, federal regulations, administrative law decisions, topical databases, legal periodicals, West's Insta-Cite, West's Quick-Cite, Shepard's Citations, Shepard's PreView, Black's Law Dictionary, DIALOG on WESTLAW, and gateway access to QUICKLAW (Canadian Law). It also includes synopses, prepared by lawyer-editors, that accompany the full text of federal and state court decisions.

---

79. See http://www.textwise.com/.
80. See http://www.thomasregister.com/.
81. See http://www.thomson-thomson.com/.
82. See http://www.westpub.com/WLAWInfo/wlawhome.htm.

9.5   Industry-Specific Content Providers

This section covers content providers that specialize in specific industries. Again, only a sampling of these providers is given below. Consult the indexes in Yahoo! and other directory services for other specific industries.

9.5.1   Electric Power Research Institute

The Electric Power Research Institute (EPRI)[83] hosts Energysearch, a resource center devoted to the electric industry. EPRI believes that a topic-specific search site can give "more precise results for users in the energy industry than generic WWW services."

9.5.2   MediaTrak

MediaTrak[84] is an online subscription database of information on journalists for PR professionals.

9.5.3   PaperChase

PaperChase[85] provides access to medical information in MEDLINE, AIDSLINE, HealthSTAR, CANCERLIT, and CINAHL.

9.5.4   Pharmsearch

Pharmsearch offers access to a pharmaceutical patents database of European Patent Office, British, French, German, U.S., and WIPO patents accessible by full indexing or by Markush Structure within 6 to 14 weeks of publication.

9.5.5   Trade Dimensions

Trade Dimensions[86] is a publisher of site-specific directories and databases for the retail, food, and consumer-packaged-goods industries.

---

83. See http://www.energysearch.com/.
84. See http://www.pitchingtips.com/.
85. See http://www.paperchase.com/.
86. See http://www.tradedimensions.com/.

9.6   Market Research Firms

This section covers the content providers that specialize in market research. Usually their products are wrapped with extensive services to investigate a specific market.

Some market research firms are described below. Others include A.C. Nielsen,[87] International Data Corporation[88] (which we have described previously), PR Wire,[89] and Business Wire.[90]

9.6.1   Dataquest

Dataquest[91], part of the Gartner Group, is a leader in the market intelligence industry. It provides clients with access to an international network of research, information, custom consulting, and analysis. Dataquest's products and programs cover all aspects of IT, including semiconductors, computer systems and peripherals, telecommunications, software, and services.

9.6.2   Harte-Hanks Direct Marketing

The Direct Marketing Division of Harte-Hanks[92] is based in San Antonio, Texas, and offers a full range of specialized and coordinated services.

Harte-Hanks Communications, Inc., is a diversified communications company traded on the New York Stock Exchange (symbol: HHS). The company's mix of targeted and mass media businesses is unique within the industry.

Harte-Hanks Direct Marketing is one of the nation's premier direct marketing companies. North America's largest publisher of advertising shoppers, Harte-Hanks Shoppers, publishes 570 separate editions with almost 7 million total circulation each week in four major markets.

9.7   Library Services

This section covers the services offered by research and corporate libraries throughout the world. There is a vast array of available information here, especially given the growing movement toward digital libraries.

---

87. See http://www.acnielsen.com/.
88. See http://www.idcresearch.com/.
89. See http://www.pr-wire.com/.
90. See http://www.businesswire.com/.
91. See http://www.dataquest.com/.
92. See http://www.harte-hanks.com/.

For current information, see the Yahoo! directory on Library Services.[93] Services that are not described below are the Library of Congress,[94] Digital Library,[95] Internet Public Library,[96] and UCI Virtual Reference Collection.[97] In addition, several corporate libraries are accessible to the public, such as those of Lucent, Rand Corporation, IBM, HP, Digital Equipment, and Xerox PARC.

9.7.1 Alexandria Digital Library

The Alexandria Digital Library[98] explores the problems related to a "distributed digital library for geographically referenced information."

9.7.2 Berkeley Digital Library SunSITE

Berkeley Digital Library SunSITE[99] is a resource site where "we build digital collections and services while providing information and support to others doing the same." It has an excellent collection of information directories, especially those for intellectual property rights[100] and metadata[101] by the International Federation of Library Associations (IFLA).

9.7.3 CARL Corporation

CARL Corporation[102] was founded as the Colorado Alliance of Research Libraries to market and support library management systems.

9.7.4 Internet Archive

Internet Archive,[103] one of the more unusual Web resources, is collecting and storing public materials from the World Wide Web. The Archive will provide historians, researchers, scholars, and others access to this vast collection of data (reaching 10 terabytes) and will ensure the longevity of this information.

---

93. See http://www.yahoo.com/Business_and_Economy/Companies/Information/Library_Services/.
94. See http://www.loc.gov/.
95. See http://elib.cs.berkeley.edu/.
96. See http://www.ipl.org/.
97. See http://www.lib.uci.edu/.
98. See http://www.alexandria.ucsb.edu/.
99. See http://sunsite.berkeley.edu/.
100. See http://sunsite.berkeley.edu/Copyright/.
101. See http://www.nlc-bnc.ca/ifla/II/metadata.htm.
102. See http://www.carl.org/.
103. See http://www.archive.org/.

9.7.5 Microsoft Corporate Library

The Microsoft Library Home Page[104] is a public site that provides some current and in-depth links. The purpose is to give "Microsoft employees an efficient means of accessing information relevant to their business concerns on the Internet." As a public site, it constitutes a technology-savvy librarian's view of Web resources for a very high-tech company. Check out the section on Internet resources.

9.7.6 Online Computer Library Center (OCLC)

The Online Computer Library Center (OCLC)[105] is a nonprofit service and research organization with the goal of furthering access to the world's information and reducing the costs of that access. OCLC supports WorldCat, the world's largest bibliographic database, containing over 36 million records representing 370 languages and growing by two million records per year. OCLC Research is involved in various projects, including the Dublin Core and the Resource Description Framework described in Chapter 7, Standards.

9.8 General News Agencies

This section covers general news agencies, which make up a huge number of sites. Some examples are the *Chicago Tribune, The Miami Herald,* CNN,[106] MSNBC[107], *The New York Times, The San Jose Mercury News, USA Today,*[108] and *The Washington Post.*

9.8.1 Wall Street Journal Interactive Edition[109]

The WSJ Interactive Edition has over 150,000 paid subscribers and covers the same extensive content as its hard-copy counterpart. An example of a Company Briefing Book is shown in Figure 9-9.

---

104. See http://library.microsoft.com/.
105. See http://www.oclc.org/.
106. See http://www.cnn.com/.
107. See http://www.msnbc.com/.
108. See http://www.usatoday.com/.
109. See http://interactive.wsj.com/.

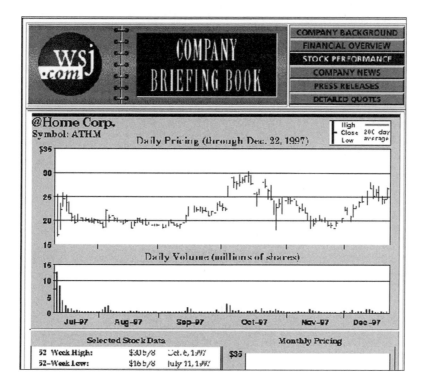

Figure 9-9 WSJ Briefing Book on a Company

9.9 IT Trade Publications

An important category of resources is IT trade publications, which also constitute a huge number of sites. Some examples are *BYTE, ComputerWorld, Datamation, InformationWeek, InfoWorld, Internet Week, PC Magazine, PC Week, TechWeb Wire,* and *ZD Net News.*

9.10 Investment Services

This section covers investment services, which also make up a huge number of sites. Some examples are Big Charts, Individual, InfoBeat, IPO Central, Microsoft Investor, Quote.Com, Smart Money, and TechInvestor.

9.10.1 IPO Central

IPO Central[110] provides EDGAR access to companies that have filed to go public via SEC Form S-1 and so on. It is owned by Hoover's Inc.

9.11 Related Publications

This section describes a sampling of publications that cover various aspects of Web farming.

9.11.1 CyberSkeptic's Guide to Internet Research

CyberSkeptic's Guide to Internet Research is a monthly newsletter from Biblio-Data,[111] priced at $99 per year.

9.11.2 D-Lib Magazine

D-Lib Magazine,[112] a monthly magazine on research about digital libraries, is a forum for researchers and developers of advanced digital libraries. A DARPA-sponsored project, *D-Lib Magazine* is coordinated by the Corporation for National Research Initiatives[113] for the NSF/DARPA/NASA Digital Libraries Initiative.[114] Its objectives are

- To stimulate the development of a common infrastructure for digital libraries and to coordinate research into those aspects that require consensus
- To provide information exchange about all research and advanced development in digital libraries
- To encourage and assist the transfer of these research efforts into the creation of a national digital library system

---

110. See http://www.ipocentral.com/.
111. See http://www.bibliodata.com/.
112. See http://www.dlib.org/.
113. See http://www.cnri.reston.va.us/.
114. See http://www.cise.nsf.gov/iris/DLHome.html.

9.11.3 Fulltext Sources Online

Fulltext Sources Online (FSO),[115] published by BiblioData, covers over 7000 online sources containing full-text content, such as DIALOG, NEXIS, LEXIS, Westlaw, Dow Jones, NewsNet, DataTimes EyeQ, Ovid, STN, GBI, Genios, FT Profile, Data-Star, Info Globe, Infomart, QL, and Burrelle's. It is now available in electronic format.

9.11.4 InterNIC News

InterNIC News[116] is a monthly publication on technical issues related to the Internet. Its audience consists of Webmasters and Internet service providers.

9.11.5 Information Today

Information Today, Inc.[117] is the publisher of Information Today, along with several other periodicals (*Searcher, Link-Up, IntraNet Professional, Information Science Abstracts, Computer Libraries,* and *Computer Abstracts*), conferences (National Online Meeting), and books (*Finding Statistics Online, Naked in Cyberspace, The Online Deskbook,* and *Secrets of the Super Net Searchers*). A valuable site for Web farmers!

9.11.6 Online Inc.

Online[118] is written for information professionals. It provides articles, product reviews, case studies, evaluation, and informed opinion about selecting, using, and managing electronic information products, plus industry and professional information about online database systems, CD-ROM technology, and the Internet. Subscriptions are $55.50/year for six issues.

The same organization publishes DATABASE, which is written for "hands-on" searchers, managers of information facilities, and others who use information technology. It provides practical, how-to advice on effective use of databases and systems, plus innovative tips and techniques, reviews, and product comparisons. It covers databases in online, CD-ROM, disk, and tape formats, and resources on the Internet. Subscriptions are $55.50/year for six issues.

---

115. See http://www.bibliodata.com/fso/fsodata.html.
116. See http://rs.internic.net/nic-support/nicnews/.
117. See http://www.infotoday.com/.
118. See http://www.onlineinc.com/onlinemag/.

9.12 Professional Societies

This section covers the various professional societies related to Web farming. Note especially the publications, membership lists, annual conferences, and special interest groups.

Professional societies that are not described below include IEEE and DAMA.

9.12.1 American Society of Information Science

The American Society of Information Science (ASIS)[119] was founded in 1937 for "information professionals leading the search for new and better theories, techniques, and technologies to improve access to information." Its membership of over 4000 is drawn from science, mathematics, law, and medicine. ASIS offers a full set of services and programs, including an annual conference, the *Journal of the American Society for Information Science,* and the *Annual Review of Information Science and Technology.*

9.12.2 Association for Computing Machinery

The Association for Computing Machinery (ACM)[120] is the oldest society in the computer science profession, ranking alongside the IEEE Computer Society. The ACM offers both hard-copy and electronic versions of their publications, along with an extensive full-text ACM digital library. There are numerous special interest groups, such as the SIG for Information Retrieval, the SIG for the Management of Data, and the SIGLink. In addition, there are numerous conferences and workshops on topics relevant to Web farming.

9.12.3 Association for Information and Image Management

The Association for Information and Image Management (AIIM)[121] has focused on the document management industry for over 50 years. It has over 9000 individual members and 900 corporate members. AIIM has a large annual conference, a trade show, local chapters, and international events.

---

119. See http://www.asis.org/.
120. See http://www.acm.org/.
121. See http://www.aiim.org/.

9.12.4   Association of Independent Information Professionals

The Association of Independent Information Professionals (AIIP)[122] is "an international association of owners of information businesses" providing such information services as "online database searching, market and industry surveys, document delivery, library services, general research services, public records research, thesaurus building, indexing and abstracting services, digital library development, competitive intelligence, and specialized research in specific subject areas." AIIP was founded in 1987 by Marilyn Levine, a professor at the University of Wisconsin. It now has more than 800 members in 21 countries. AIIP holds an annual conference with vendor exhibits. The AIIP Code of Ethical Business Practice emphasizes "honesty, competence, and confidentiality."

9.12.5   Association of Research Libraries

The mission of the Association of Research Libraries (ARL)[123] is to "shape and influence forces affecting the future of research libraries in the process of scholarly communication" and "promote equitable access and effective use of recorded knowledge in support of teaching, research, scholarship, and community service." Its membership consists of over 200 research libraries in North America.

9.12.6   Coalition for Networked Information

The Coalition for Networked Information (CNI)[124] was formed in 1990 by ARL, CAUSE, and EDUCOM to "advance scholarship and intellectual productivity by promoting the provision of information resources on existing and future telecommunications networks." The executive director of CNI is Clifford Lynch, who has worked very actively on the tough issues of metadata and digital identifiers.

9.12.7   European Information Researchers Network

The European Information Researchers Network (EIRENE)[125] is a professional association representing information brokers from the European Union, EFTA, and Eastern European countries to promote communication among themselves. Their goal is "to increase access to information and develop information brokerage as a commercial activity, whilst working towards raising the quality of service to clients."

---

122. See http://www.aiip.org/.
123. See http://www.arl.org/.
124. See http://www.cni.org/.
125. See http://www.eirene.com/.

9.12.8 Information Professionals Institute

The Information Professionals Institute (IPI)[126] provides "products and services to help information brokers develop industry-specific skills and business savvy." IPI was founded in 1992 by information broker pioneers Sue Rugge, Helen Burwell, and Ruth Orenstein. IPI offers a set of interesting seminars, including *Information Broker's Seminar: How to Make Money as an Information Broker; Comparative Online Searching; Using Public Records for Informed Business Decisions;* and *Competitive Intelligence: Online and Internet Sources.*

9.12.9 Internet Society

The Internet Society[127] is a "non-profit, non-governmental, international professional membership organization that brings diverse interests and factions together to hammer out reasonable solutions that generate progress and growth for the Internet. Its more than 100 organizational and 7000 individual members from more than 150 countries represent a veritable *Who's Who* of the Internet community."

The Internet Society is heavily involved with defining and setting Internet standards. These standards are developed by the Internet Engineering Task Force.[128] The standards are then considered by the Internet Engineering Steering Group,[129] with appeal to the Internet Architecture Board,[130] and promulgated by the Internet Society as international standards. The RFC Editor[131] is responsible for preparing and organizing the standards in their final form. The standards may be found at numerous sites distributed throughout the world, such as InterNIC.[132]

Web Farmers

Join ISOC and become a good net citizen!

9.12.10 Library and Information Technology Association

The Library and Information Technology Association (LITA)[133] is concerned with "the impact of emerging technologies on library service and with the effect of automated technologies on people." As stated in their strategy statement, LITA "provides educational opportunities for learning about information technologies, monitors new

---

126. See http://www.ipn.net/ipi/.
127. See http://www.isoc.org/.
128. See http://www.ietf.org/.
129. See http://www.ietf.org/iesg.html.
130. See http://www.iab.org/iab/.
131. See http://www.isi.edu/rfc-editor/.
132. See http://ds.internic.net/ds/dspg1intdoc.html.
133. See http://www.lita.org/.

technologies with potential applications in information science, encourages and fosters research, promotes technical standards, and examines the effects of library systems and networks."

9.12.11 Society for Competitive Information Professionals

The Society for Competitive Information Professionals (SCIP)[134] fosters the profession of competitive intelligence gathering and analysis. Founded in 1986, SCIP has 5700 members in 44 countries.

> From fierce new competitors to changing technologies, the competitive environment is never the same from day to day. In the cutthroat global marketplace, companies need more than one tool to succeed. And while strategy and planning can tell you which direction to head and where your journey should end, only competitive intelligence (CI) can show you the storms on the horizon and allow you to benefit from the strongest winds.[135]

9.12.12 Society for Insurance Research

The Society for Insurance Research (SIR)[136] is a not-for-profit professional organization whose purpose is to stimulate research affecting the insurance industry and to advance the profession of insurance research. It publishes *Research Review,* a quarterly journal for professional researchers in the insurance and financial services industries.

9.12.13 Special Libraries Association

The Special Libraries Association (SLA)[137] caters to special librarians, who are "information resource experts dedicated to putting knowledge to work to attain the goals of their organizations, such as corporations, private businesses, government agencies, museums, colleges, hospitals, associations, and information management consulting firms."

---

134. See http://www.scip.org/.
135. See http://www.scip.org/about.html.
136. See http://www.connectyou.com/sir/.
137. See http://www.sla.org/.

9.13 Book Distributors

This section lists the major providers of book information on the Web. These sites are useful in finding current texts on specific topics. Some examples are the American Library Association,[138] *Publisher's Weekly*,[139] the American Booksellers' Association,[140] Amazon.Com,[141] and Barnes and Noble.[142]

9.14 Intelligence and Investigative Resources

This section lists some providers from the intelligence-gathering field. Their information covers the military, cultural, and political arenas on a global scale.

For current information, see the Yahoo! directory on Intelligence[143] (especially the indexes) and the Yahoo! directory (over 500 entries) on Investigative Services.[144]

9.14.1 Avert, Inc.[145]

Avert (NASDAQ: AVRT) provides employment background checking "to help employers hire safe, honest and competent employees." Services include SSN validation, name/address links, criminal court records, reference checking, education and credential confirmation, workers compensation claims, driving records, credit link, civil and bankruptcy court records, employment application forms, and custom requests. Avert offers online access via Web browser and requires an initial registration to certify the user's lawful purposes according to the Fair Credit Reporting Act.

9.14.2 Jane's Information Group[146]

For a hundred years, the legacy of Fred T. Jane has lived in the information resources provided by his company. His first publication, *Jane's All the World's Fighting Ships*, was an instant success with ship's captains who needed to distinguish other ships quickly and accurately. Jane's describes itself as "the leading unclassified information supplier and integrator for military, government and related commercial organizations worldwide." It can deliver information via CD-ROM or internal data feeds. Its

---

138. See http://www.ala.org/booklist/.
139. See http://www.bookwire.com/pw/pw.html/.
140. See http://www.bookweb.org/.
141. See http://www.amazon.com/.
142. See http://www.barnesandnoble.com/.
143. See http://www.yahoo.com/Government/Intelligence/.
144. See http://www.yahoo.com/Business_and_Economy/Companies/Information
    /Investigative_Services/.
145. See http://www.avert.com/.
146. See http://www.janes.com/.

coverage has grown beyond the military to cover geopolitical topics, terrorism, and global technology. Jane's recently acquired IntelWeb,[147] which is the Web site for the *Intelligence Watch Report.*

This Web site is valuable for any multinational company seeking to understand the regions where it does business.

9.14.3 Strategic Forecasting Intelligence Services

Strategic Forecasting Intelligence Services (SFIS) is part of STRATFOR Systems, Inc.[148] SFIS provides corporate intelligence services to firms needing "industry-specific, technology-specific or country-specific intelligence" created by combining "collection expertise with systematic analytic practices."

9.15 U.S. Government Agencies

An amazing amount of information is available from the U.S. government. That is the good news. The bad news is that you must understand its background before the information can be meaningful.

For current information, see the appropriate Yahoo! directories on the U.S. government and scan an exhaustive list, from the General Accounting Office of about 4500 web sites within the federal government. The *Washington Post* offers a version with hyperlinks at http://wp4.washingtonpost.com/wp-srv/national /longterm/edguide/gao.htm. Also, see the book by Bruce Maxwell, *How to Access the Federal Government on the Internet 1998: Washington Online,* Congressional Quarterly Books, 1997. It identifies over 600 federal government sites.

9.15.1 Federal Web Locator[149]

Based on the organization of the U.S. Government Manual, the Federal Web Locator is a one-stop shopping center for U.S. government information. It is supported by the Villanova Center for Information Law and Policy.

9.15.2 THOMAS

To make legislative information about the U.S. Congress freely available, the Library of Congress brought the THOMAS Web site online in January 1995. Its home page has one of the best designs for compacted information access. Moreover, most content is updated daily, and an excellent search engine is available. There are links to numerous other government sites, along with historical documents from

---

147. See http://www.awpi.com/IntelWeb/.
148. See http://www.stratfor.com/.
149. See http://www.law.vill.edu/fed-agency/.

1774. There is even an explanation of the legislative process for those who have forgotten their U.S. government studies from high school.

The THOMAS databases cover Congressional House and Senate floor activities and actions; bill summaries and full text (in both plain text and PDF); roll call votes; public laws since 1973; full text of the Congressional Record and Index; House and Senate committee reports.

This is definitely a great source of U.S. government information.

9.15.3 PACER—Public Access to Court Electronic Records

PACER[150] is the public access to the records of the U.S. Federal Courts, which started in 1990. The service is not via the Internet but by direct dial into the district U.S. Court. Usually there is a $.60 per minute access fee to retrieve case information and court dockets.

9.15.4 U.S. Securities and Exchange Commission

U.S. SECURITIES
AND EXCHANGE
COMMISSION

"We are the investor's advocate."
William O. Douglas
SEC Chairman, 1937-1939

The U.S. Securities and Exchange Commission (SEC)[151] is an independent and nonpartisan regulatory agency that monitors and regulates any public exchange of securities. The objective is to protect investors in securities markets that operate fairly and to ensure that investors have access to all information concerning publicly traded securities.

EDGAR[152] (the Electronic Data Gathering, Analysis, and Retrieval system) performs automated collection, validation, indexing, acceptance, and forwarding of submissions by companies and other entities that are required by law to file forms with the SEC. As of January 1, 1998, the SEC does not accept any paper filing that is required to be filed electronically unless there is a hardship exemption.

The more important SEC forms are

- 3,4,5: a statement of ownership regarding security held by every director, officer, or owner of more than 10% of a class of equity securities
- 8-K: time-sensitive report of any event or corporate change which can be of importance to investors
- 10-K: an annual (audited) report providing a comprehensive overview of the registrant's business
- 10-Q: a quarterly (unaudited) financial report filed within 45 days of the quarter close
- 11-K: a special annual report for employee stock purchase, savings, and similar plans

---

150. See www.uscourts.gov/PubAccess.html.
151. See http://www.sec.gov/.
152. See http://www.sec.gov/edgarhp.htm.

- 13D: report that more than 5% of a class of registered equity securities are owned by any person or group of persons
- DEF 14A: proxy statement that provides information necessary to enable investors to vote in an informed manner on matters to be acted upon at security holders' meeting
- DEFC 14A: report that someone is attempting to gain control of a company's board
- S-1: registration statement for initial public offerings
- S-3: public offering of securities
- S-4: public offering of securities to register securities in connection with business combinations and exchange offers
- S-8: public offering of securities to be offered to an issuer's employees

The following specific information about companies can be found in SEC forms:

- Salaries of top executives and directors in the Proxy Statement of form DEF 14A.
- Significant changes in a company's ownership and finances, including transfers of control, major purchases of other companies, hiring of new auditors, or bankruptcy or receivership proceedings. In a company's 8-K filing.
- Competitive issues, corporate structure, details of major lawsuits, biographical backgrounds of officers and directors, financial data. In a company's 10-K.
- Names of people buying more than 5% of the securities of a publicly held company. In a 13-D filing.
- Insider selling of a company's stock by officers, directors, and other major holders. In Form 3, Form 4, and Form 144.

Numerous content providers provide custom access to and specialized transformation of the EDGAR database. Reports directly from EDGAR are difficult to understand and are several days old. The following fee-based services provide easy-to-use enhancements, along with customized alerts: Smart Edgar,[153] FreeEDGAR,[154] Disclosure,[155] EDGAR-Online,[156] and IPO Central.[157] Consult Yahoo![158] and Investor Guide[159] for a current list of EDGAR providers.

---

153. See http://dbc.smart-edgar.com/.
154. See http://www.freeedgar.com/.
155. See http://www.disclosure.com/.
156. See http://www.edgar-online.com/.
157. See http://www.ipocentral.com/.
158. See http://www.yahoo.com/Business_and_Economy/Finance_and_Investment/Corporate_Reports /SEC_EDGAR_Filings/.
159. See http://www.investorguide.com/EDGAR.htm.

9.15.5   U.S. Social Security Administration

The U.S. Social Security Administration[160] manages a large domestic government program to provide economic protection for Americans of all ages, especially with retirement benefits. Because a large portion of persons are living to older ages, the program is under pressure for reforms.

Supplying information to add realism to the debates, the Office of Research, Evaluation, and Statistics (ORES)[161] provides statistical data and analyses of the old-age, survivors, disability insurance (OASDI), and Supplemental Security Income (SSI) programs. In quarterly, annual, and one-time publications (usually in Adobe Acrobat PDF format), ORES makes available the majority of its publications and tables.

U.S. Census Bureau *the Official Statistics*

9.15.6   U.S. Bureau of the Census

The U.S. Bureau of the Census[162] is the official source of social, demographic, and economic information for the U.S. and for some areas of the world. This is a large site that requires time to explore, but is well worth the effort. Spend time in the CenStats and CenStore areas. The CenStats is a subscription service with access to County Business Patterns, USA Counties, Annual Survey of Manufacturers, ZIP Business Patterns, Census Tract/Street Index, Building Permits, International Trade Data, Occupation by Sex, Race and Hispanic Origins, and the Consolidated Federal Funds Report. Also, try the Java version of the "population clock."

9.15.7   U.S. Intelligence Community[163]

There are over 14 agencies within the U.S. Government that deal with intelligence in various forms. (See Figure 9-10.) The more visible agencies, such as the Central Intelligence Agency (CIA), have excellent (unclassified) resources; however, a corporate Web farmer may be more interested in non-DoD agencies, such as the FBI and Justice.

An excellent overview and indexes are available at Columbia University[164] and Loyola College;[165] you can also check Yahoo:Government:Intelligence[166] periodically.

---

160. See http://www.ssa.gov/.
161. See http://www.ssa.gov/statistics/ores_home.html.
162. See http://www.census.gov/.
163. See http://www.odci.gov/ic/.
164. See http://www.columbia.edu/cu/libraries/indiv/dsc/intell.html.
165. See http://www.loyola.edu/dept/politics/intel.html.
166. See http://www.yahoo.com/Government/Intelligence/.

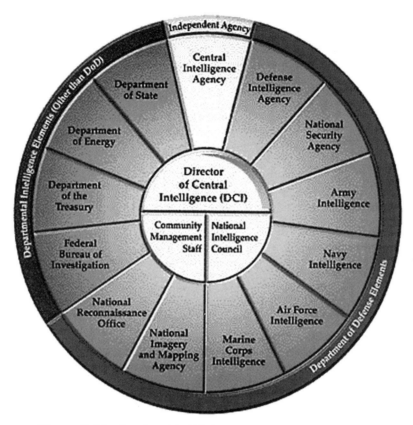

Figure 9-10   Overview of the U.S. Government Intelligence Community

The CIA[167] World Fact Book contains information drawn from many government agencies about each country in the world, covering geography, people, governments, economics, communications, transportation, and defense. It also includes abbreviations for international organizations, selected international environmental agreements, weights and measures, estimates of gross domestic products on an exchange-rate basis, and regional maps.

167. See http://www.odci.gov/cia/.

9.15.8   U.S. Patent and Trademark Office

The U.S. Patent and Trademark Office[168] is a noncommercial federal entity whose role has not changed for over 200 years:

> to promote the progress of science and the useful arts by securing for limited times to authors and inventors the exclusive rights to their respective writings and discoveries.

The PTO does so by issuing patents and trademark registrations. Registered trademarks enable the providers of goods and services to build reputations based on consumer expectations and to win share in the marketplace. The PTO's operations are fully funded by its customers through fees paid for its product and services.

---

168. See http://www.uspto.gov/.

## Chapter Ten

Techniques

Knowing the right techniques is a critical part of being a good farmer. Plowing the right contours is essential for soil conservation and crop productivity. Likewise, Web farming requires the farmer to develop good techniques in working with Web content.

This chapter describes an assortment of useful techniques for Web farming—secrets of the trade. From the perspective of the Web analyst, this chapter is important for honing the skills needed for discovering and acquiring useful content. From the perspective of the agent-programmer, this chapter is important for creating the algorithms for systematic farming. From the perspective of the system administrator, this chapter is important for knowing where things can go wrong.

The chapter contains the following sections

- Discovery: Finding Web content that is relevant to business factors
- Acquisition: Retrieving content and maintaining its historical context
- Structuring: Transforming and packaging content to enhance its value

10.1 Discovery

This first section concentrates on techniques for discovery—finding relevant Web content amid the jungle of cyberspace.

10.1.1 The Terrain of Cyberspace

The Web (as defined for the purposed of this book) is not a flat expanse where your vision is unbounded. The Web is, rather, a jungle where the terrain is treacherous and surprises spring out unexpectedly.

For the casual surfer of the Web, a quick visit to a favorite search site may inspire a false hope of discovery. With numerous "hits," the desired information seems only a few clicks away. Yet you can spend hours on entertainment and find only a few brief moments of real value. Occasionally when you do discover useful information, it seems to slip through your fingers like grains of sand. Clicking on the Print button inspires a false hope of preservation; the result is only taller stacks of yellowing paper.

You can (and should) feel depressed about the difficulty of productive discovery of Web content. We often wander into the Web jungle with only a dumb browser for assistance.

The varied terrain of cyberspace is as follows:

- *On-ramp:* Content that is directly referenced by the "on-ramps to the Information Highway" (also called portals or starting places). Examples are the Netscape start page, Yahoo!, and the Microsoft Internet Explorer start page. Not only do the on-ramps influence marketing exposure for products and services, but they also control exposure to basic information content. The content of the on-ramp's terrain is mainly in their index databases (for AltaVista, HotBot, etc.) or directory structures (for Yahoo! and Magellan).

- *Glamour Central:* Often called the visible Web, this is the content that is indexed by most global search sites and is well linked from other sites. This terrain makes up the bulk of Web content, but it may not contain the most important content from a specific business perspective. The visible Web is also quite chaotic; participants are driven by marketing motivation to have their Web sites listed favorably by the major search sites. The attention economy is overly healthy in this terrain, delivering more noise than content for the Web farmer.

- *Specialty Boutique:* This content usually comes from a single person who is an expert and is very interested in a specific topic. Maintained manually and infrequently, this content tends to consist of annotated lists of URLs with little original content. The experts here are university professors and bright (but struggling) individual consultants.

- *Not Esteemed:* Content that is generally unknown to the *On-ramp* and thus is considered of little value. This lack of esteem may result from a lack of links to the site or a request for robot exclusion. The Webmaster has not submitted its URL for indexing. This content tends to be from smaller sites that lack technical expertise, such as nonprofit companies, volunteer organizations, small professional groups, and personal Web sites.

- *Just Hatched:* Content that has been created in the last month or so, as a large portion of current content has been. Some studies indicate that the average age of a Web page is slightly more than a month. Since the cycle for index crawling by the major search sites is usually three months or more, the *Just Hatched* content is often not indexed nor directly referenced. Only by periodically checking (or subscribing to) specific content producers can you discover this content in a timely manner.

- *Not My Language:* Content that is displayed and indexed in a language other than your own. English has been the dominant language of the Web in the past. However, content created in various European languages, along with Japanese, constitutes a rapidly growing portion of Web content. The Web is increasingly global, so our "discovery scope" should be too.

- *Behind the Peephole:* Content generated from a database whose only visible part is a few META keywords and a cryptic FORM section. Much to our frustration, behind the peephole often lie huge and valuable databases (such as SEC EDGAR). This terrain is the vast undiscovered territory of cyberspace and is in dire need of metadata standards (such as XML and RDF).

- *For Members Only:* Content that can be viewed only by members, who may have to have paid a membership fee. The entry barrier may range from a free registration procedure, capturing personal identification, to a multitier monthly subscription. In many cases, there is a 30-day trial period, leading to a fixed monthly subscription. In all cases, the restricted-entry content bars global indexing and tends to consist of Web-enabled databases (thus having the problems of the *Behind the Peephole* terrain). However, content from *For Members Only* terrain constitutes a major source for a Web farming system because the content is reliable, validated, and managed.

- *Pay-Per-View:* Content that is also restricted and is delivered only on a per-use basis. Such sites usually require prior signing of licensing agreements establishing the proprietary nature of the content. In some cases (such as Dialog), the cost of entry is quite steep and complex (e.g., *dialunits*). However, the *Pay-Per-View* terrain will also be a major source of content because of availability and reliability.

- *Community Discussions:* Content consisting of continuous discussion in a community of people. Although not considered technically part of the Web, the *Community Discussion* terrain is extremely important for monitoring current trends in rumors, perceptions, opinions, and other soft information. Sources include newsgroups (Usenet), list servers (Listserv), email streams (InfoBeat), email newsletters (e-zines), Internet Relay Chat (IRC), and now newer "chat" technologies (such as NetMeeting).

- *Forgotten Territory:* Content that is contained in, and still maintained with, older Internet technologies, such as FTP directories, Archie, Gopher, WAIS (ANSI/NISO Z90.50-1995), and direct library catalogs (via telnet).

- *Spinning the CD:* Content that is stored on CD-ROM (and in other electronic formats, such as magnetic cartridges). Although these media are not part of the Web, they are part of cyberspace and can be an important source. The real issue is the trade-off between the cost of storage media and the cost of bandwidth, balanced with the volatility of the content. As volatility increases, the cost of reproducing and replacing storage media swings the choice of a delivery mechanism toward the Web. Likewise, as the cost of bandwidth declines, the preference swings toward the Web. In any case, CD-ROM content (especially with the newer DVD medium) will increasingly become complementary to Web content by providing a stable base for nonvolatile content.

- *Yellowing Hardcopy:* Content that is contained as color variations on sheets of organic material. Lest we forget, most of the world's knowledge is still stored on paper. Whether the content consists of photographic images or of print digitized by optical character recognition, Web farming systems must be able to incorporate hardcopy content as a practical matter.

The varying terrain of cyberspace requires different discovery strategies. Ignoring any one of the above categories can have significant impacts on the value created for your business. The challenge is to design the system and procedure that adequately integrate the various discovery strategies.

10.1.2 Discovery Skills

This section highlights the artistic nature of discovery rather than its technical practice. Effective discovery skills come from some combination of creative curiosity and insightful detective work. In-depth knowledge of Web technology and tools is certainly helpful but is not a necessary requirement. Each index engine and each content provider is a world unto itself—with a unique history, personality, and motivation. You will be like a backpacker hiking in the Grand Canyon for the first time. Regardless of your backpacking expertise, your knowledge of the terrain is of the utmost importance. In particular, Web farmers can learn much from the library science and information brokering professions.

Effective discovery skills come from some combination of creative curiosity and insightful detective work.

Here are some professional texts that are useful in enhancing discovery skills:

- *Naked in Cyberspace*, Lane, 1997: Excellent! A must reference for the Web farmer. It is written from the perspective of finding information about persons, rather than corporations or industries. A sobering and balanced description of the privacy and need-to-know issues.

- *Finding Statistics Online*, Berinstein, 1998: Compilation of sources for various online resources. It lacks details on specific content providers, but does present a broad spectrum of information.

- *Secrets of the Super Net Searchers*, Basch, 1996. Many little nuggets sprinkled through interviews with experienced Web searchers.

- *Search Engines for the World Wide Web*, Glossbrenner and Glossbrenner, 1998: Nice, compact guide to using the global search services. The book covers AltaVista, Excite, HotBot, Infoseek, Lycos, and Yahoo!, along with newsgroup and email lists.

- *The Online Deskbook*, Bates, 1996: A nice companion to the Berinstein book because of its coverage of specific content providers (such as Dialog, Dow Jones News, Lexis-Nexis, and so forth). However, the book is starting to show its age.

- *The Information Broker's Handbook*, Rugge and Glossbrenner, 1997: Although written from the perspective of establishing an information brokering company, it contains valuable descriptions of critical information resources.

- *Online Resources for Business*, Glossbrenner and Rosenberg, 1995: This book is a bit dated, but it does integrate the various information resources in a how-to manner.

- *Web Search Strategies*, Pfaffenberger, 1996: An early text that overlaps with Glossbrenner and Glossbrenner (1998) and Glossbrenner and Rosenberg (1995). It omits AltaVista, but it does contain lots of examples.

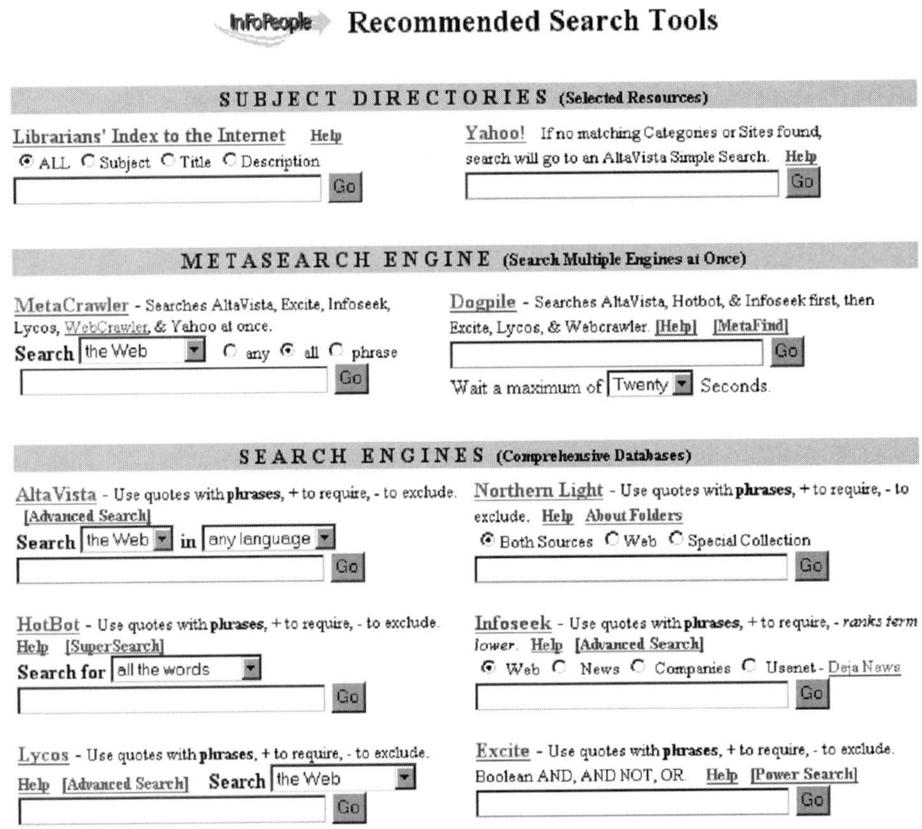

Figure 10-1 Recommended Search Tools from InfoPeople

10.1.3 Start Page

The Start Page is the Web page from which you start your searching. For many, the Start Page is whatever appears when you press *Search* on your browser, which in most cases is satisfactory for generic searches. The recommended approach is to construct your own customized Start Page. For fast rendition, store the page in a convenient hard-disk location, and set it as the default Start Page for your browser.

A favorite is the UCB Recommended Search Tools,[1] authored by Carole Leita of the InFoPeople project, as shown (circa July 1998) in Figure 10-1.

---

1. See http://infopeople.berkeley.edu:8000/src/srctools.html.

Note the categories of Subject Directories, Metasearch Engine, and Search Engines. Also note the creative use of FORM tags as entry points into the various services. Revisit this site every few months for revisions.

10.1.4   What Is Indexed?

Here lies a long tale. Indexing to one engine may be very different from indexing to another. You may think that the index engines index only the text visible in a browser. However, there are many variations, and indexing of the full text is often not done. Sometimes only the URL, the page title, and the first 100 words of visible text are indexed. At other times, the invisible text in the HEADER section (such as META keywords and the like) is also indexed. And then there are headings (in H tags), hyperlinks (in HREF tags), and so on. The specific combination of these, along with their relative importance, can be a mystery to the user of the search service.

For further information, see Danny Sullivan's Search Engine Watch[2] and, in particular, the section "Webmaster's Guide to Search Engines." Besides unraveling some of the mysteries of how a search engine indexes a site, it provides tips on improving ranking within those indexes.

10.1.5   Refining the Search

The effective refining of search results is a necessary part of discovery. We will give two examples of refining a search, using Northern Light and AltaVista.

The effective refining of search results is a necessary part of discovery.

First, let's query Northern Light for content on "information visualization" as shown in Figure 10-2.

The result is 73,855 items, of which the first 10 are displayed. Assuming that you could scan three sets of 10 items per minute, it would take 41 hours to scan all of the items—not a productive use of your time.

Note (in Figure 10-3) that Northern Light has categorized those 73,855 items into 11 subtopics (called "custom search folders" on the left). An important (but unanswered) question is how was this categorization performed.

If we click on the Conference search folder, we get the display shown in Figure 10-4. Note that there are now 806 items related to "conferences" on "information visualization," quite a reduction from 73,855 items. However, the question arises of how this folder was clustered and how over 73,000 items were eliminated. Remember the missing-mystery problem and the related recall-precision trade-off.

---

2.   See http://searchenginewatch.com/.

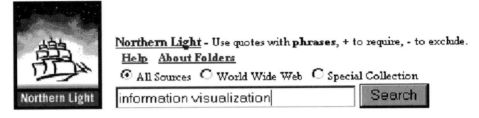

Figure 10-2 Query for Northern Light

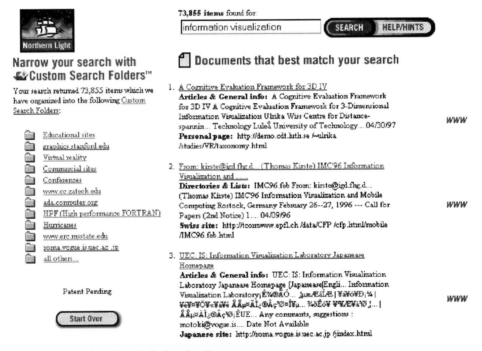

Figure 10-3 Query Results for Iteration #1

Let's take the process through one more step. Let's click on "Information search and retrieval" folder (Figure 10-5).

Now we have nine items related to "information search and retrieval" "conferences" on "information visualization." It is interesting to notice that each refinement has caused a hundredfold reduction in the number of items.

Second, let's try using LiveTopics at AltaVista. If we query on "information visualization" again, we get the display shown in Figure 10-6.

Note that we now have a mere 645,080 items obviously taking more than 41 hours to scan.

Figure 10-4 Query Results for Iteration #2

Figure 10-5 Query Results for Iteration #3

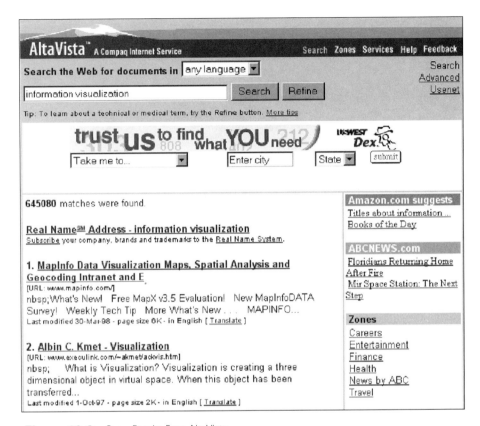

Figure 10-6   Query Results From AltaVista

Now let's click on the Refine button, which gives us the display shown in Figure 10-7.

Based on the frequency of terms appearing together in the various items, a list of subtopic clusters is presented. For example, one cluster is "Analysis, optimization, statistical, multivariate." You can then include or exclude that cluster and refine the search. In the above example, refining this query resulted in 80,733 items, an eight-fold reduction.

In contrast, you can include or exclude clusters in a graphical fashion by clicking on the Graph button in the upper right. Figure 10-8 shows the result.

This is the LiveTopics facility[3] (now called the graphic version of the Refine tool) within AltaVista. Based on COW9 collaboration[4] with François Bourdoncle of École des Mines de Paris, it consists of a Java applet that draws a graph based on a simple data file containing the subtopic clusters. There is additional information in

3.   See http://altavista.digital.com/av/content/help_refine.htm.
4.   See http://altavista.digital.com/av/content/about_our_technology_cow9.htm.

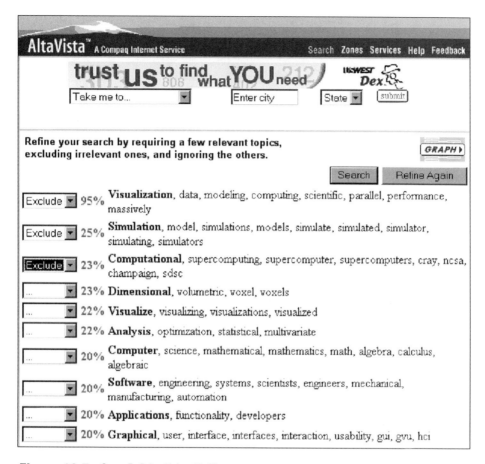

Figure 10-7   Query Refining Using AltaVista

the linking of clusters to show which ones are more closely associated with others. When the cursor passes over one of the clusters, it opens into a list of topics. Each topic can then be included or excluded in a refined search.

As suggested by AltaVista, try the following: Check out the topics contained in your company's Web site and then compare them with those of your competition. First search for `host:yourcompany.com`, then search for `host:yourcompetition.com` using the Refine tool.

Although this dynamic categorization facility seems powerful, the interpretation of the refinement among the underlying items is not intuitive. It requires some practice.

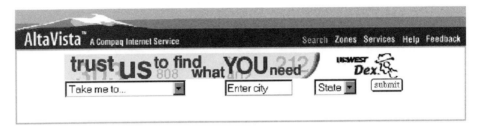

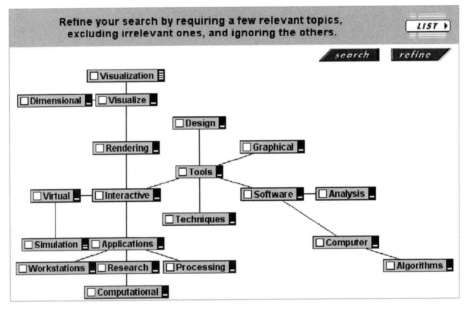

Figure 10-8 Graphical Query Refining by AltaVista

10.1.6 Advanced Searching

Most discovery services have an advanced set of search commands, which vary from service to service. For example, AltaVista has extensions that allow full Boolean expressions, date ranges, link/URL searches, and so on.

Web farmers should be well acquainted with the advanced search facilities of the major discovery services.

As an example of advanced queries useful to Web farming, the following procedure would find the current new material related to a company called xxx:

To find new material at a site

```
host:xxx.com and title:new
```

To find new pages at a site

```
host:xxx.com and (date > today-30)
```

To find a map of the entire site

```
host:xxx.com and title: (index or content)
```

To find URL references to a site

```
link:xxx.com and not host:xxx.com
```

The following *Where-Linked* query is useful to determine what other Web pages have links pointing to your Web site. An example of using the Where-Linked query is to add the following FORM code to your page:[5]

```
<FORM method=GET action="http://www.altavista.digital.com/cgi-bin/query">
<INPUT TYPE=hidden NAME=pg VALUE=aq>
<INPUT TYPE=hidden NAME=what VALUE=web>
<INPUT TYPE=hidden NAME=q VALUE=
"link:yourdomain.com AND
 ( NOT host:yourdomain.com ) AND
 ( NOT host:othergarbagesites.com )
">
<INPUT TYPE=submit VALUE="Click here to see links from other sites
  (courtesy of Alta Vista)">
</FORM>
```

With a little HTML scripting code, you can create some interesting and powerful queries against specific search engines.

10.1.7 Profiling Web Pages

This section suggests a quick way to categorize a Web page in terms of a profile of technical characteristics. The objective of the page profile is that through a quick text scan of the HTML file, a useful profile of a given Web page can be obtained. When you are dealing with thousands of pages, this quick profiling can be a useful way of categorizing massive amounts of data quickly.

---

5. Adapted from http://nano.xerox.com/nano/.

Some suggestions for a technical profile are

- Size of HTML text (in kilobytes)
- Number of image objects (GIF and JPEG)
- Total size of image objects (in kilobytes)
- Number of mapped images
- Number of TABLE tags (yes/no)
- Number of FRAME tags
- Number of URL links to same page
- Number of URL links to pages at same site
- Number of URL links to pages at different sites
- Presence of site search or indexing features
- Number of MailTo URL links
- Use of FORM tags (yes/no)
- Use of Java (or equivalent) applets
- Use of JavaScripts (or equivalent) in-line code

Lincoln Stein, who coordinates informatics at the MIT Genome Center, commented that Web sites seem to be of two types: information-rich and link-rich.[6]

> Each type has its place in the world. The link-rich sites give you the road map; information-rich sites provide the payoff at the end of the journey. While all sites provide some mixture of links and information, a few specialists are skewed to one extreme or another.

Stein proposes an Information Index composed of a ratio of text inside links to text in the body. A typical Yahoo! page would score close to 100, while a page from EGDAR would score zero. He continues by suggesting indexes for graphics, Doo-dad, TutieFrutie, Frames, and so on. However, an Information Index may be a quick way of sifting the wheat from the chaff in thousands of Web pages.

A final area that would be useful in this technical profile is the volatility of the Web page. By scanning at periodic intervals, you could construct an index of changes to content and to links.

6. L.D. Stein, Sifting the Wheat from the Chaff, *Web Techniques*, May 1997, 8–11.

10.2 Acquisition

This section focuses on the techniques for acquisition—acquiring Web content once it is discovered.

10.2.1 Web Crawling

A Web crawler (or spider or worm) is a program that automatically traverses the hypertext structure by retrieving a Web document and then recursively retrieving all documents that are referenced. One might say that a typical Web browser is a one-level Web crawler, since it crawls a specific link and identifies links in the resulting object.

The HTTP Tutorial,[7] by James Marshall, is useful in understanding the hidden interactions of Web servers. Martijn Koster at Excite's WebCrawler is also a good resource site,[8] containing a FAQ list and an implementation list on Web crawlers.

Marshall has issued this cogent warning to would-be crawlers:

> In particular, don't be tempted to write programs that automatically follow Web links (called robots or spiders) before you really know what you're doing. They can be useful, but a badly-written robot is one of the worst kinds of programs on the Web, blindly following a rapidly increasing number of links and quickly draining server resources. If you plan to write anything like a robot, please read more about them. There may already be a working program to do what you want.... Definitely support the current Standard for Robot Exclusion, and stay tuned for further developments.

Another reference is the *Guide to Search Engines,* by Sonnenreich and Macinta, 1998. It is a comprehensive and knowledgeable explanation of search engines as applied to intranets. This is not a description of the global search services (such as AltaVista).

The Robot Exclusion Standard is a convention to limit and direct a Web crawler to content on a specific site.[9] The following is the robot exclusion file for the IBM Web site. Note the disallow statement for the Stretch area (which has some interesting information not globally indexed) and the quasi-use of XML for the Webmaster information.

---

7. See http://www.jmarshall.com/easy/http/.
8. See http://info.webcrawler.com/mak/projects/robots/robots.html.
9. See the Web Robots Page at http://infor.webcrawler.com/mak/projects/robots/robots.html or http://www.archive.org/robotexclusion.html.

```
#This is a file retrieved by webwalkers a.k.a. spiders that
#conform to a defacto standard.
# See <URL:http://info.webcrawler.com/mak/projects/robots/robots.html>
# The webmaster for this site is:
#   <name>Ed Costello</name>
#   <address>epc@www.ibm.com</address>
#
#Format is:
#       User-agent: <name of spider>
#       Disallow: <nothing> | <path>
# Flag  Date    By      Reason
# $11-  950130  epc     finally understood what the file was for!
# $L2=  960909  epc     fixed url since mak moved to Webcrawler...
# $L3=   970811 epc     drop /Stretch/
#
#-----------------------------------------------------------------------
# following prevents access to /misc/ for spiders
User-Agent: *
Disallow: /Admin
Disallow: /Features
Disallow: /stage
Disallow: /Stage
Disallow: /images
Disallow: /Search
Disallow: /search
Disallow: /Stretch
Disallow: /globalnetwork/customer
```

For the Microsoft Web site, the robot exclusion file is simply this:

```
# robots.txt for http://www.microsoft.com/
# do not delete this file, contact MSCOMSYS for edits!!!!
#
User-agent: *
Disallow: /isapi/        # keep robots out of the executable tree
Disallow: /scripts/
```

A casual sampling of several major Web sites indicates that many sites, surprisingly, do not have robot exclusion files, implying that their Webmasters desire complete global indexing.

10.2.2   Accessing Dynamic Pages

Welcome to the *Behind the Peephole* terrain of the Webscape. The good news is that a single request can access an enormous database behind a Web site. The bad news is that you often do not know the characteristics and structure of that database. However, there are implicit clues to the contents of that database buried in the FORM tag.

Consider the following example from Yahoo!'s stock page,[10] as shown below.

The FORM tag that actually obtains a stock quote is shown here:

```
<form method=get action="/q">
<input type=text size=25 name=s>
<input type=submit value="Get Quotes">
<select name=d>
<option value=f selected>Basic
<option value=t>Detailed
<option value=1y>Chart
<option value=r>Research
</select>
<a href="/l">symbol lookup</a>
</form>
```

The FORM tag uses the GET method to invoke the 'Q' procedure on the server. The procedure is passed the parameters for stock name (as 'S=') and display type (as 'D='). The stock name is entered as a free-form text field, while the display type is a pop-down list. Entering 'INTC' for the stock symbol for Intel Corporation and clicking on the Get Quote button results in the following URL, issued to the Yahoo! server:

```
http://quote.yahoo.com/q?s=intc&d=f
```

---

10. See http://quote.yahoo.com/.

Note the use of the question mark to initiate the parameter list (called the "query string"). The result is a basic display of quote information, as shown below.

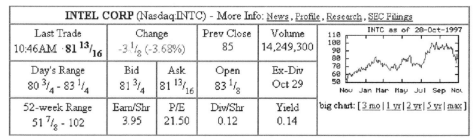

Wed Oct 29 10:53AM Eastern U.S. Time -- U.S. Markets close in 5 hours 7 minutes.

Symbol	Last Trade		Change	Volume	More Info
INTC	10:37AM	82 $\frac{1}{4}$	-2 $\frac{11}{16}$ -3.16%	13,209,900	Chart, News, Profile, Research, SEC Filings

Select a Symbol for a detailed quote. Quotes delayed 15 minutes for Nasdaq, 20 minutes otherwise.

If the display type "detailed" has been selected instead, the following URL is generated and sent to the Yahoo! server for processing:

```
http://quote.yahoo.com/q?s=INTC&d=t
```

The resulting display of stock information is shown below.

INTEL CORP (Nasdaq:INTC) - More Info: News, Profile, Research, SEC Filings				
Last Trade 10:46AM ·81 $\frac{13}{16}$	Change -3 $\frac{1}{8}$ (-3.68%)	Prev Close 85	Volume 14,249,300	INTC as of 28-Oct-1997
Day's Range 80 $\frac{3}{4}$ - 83 $\frac{1}{4}$	Bid 81 $\frac{3}{4}$ · Ask 81 $\frac{13}{16}$	Open 83 $\frac{1}{8}$	Ex-Div Oct 29	
52-week Range 51 $\frac{7}{8}$ - 102	Earn/Shr 3.95 · P/E 21.50	Div/Shr 0.12	Yield 0.14	big chart: [3 mo	1 yr	2 yr	5 yr	max]

Non-Tables Version ~ Download Spreadsheet Format
Basic Quotes for All Above Symbols ~ Yahoo! Finance Home

Note the option to download "spreadsheet format" above. The resulting URL is as follows:

```
http://quote.yahoo.com/d/quotes.csv?s=INTC&f=sl1d1t1c1ohgv&e=.csv
```

It returns the following comma-delimited file (where its MIME type is CSV) to the browser:

```
"INTC",81.6875,"10/29/1997","10:49AM",-3.25,83.125,83.25,80.75,14535500
```

As shown below, the Microsoft Internet Explorer displays an embedded Excel spreadsheet to handle this MIME type.

	A1		=	INTC					
	A	B	C	D	E	F	G	H	I
1	INTC	81.6875	10/29/97	10:49AM	-3.25	83.125	83.25	80.75	14535500
2									
3									

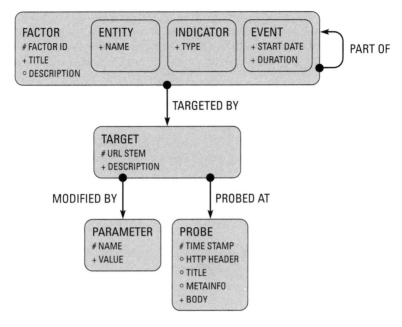

Figure 10-9 Schema for Control Database

The point of this example of Yahoo! quotes is twofold. First, you can interpret the parameters of the FORM tag in terms of database content or format. Thus, you could construct programs that generate the appropriate URL request, rather than relying on the human interface of the FORM tag. Second, it is relatively easy to deliver the data in a concise format (such as CSV), as opposed to some fancy presentation. Thus, you could import the resulting data directly into a database, rather than parsing some cryptic HTML file.

The next advance with dynamic pages from Web-enabled databases would be to set standards in the use of XML to define the database interface, query the database, and deliver the data back in a structured format.

10.2.3 Organizing Dynamic References

As described in Chapter 5, Architecture, the database that controls the Web farming system is a critical component. This database should monitor each probe of Web content and relate it back to its associated Critical External Factor (CEF).

A suggestion for such a database design is shown in Figure 10-9.

Each FACTOR entity is specialized into ENTITY, INDICATOR, and EVENT subtypes and can be related to each other by the relation PART OF. However, the important part is the management of targets for specific factors.

For each FACTOR, there can be one or more TARGET instances, each with a URL STEM that may be either a static or a dynamic URL reference.[11] If it is a dynamic URL, there are one or more instances of PARAMETER. For example, a dynamic URL to obtain the stock quote for Intel Corporation would have this URL STEM:[12]

```
http://quote.yahoo.com/q
```

And the PARAMETER instances would be

```
NAME = "s" and VALUE = "intc"
NAME = "d" and VALUE = "f"
```

The probing process would generate the actual URL as

```
http://quote.yahoo.com/q$s=intc&d=f
```

For dynamic URL targets that probe databases, the decomposition of parameters allows the retrieval of a range of result sets. We might call this a "poor man's" query facility.

For each TARGET instance, there will be many PROBE instances, one for every periodic retrieval of the Web page referenced. Each PROBE instance records the time that the HTTP GET method returned the initial HTML file, along with HTTP header information, page description from the HTML META tags, TITLE text from the HTML TITLE tag, and a compressed version of the BODY text.[13]

10.2.4   Other Acquisition Techniques

Some of the techniques required for effective acquisition of Web content are the following:

- Dealing with HTML frames
- Dealing with Java applets and ActiveX controls
- Handling Delta analysis of static pages
- OCR of graphical images
- Handling continuous data feeds
- Preserving persistent connections
- Handling secure connections
- Automating authentication of restricted resources

11. See the section "Build Selection and Extraction Filters" in Chapter 4, Methodology, for more on URL selection methods.
12. See the full example in the section "FORM Tags" in Chapter 7, Standards.
13. See the sections "Maintain Historical Context" and "Build Selection and Extraction Filters" in Chapter 4, Methodology, for more on compression and extraction.

Keeping the Goals Clearly in Sight

After a year of intense effort, the team had grown to five persons on-board and another was being hired. People were in high spirits, but, unfortunately, the team was lost in a deluge of technical problems. Every new addition to the system seemed to cause other components to fail. Management became concerned that the business intelligence activity was out of control, or at least pushing the envelope too far.

It was Alice who brought some sense back to the team. "Remember that our goal is quite simple," she said. "Find useful business information, and get it to the people who need it."

The team began to spend less time in front of their monitors and more time visiting with people throughout the company. They even traveled to several key customers to see for themselves what they had been studying. Alice reflected on that experience. "That period brought a fresh perspective to the whole team; we wanted to start from scratch and rebuild the entire data collection. Although we didn't do that, our users seemed to feel that we had!"

Next installment is on page 325.

10.3 Structuring

This section focuses on the techniques of structuring—relating, transforming, and packaging content to add business value.

10.3.1 Organizing Web Content

Some mechanism is required for organizing Web content once it has been discovered and acquired. Otherwise, our content database would consist of a myriad of little pieces without a coherent structure. Possible avenues for this organizing are suggested below.

1. Organize the Critical External Factors (or simply factors) that were identified in the first task of Getting Started (as described in Chapter 4, Methodology). Give each factor a unique label (50-character maximum) and a description (one or two sentences in a MEMO field). Depending on your level of effort in documenting factors, you could have hundreds of entries, or even a thousand entries, for factors. Consider using a personal database tool (such as Microsoft Access) or a spreadsheet utility (such as Lotus 1-2-3 or Microsoft Excel) to assist.

2. As much as possible, structure the list of factors hierarchically so that the factors are grouped based on their impacts on the enterprise. Use the notation of Yahoo! and others, which concatenates higher-level factors, such as *"top: second: third: leaf."* The top-level factor should be related back to the overall market structure of your business environment. The factors at the leaf (or bottom) level would be used to guide the discovery process.

3. Include a priority field (number from 1 to 5, with 1 being "absolutely critical"). Do a frequency distribution on the priority field, and attempt to even out the distribution to eliminate gross lumps. Enlisting your colleagues or even a few executives, you could ask them, in a questionnaire, to rate the priorities of the factors and assign the average rating to a decimal field. The goal is focusing subsequent effort on the factor entries with higher priority. There is probably an 80-20 rule in which 20% of the factors will determine 80% of the impacts on your enterprise.

4. Pick the first factor entry. As described in later chapters, use your existing browser and other Web tools with various generic discovery services (e.g., Yahoo! and AltaVista) to discover Web content about this first factor.

5. When a search query returns useful results, save the query. For instance, save the URL for the query as a favorite in a folder labeled with the factor name and located in the factor PROBES folder.

6. When useful Web content is discovered, save the content. For instance, save the URL for the Web page as a favorite in a folder labeled with the factor name and located in the factor CONTENT folder.

7. Explore back to the root of the URL (i.e., upstream in the Web structure) to determine how much of the entire Web site is relevant. Relevant pages could include the root page but could also include the pages containing What's New, Site Search, Table of Contents, Site Index, Today's Announcements, Related Links, and the like. Explore links at a Web site to other sites to determine whether these other sites are relevant. With megasites (such as Microsoft, IBM, Digital Equipment, and Hewlett-Packard), you may want to consider each one a collection of separate Web sites.

8. Continue to process the next few factor entries, while recording notes on the following questions:
   - How often should a specific site be probed to maintain currency with its content? In other words, what is the volatility of the Web content?
   - How can the query be fine-tuned to eliminate extraneous sites? In other words, how can we increase precision with a reasonable penalty on recall? This is the wheat-chaff dilemma.
   - Is the query missing relevant content? In other words, how can we increase recall with a reasonable penalty on precision? This is the missing-mystery dilemma.

9. Continue to formulate discovery plans by researching the remaining factors as time and energy permits. After you research 10 to 20 factors, an initial discovery plan should emerge.

10.3.2 Parsing Semistructured Data

A promising area of research is the "wrapper" approach to handling semistructured data, such as the typical Web paper. An article[14] in the ACM *SIGMOD Record* describes how the underlying structure of the Web page can be deduced from the formatting data (e.g., header H tags). The effort and reliability of generating a wrapper for a specific Web page is the issue addressed by this article. Using parsing tools (such as YACC and LEX from UNIX), tokens for the HTML heading tags are identified and used to parse the structured values. Results are given for 14 Web sources, with the time to specify the wrapper at six minutes or less.

This chapter has described a few techniques that are useful in Web farming. These techniques suggest an evolving (and, perhaps, maturing) process of business intelligence. You are encouraged to adapt those techniques you find useful and to create new ones as required. The remaining chapters delve into the societal issues of, and future challenges for, Web farming.

14. N. Ashish and C.A. Knoblock, Wrapper Generation for Semistructured Internet Sources, *SIGMOD Record,* vol. 26, no. 4, December 1997, 8–15. Other articles in this same issue report on a Workshop on Management of Semi-Structured Data in May 1997. Papers are also available at http://www.research.att.com/~suciu/workshop-papers.html and are supported through NSF grant number IRI93-18791.

## Part Four

Harvesting the Crop

## Chapter Eleven

Society

Society is an important part of being a successful farmer. Fellow farmers, along with other community folks, discuss and resolve issues affecting the entire community.

This chapter discusses the societal issues related to Web farming. In particular, we first focus on the information ecology formed by the Internet and then touch on the sensitive issues of privacy and intellectual property rights, along with competitive intelligence, industrial espionage, and information warfare. The chapter closes with a suggested code of ethics for Web farming.

11.1 Information Ecology

We have used the term *information ecology* to emphasize the stewardship role of IT professionals toward a valuable resource within the enterprise—information. We return to this theme now, but at the societal level. The principles are much the same.

Information ecology is the understanding of the complex interactions among information creators and information consumers. At various times, every business, government agency, and individual is both a creator and a consumer of information. The exchange of information is at the core of many industries, from entertainment to advertising, stock markets, newspapers, and book publishing.

As Tom Davenport of the University of Texas points out, information ecology requires a holistic approach to thinking about people and their behavior toward information.[1] Biological ecology thrives on diversity; information ecology also thrives on diversity. The Web is an excellent example of information diversity for society.

The Web is an excellent example of information diversity for society.

11.1.1 Public Good or Private Property

Imagine a society in which there is little or no exchange of information. For some people, such an image may conjure thoughts of a repressive totalitarian society or of Orwell's *1984*. For others, the image reminds one of a week-long backpack trip (without a radio or a cellular phone) bringing a needed rest from the continuous stream of sales calls, national disasters, political infighting, international unrest, highway accidents, and so on. We know that as a free society we cannot live without the open exchange of information, yet we often wonder how we can live with it.

Web farming puts a special twist on the information ecology within our society. In the near future, the progress of IT technology will allow every enterprise immediate access to the most current details about customers, suppliers, competitors, and so on. No longer can details hide in masses of data. No longer can ignorance be an acceptable option.

No longer can details hide in masses of data.
No longer can ignorance be an acceptable option.

Laptops will have storage equal to that of small libraries, but will weigh only a few pounds. Network connections will transfer an entire database in seconds. Every business transaction that ever occurred will be archived for pennies. (The operating

---

1. Davenport, 1997, 28ff.

system of your workstation will operate without crashing for years!) Is this picture our technology dream or our nightmare?

Regardless of the technology, will the political, legal, and economic dynamics of our society permit an open exchange of information? In particular, how will the balance sway between information as a public good and as private property? In addition, how will the tension be resolved between right-to-know and need-to-know practices?

It could be argued that a totally open exchange is the best path to a fair and efficient market that will benefit everyone. It could also be argued that a totally open exchange is a major disaster in eroding personal freedoms. Or, it could be argued that a totally open exchange is a recipe for chaotic behavior—wild swings driven by the lack of time to think properly. All these views have some validity.

When a business transaction occurs among several parties, who owns the information about that transaction? Every enterprise is a major creator of information. In the collection and organization of information about specific industries, new markets will be created and old ones rejuvenated.

11.1.2 Attention Economics

Another approach to information ecology is to focus on attention, rather than on the information itself. This new approach is called *attention economics*. In an article in *Wired* magazine,[2] Michael Goldhaber, a visiting scholar at the UCB Institute of the Study for Social Change, argues that the new economics of cyberspace should be based on attention.

> By definition, economics is the study of how a society uses its scarce resources. And information is not scarce—especially on the Net, where it is not only abundant but overflowing.... The economy of attention—not information—is the natural economy of cyberspace.... The flow of attention will not only anticipate the flow of money, but [will] eventually replace it altogether.[3]

Attention is a scarce resource since each of us has only 16 or so hours per day to devote to all the topics there are. As Goldhaber points out, the total size of global attention grows as the size of the world audience grows. However, the total available attention per person stays constant. The demand upon the attention of the persons surfing the Internet will steadily increase. Likewise, these persons will devote increasing attention to how they are allocating their attention.

The implications for Web farming are slightly different. The fixed amount of attention comes from the users of the data warehouse, into which the Web farming system is feeding information. Through publish-and-subscribe and similar mechanisms, the dissemination from the warehouse should be constantly tuned to maximize the "attention benefit" to these people.

---

2. M.H. Goldhaber, Attention Shoppers, *Wired*, December 1997.
3. Ibid.

On the other hand, the attention management of the Web farming system itself is a separate issue. Its capacity is not limited by 16 hours per day and one pair of eyes. However, the total content of the Web is far beyond that capacity, even if all of it could be accessed. Finding the best method of allocating system attention is central to operating a successful Web farming system.

11.2 Privacy and Confidentiality

Today, an enormous amount of information about our personal lives is available. With a few exceptions, all this personal information is freely available to anyone with some motivation, skills, and money. Every year, the amount of recorded information increases, and the effort required to access that information decreases.

Keeping your personal information secret has developed a negative image in today's society. The prevailing attitude is that you're guilty (or at least suspect) until all is disclosed. Openness is popular, even at the cost of intruding on the privacy of the individual. An article in the *Wall Street Journal* highlights this shift in public opinion toward secrets:

> Secrets—knowledge kept intentionally concealed—are under siege; they are easier to learn and quicker to spread than ever.... Secrets zip around the globe by satellite, electronic media, and tabloid television. And the public eats them up.... In recent decades, keeping secrets has become synonymous with repression and shame. Openness is the mantra of modern America.... The very word *secret,* as opposed to *private, silent, reticent* or *confidential,* seems pejorative to many people.[4]

One of the more sobering books to read is Carole Lane's *Naked in Cyberspace,*[5] in which the author lays bare the available resources for finding information about specific individuals. In Chapter Four, she gives a few sample searches for personal information that provoke one's thoughts about privacy and confidentiality. From local courthouses, records of birth, death, marriage, divorce, adoption, and court cases are compiled with records of telephone numbers, mailing addresses, social security numbers, driver's licenses, email addresses, newspaper articles, fishing licenses, immigration records, tax records, census data, genealogy, vehicle registrations, insurance records, criminal history, and credit ratings—all available from commercial databases and various Web sites.

---

4. C. Crossen, "In This Tell-All Era, Secrets Just Aren't What They Used To Be, *WSJ*, March 31, 1998, A1.
5. Lane, 1997.

Read Carole Lane's *Naked in Cyberspace*. It will give you a professional, balanced view of the emotion-charged privacy issue, plus useful intelligence-gathering skills and some ethical guidelines for the use of those skills.

The technology that supports Web farming is the same technology that erodes our privacy. In the past, much of our personal information was stored in typed or printed records; that limited our ability to search for and retrieve the information. Acquiring those records involved lots of hard work traveling to specific government agencies, scanning microfiches, and copying data. Only the most diligent were able to compile a significant dossier of personal information.

> *The technology that supports Web farming*
> *is the same technology that erodes our privacy.*

With today's technology, the barriers of old are rapidly disappearing. With a few clicks on a Web site and a few blocks of text pasted into a document, a personal dossier is ready for instant delivery as an email attachment.

> *With a few clicks on a Web site and a few blocks of text*
> *pasted into a document, a personal dossier is ready for*
> *instant delivery as an email attachment.*

The right to privacy is neither a simple issue nor one that is easily solved with extreme alternatives. Carole Lane describes clearly the delicate balance between our right to privacy and our right to know:

> This is a subject that invites an emotional response. Few of us relish the fact that others have access to a great deal of personal information about us, or could have it with surprisingly little effort. However, most of us would claim the right to investigate the background of others, at least under certain circumstances.... Much as we all wish to protect our own right of privacy, we all accept that this right is not absolute. Whether it is appropriate for us to invade someone's privacy, or for them to invade ours, sometimes calls for delicate judgment.[6]

---

6. Ibid, 41.

Our purpose here is not to critique the broad issues of privacy and confidentiality in general society, or even in cyberspace. Our focus is on Web farming, which at times will involve the acquisition, analysis, and dissemination of information that is of a personal nature. At the very least, persons involved with Web farming should thoroughly understand their legal responsibilities as they are related to personal information. Even better, persons involved with Web farming should explicitly state to anyone affected their policies for handling personal information and then abide by those policies.

The following sections describe the major laws regulating personal privacy in the U.S., followed by industry efforts at self-regulation and standards.

11.2.1 U.S. Freedom of Information Act

The Freedom of Information Act[7] replaces a *need-to-know* criterion with a *right-to-know* one for determining whether an individual can access certain government records. Before the enactment of this law, the burden was on the individual to establish a right to examine government records. Now the government has to justify the need for secrecy.

The law sets standards for determining which records must be disclosed and which may be withheld, along with administrative and judicial remedies for those denied access. In general, the U.S. government is expected to provide the fullest possible disclosure of information to the public.

The good news for Web farming is that government Web sites, from EDGAR to THOMAS, are becoming primary information sources.

11.2.2 U.S. Federal Privacy Act

Complementing the Freedom of Information Act, the Federal Privacy Act further regulates government recordkeeping and disclosure practices when the information is about an individual. The law requires that personal information in government records be accurate, complete, relevant, and timely. The subject has the right to know about her information and to challenge its accuracy.

The law requires that agencies gathering information for one purpose cannot use that information for another purpose. Each agency must publish a description of all personal information it maintains, so agencies are prevented from keeping secret records.

Marc Rotenberg, director of the Electronic Privacy Information Center, described the two-sided nature of privacy concisely:

> Privacy is not simply about preventing others from getting information about you. It's also about your right to get access to information about yourself.[8]

---

7. FOIA 5 US Code Section 552. However, everyone who is not a lawyer should consult *The Citizen's Guide to Using the Freedom of Information Act* (1997), a copy of which can be found at http://www.epic.org/open_gov/citizens_guide_97.html.
8. *Washington Post,* April 8, 1997.

Together with the Freedom of Information Act, the Privacy Act permits disclosure of most personal information to the individual and restricts disclosure of personal information to others when disclosure violates the individual's privacy. Both laws also recognize the legitimate need to restrict any disclosure of certain information, such as that related to national defense, foreign policy, and criminal investigations.

11.2.3 Code of Fair Information Practices

The foundation of the Privacy Act is the Code of Fair Information Practices, which evolved from earlier work with privacy regulations.

The initial version came from a report in 1973 from the Advisory Committee on Automated Data Systems for the U.S. Department of Health, Education, and Welfare. Later contributions came from the Organization for Economic Cooperation and Development (OECD) in 1981, and from the Council of European Convention, also in 1981, becoming "the core of all data protection in Europe and elsewhere."[9]

The FIP version reprinted below is from a congressional report[10] authored by Robert Gellman[11] in 1994. Government agencies and companies often use this version of the Code of Fair Information Practices as a template for their specific privacy policies.

- Principle of Openness, which provides that the existence of record-keeping systems and databanks containing data about individuals should be publicly known, along with a description of the main purpose and uses of the data.

- Principle of Individual Participation, which provides that each individual should have a right to see any data about himself and to correct or remove any data that is not timely, accurate, relevant, or complete.

- Principle of Collection Limitation, which provides that there should be limits to the collection of personal data, that data should be collected by lawful and fair means, and that data should be collected, where appropriate, with the knowledge or consent of the subject.

- Principle of Data Quality, which provides that personal data should be relevant to the purposes for which it is to be used, and should be accurate, complete, and timely.

- Principle of Use Limitation, which provides that there must be limits to the internal uses of personal data and that the data should be used only for the purposes specified at the time of collection.

---

9. Email message from Robert Gellman, March 12, 1998.
10. H.R. Report No. 103-601, Part 5, 103rd Congress, 1994.
11. A privacy and information policy consultant at rgellman@cais.com.

- Principle of Disclosure Limitation, which provides that personal data should not be communicated externally without the consent of the data subject or other legal authority.

- Principle of Security, which provides that personal data should be protected by reasonable security safeguards against such risks as loss, unauthorized access, destruction, use, modification, or disclosure. Sufficient resources should be available to offer reasonable assurances that security goals will be accomplished.

- Principle of Accountability, which provides that record keepers should be accountable for complying with fair information practices.

These principles should guide every information provider toward respect for personal privacy. In particular, Web farming systems should be aware of any content that identifies a specific person (by name, social security number, address, telephone number, or so on). If such content exists, the management of that system should interpret each of the above principles in its unique situation and create a statement of its responsibilities in handling personal information.

11.2.4   U.S. Fair Credit Reporting Act

The Fair Credit Reporting Act[12] is an interesting contrast to the two laws we have discussed. The purpose of this law is to ensure fair and equitable procedures for the consumer who is seeking credit, employment, insurance, and other financial transactions. The law is aimed at the provider of personal financial information (called the consumer reporting agency, or CRA) and at the persons requesting and using that information. The major CRAs in the U.S. are Equifax,[13] Experian (formerly TRW Credit),[14] and TransUnion.[15]

Web Farmers

Order a copy of your credit report from a CRA to better understand the FCRA law.

If Web farming systems seek to acquire financial credit reports on individuals, the Fair Credit Reporting Act is highly relevant. In particular, there are specific allowable reasons ("permissible purposes") for legitimately requesting credit information and obligations regarding the use and dissemination of that information.

---

12. FCRA 15 U.S. Code 1681-1681u. A complete copy, merged with current amendments, is available at http://www.ftc.gov/os/statutes/fcra.htm. In particular, see Section 604 on Permissible Purposes of Consumer Reports for the criteria you must meet to legally get access to the credit report of another person.
13. See http://www.equifax.com/.
14. See http://www.experian.com/.
15. See http://www.tuc.com/.

The CRA may furnish credit reports only to a person who intends to use the report for the following:

- Credit transaction involving the consumer
- Employment involving the consumer
- Insurance involving the consumer
- Eligibility for a license conferred by the government involving the consumer
- Another "legitimate business need for the information with a business transaction"

If the consumer is denied services because of the credit report, the consumer must be informed of the situation and must be told which agency supplied the report.

The criminal penalty for obtaining information under false pretenses is a fine of not more than $5,000 or imprisonment for not more than one year, or both. Ouch!

Web farming systems should be especially sensitive to acquiring and handling financial information about specific persons. The dissemination of that information may classify your system as a credit reporting agency and, hence, make it subject to the restrictions of this law.

The next five sections deal with self-regulation and standards related to privacy protection.

11.2.5 TRUSTe

TRUSTe[16] is an independent non-profit organization with the purpose of stimulating Internet commerce through self-regulation of privacy and forestalling government regulation of Internet privacy. The point is that e-commerce is dampened by privacy concerns about giving one's name, address, and credit card information over the Internet. Unless these concerns are addressed, e-commerce will be for only a few brave souls (or a mass of apathetic ones).

The TRUSTe program ensures consumer privacy through a system of "Trust-marks," displayed on the home page of a company's Web site. By clicking on this trustmark, the person is given the stated privacy policy of the Web site. These policy statements must include the following:

- The type of personally identifiable information that the site gathers
- How this information will be used and processed
- How the security of this information will be ensured
- With whom this information will be shared

---

16. See http://www.truste.org/.

- How visitors to the site may opt out of having their information disclosed
- How visitors may change or update their information once it is disclosed
- How visitors may delete or deactivate their information from the site database

Compliance with the TRUSTe program is monitored by a process consisting of

- Initial and periodic reviews by TRUSTe staff
- Seeding of personal information by TRUSTe staff to detect violations
- Random audits by independent firms, such as PricewaterhouseCoopers
- Feedback from users

Fees for the TRUSTe program range from $249 to $5,000, depending on the company's annual revenues.

See the policies of Lands-End[17] (which heavily emphasizes e-commerce) and MatchLogic[18] (which has a multilevel policy dependent on specific areas of its Web site).

11.2.6 Firefly Network Privacy Policy

As a collaborative service, Firefly collects personal preferences, allowing people to specify their interests and information they would like to receive. Firefly has been acquired by Microsoft, which stated that the acquisition will enable it to "deliver more privacy-rich products and services on the Internet."

The network privacy policy of Firefly is simple and straightforward:

> Your e-mail address will not be shared outside of the Firefly Network for marketing purposes without your consent. Profile information will be used to create personalized content, services and advertising on sites in the Firefly Network. In addition, Firefly and third-party licensees may use your profile to generate aggregate reports and market research. You may inform Firefly Network, Inc. at cancel@firefly.net at any time if you would like to cancel your account and have your contact information deleted from Firefly's records.[19]

---

17. See http://www.landsend.com/.
18. See http://www.matchlogic.com/.
19. See http://www.firefly.com/PrivacyPol.html.

11.2.7 IBM Fair Information Practices

On its home site, IBM offers a Privacy section containing the following simple and understandable policy:

> At IBM, we intend to give you as much control as possible over your personal information. In general, you can visit IBM on the Web without telling us who you are or revealing any information about yourself. There are times, however, when we may need information from you, such as your name and address. It is our intent to let you know before we collect personal information from you on the Internet. If you choose to give us personal information...it is our intent to let you know how we will use such information. If you tell us that you do not wish to have this information used as a basis for further contact with you, we will respect your wishes. We do keep track of the domains from which people visit us. We analyze this data for trends and statistics, and then we discard it.[20]

IBM summarizes its interpretation of the Code of Fair Information Practices as follows:

- "Consumers being informed that their information is being collected"
- "Choice whether or not to share their personal information"
- "The use of appropriate security as desired by the consumer"
- "Where access to such personally identifiable data is allowed"[21]

11.2.8 Platform for Privacy Preferences Project of W3C

In contrast to TRUSTe, another effort to deal with privacy on the Internet is the Platform for Privacy Preferences Project of W3C.[22] The objective of this project is to standardize the statements of privacy practices for a Web site and of privacy preferences for a visitor to that Web site.

When a person visits a Web site that does not agree with his privacy preferences, he is notified of the mismatch and is asked whether he wishes to continue. If he shares personal information with the Web site, the interactions with that site can be customized, increasing convenience and quality to the person. However, the cost is that he provides some of his personal information, such as a "cookie," an email

---

20. See http://www.ibm.com/Privacy/.
21. IBM, *Business Intelligence—Executive Questions and Answers*, February 26, 1998.
22. See http://www.w3.org/P3P/Overview.html.

address, a mailing address, purchasing patterns, and a credit card account number. By explicitly stating the privacy practices of a Web site, the Webmaster is assuring visitors that personal information will be used only for certain purposes. Of course, there is no legal obligation to do so at the current time.

One proposal for the Privacy Preferences Project is the Open Profiling Standard proposed by Firefly, Netscape, and Verisign Inc. and backed by Microsoft.

11.2.9 Further Information about Privacy

For further information on privacy, consult the following Web resources:

- The Electronic Frontier Foundation,[23] whose goal is "to protect privacy rights and free expression"
- The Electronic Privacy Information Center,[24] which has broad coverage of privacy issues
- The Privacy Rights Clearinghouse,[25] which was established in 1992 by the California Telecommunications Education Trust and is associated with the Utility Consumers' Action Network, a nonprofit consumer organization in San Diego
- Privacy International,[26] which involves more than 40 countries in watching government and corporate practices

11.3 Intellectual Property Rights

An issue related to privacy is the protection of intellectual property rights. The purpose of intellectual property rights is not to hide information but to protect the information from being exploited commercially by those who have no right to its use.

There are three forms of protection for intellectual property: copyright, patents, and trade secrets. From the perspective of Web farming, copyright laws are the most relevant.

The stated purpose of the copyright is to "promote the progress of science and the useful arts" by protecting the property rights of authors. Most people mistake the means of the copyright for its ends. The purpose is to promote the benefits to society and not necessarily the rights of individuals. However, the absence of ownership protection would discourage authors from creating and publishing creative works because they would be inadequately compensated for their efforts.

Over the centuries, developed countries have wanted protection for their creative works, while undeveloped countries have argued against that protection because of

---

23. See http://www.eff.org/.
24. See http://www.epic.org/.
25. See http://www.privacyrights.org/.
26. See http://www.privacy.org/pi.

their general poverty, the lack of hard currency, and similar disadvantages.[27] In today's cyberspace, intellectual property can be exported instantaneously to haves and have-nots alike. Copyright on the Web is becoming a global issue of importance.

Copyright protection is based on the idea that information is property. There is an owner—the author or publisher—of this property. As McLuhan and Fiore argued in their classic book,[28] the concept of authorship is only a few centuries old—a creation of print technology. Before printing, authorship was a group activity in which ideas from many people were merged in an oral tradition of information creation. A technology such as that of the Web will lessen the importance of authorship, and hence of copyright, because of the benefits to society of merging many ideas from multiple sources into new products, rapidly and efficiently. Whether or not the ideas of McLuhan and Fiore are adopted, authorship and its rights will be a critical issue in determining the future dynamics of the Web and of Web farming.

Copyright protection requires that information, as the property of an author, should be *tangible (or fixed)*. The law defines information as

> ...original works of authorship fixed in any tangible medium of expression, now known or later developed, from which they can be perceived, reproduced or otherwise communicated, either directly or with the aid of a machine or device.[29]

For printed materials, the requirement of "being fixed" is simple. The work exists as lettering or a design upon a piece of paper. For electronic information, it is not as certain when and how the work is "fixed," because it exists as slight magnetic fluctuations on a disk or as photon pulses within an optical cable. Further, a typical Web page is actually a complex assembly of separate objects (text, images, and rendering tags), possibly from different Web sites. The copyright law allows for future technologies by referring to media "now known or later developed" and to "the aid of a machine or device."

11.3.1 Protection of Databases

Copyright protection also requires that information, as the property of an author, be *original* and *creative;* this brings us to the controversy surrounding the protection of electronic databases. The issue is the degree of originality and creativity present in such databases.

A U.S. Supreme Court case in 1991 involved competing telephone directories in which one party argued for copyright protection for compiling telephone numbers from the "white pages."[30] The court decided that such a database compilation involved a lot of work, but was not a creative (or original) work and, hence, was not

---

27. Lesk, 1997, 225.
28. McLuhan and Fiore, 1967. Reprinted in 1996 by Hardwired.
29. Section 102a of U.S. Code 17.
30. *Feist Publications v. Rural Telephone Service Co.,* 111 S.Ct. 1282.

covered under copyright laws. As a result, there are now many inexpensive CD-ROM products containing the entire contents of U.S. phone directories.

In later cases, the U.S. courts have lowered the standards for a creative work, so that "yellow pages" and baseball box scores are now covered. On the other hand, the courts have not considered horse racing charts and radiator parts catalogs to be creative enough.

There is considerable effort to amend the U.S. copyright laws to include the protection of all databases. In this context, databases are compilations of data that may not be creative (by literary standards) but involve considerable effort (i.e., "sweat of the brow"). The problem is that a database may be "so loosely defined that it's hard to imagine what kind of information doesn't qualify for protection," as Mike Godwin, staff counsel of the Electronic Frontier Foundation, points out.[31]

For Web farming, copyright protection of databases may be beneficial in preserving the value of a data warehouse, but such protection may also restrict access to the other database resources on the Web. This situation is the classic "two-edged sword."

11.3.2   Fair Use

A copyright infringement occurs when a copy of the "work" is made by someone other than the owner. "Fair use" is defined as the copying of copyrighted materials for limited and useful purposes and is tolerated as an exception to the law. In particular, you can freely use copyright materials under certain conditions, as judged by the following "fair use" criteria:

- Nature of the use, whether for educational or commercial purposes
- Type of copyrighted work, whether highly creative or purely factual
- Quantity used, both absolute and proportional amounts
- Impact on the economic value of the work for the copyright holder

Most court cases have judged any commercial use of copyright materials to be unfair exploitation. In one case *(American Geophysical Union v. Texaco),* the research library for Texaco was found to have illegally copied entire scientific articles for Texaco's scientists, though the copies were used for research.

Another case *(Sega Enterprises v. Accolade* in 1992) brought a different verdict. Accolade violated every one of the "fair use" criteria by reverse-engineering the Sega programming to determine how to create compatible games for the Sega machine. The court found that Accolade had met the "fair use" criteria because it "enriched the culture through the creation of new works." It is a sad commentary on what the courts think are culturally valuable works when the law is applied in this way to video games!

---

31. Mike Godwin, Copyright Crisis, *Internet World,* March 1997, 100–102.

Web farming systems usually operate for commercial gain and to enrich only their own enterprises. Therefore, these systems will probably have very limited "fair use" access to copyright materials.

For instance, it is uncertain whether crawling through a competitor's Web site is covered by the "fair use" criteria. The Web site contents are considered copyrighted materials, the purpose is commercial gain, and a large proportion of the contents is scanned, indexed, and sometimes archived. However, such an activity does not lessen the economic value of the Web site, and the contents are mainly factual, rather than creative. Is this activity a "fair use" of this information?

11.3.3 Copyright Clearance Center

The Copyright Clearance Center (CCC)[32] acts as an agent for authors and publishers to collect royalties for use of copyrighted materials. It is a not-for-profit reproduction rights organization for the U.S. For a person or company using copyrighted materials, the CCC provides an efficient licensing mechanism.

One CCC service is the Electronic Rights Management Service,[33] which specializes in securing the appropriate clearance for electronic materials, including material accessed via the Internet. Licensing with CCC currently involves a custom process of developing the user agreement and rights-holder (publisher or author) terms and conditions. Under a license for digital use, the fees set by the rights-holders may be per user, or per view, annual, or a combination of these.

For Web farming to become an effective intelligence function for an enterprise, fees and royalties for the use of copyright electronic material must be encouraged, stimulating the availability and quality of information on the Web. The use of advertisements as revenue generators and of infringement lawsuits will have negative impacts.

11.3.4 Infringements on the Web

The content of a Web site is usually considered an original work and, as such, is protected internationally by copyright laws under the 1971 Berne Convention.[34] Current copyright laws could rule the archiving of a Web site to be equivalent to the photocopying of an entire book. However, should we consider the indexing of a Web site to be the same? And what about caching Web pages on an internal disk for a Web browser? Every month we hear of a lawsuit based on new and unusual copyright infringements on the Web. Here are a few examples.

URL links to other Web sites (using HTML anchor tags) have been generally assumed to be legal and within "fair use" criteria, much like a bibliographic citation. However, a case in 1997 between Microsoft and Ticketmaster challenges this

---

32. See http://www.copyright.com/.
33. Further information can be obtained by emailing digital@copyright.com.
34. Berne Convention for the Protection of Literary and Artistic Works, Paris Text, 1971.

assumption. Sidewalk,[35] a Seattle city guide site operated by Microsoft, linked to the Ticketmaster Web site. However, before persons were connected to the Ticketmaster Web site, an intermediary Web page[36] was displayed with banner advertisements whose revenues went to Microsoft. Ticketmaster argued that Microsoft's link (with the intermediary page) constituted unfair use of its name and services. As of this writing, the case is still being decided.

A similar case involved several media giants (including the *Washington Post*) suing TotalNews,[37] a five-person company, for copyright infringement. TotalNews displayed other news sites in one frame of their Web page, while other frames concurrently displayed banner advertisements for TotalNews. The lawsuit was settled by granting TotalNews a "linking license" for the other news sites.

Restrictions on intersite linking strike at the basic nature of the Web. However, the misuse of another site's content strikes at the basic fairness of sharing content on the Web.

Another twist is the use of META KEYWORD tags that are invisible to the content consumer but can be used by search engines to properly index Web content. In 1997, Playboy Enterprises won a court victory against Calvin Designer Label, forcing it to stop using the terms "playboy" and "playmate" in META tags to lure people to its Web site.

The apparent conclusion is that any respectable Web farming function should play it safe. As a content consumer, assume that all content is covered by a valid copyright owned by the content provider, track the use of that content, request permission to distribute the content, and pay any copyright fees requested. As a content provider, do everything reasonable to protect your rights through explicit copyright notices (even though they are not required), click-through declarations, written licenses, encryption, and so on.

11.3.5 Further Information about Intellectual Property Rights

For further information on intellectual property rights, consult the following Web resources:

- Copyright Resources,[38] at the Copyright Clearance Center
- U.S. Copyright Office[39]
- W3C Intellectual Property Rights Overview[40]
- Yahoo! directory on Government:Law:Intellectual Property:Copyrights[41]

---

35. See http://seattle.sidewalk.com/.
36. See http://seattle.sidewalk.com/detail/12170/.
37. See http://totalnews.com/.
38. See http://www.copyright.com/copyright_resources/res_pages.html.
39. See http://lcweb.loc.gov/copyright/.
40. See http://www.w3.org/IPR/.
41. See http://www.yahoo.com/Government/Law/Intellectual_Property/Copyrights/.

11.4 Competitive Intelligence

We might characterize competitive intelligence as "marketing research with an attitude." For most persons engaged with competitive intelligence, it is an honorable profession in the tradition of general marketing research.

The Society for Competitive Information Professionals (SCIP) has given the proper "attitude" to its profession. In particular, the SCIP Code of Ethics[42] deserves special mention and commendation. The code consists of the following imperatives:

- To continually strive to increase respect and recognition for the profession
- To pursue one's duties with zeal and diligence while maintaining the highest degree of professionalism and avoiding all unethical practices
- To faithfully adhere to and abide by one's company's policies, objectives, and guidelines
- To comply with all applicable laws
- To accurately disclose all relevant information, including one's identity and organization, prior to all interviews
- To fully respect all requests for confidentiality of information
- To promote and encourage full compliance with these ethical standards within one's company, with third-party contractors, and within the entire profession

The disclosure of your identity is a point that is quite relevant to Web farming. Crawling Web sites can be performed clandestinely. Each HTTP GET request reveals only the general domain issuing the request and even that information can be distorted. A Web farming system should clearly identify itself when acquiring Web content and should reply honestly to any inquiries as to its purpose.

11.5 Industrial Espionage

The topic of industrial espionage conjures up images from the scenes of a James Bond movie. It sounds glamorous, but it is gold trim on simple theft.

Industrial espionage is gold trim on simple theft.

---

42. See http://www.scip.org/ethics.html.

Carole Lane puts it well in her characterization of a data thief:

> Somewhere between the sport hackers and the destructive hackers
> lies the data thief. These specialists break into computer systems for
> the specific purpose of obtaining the information stored inside. They
> may not harm the data or the computer systems that they invade; it
> usually is in their interests to leave no trace of their activities. How-
> ever, they do invade our privacy and steal information to which they
> have no right.[43]

Industrial espionage has become a major problem for high-tech companies
worldwide, as a *Wall Street Journal* article reveals:

> **Corporate Spying Is Real**—Victor Lee, a senior chemical engineer for
> Avery Dennison Corp., passed confidential product plans to a Taiwan-
> ese rival. For over seven years, Dr. Lee periodically mailed packages to
> Taiwan in exchange for payments of $10,000 to $15,000. On annual
> trips, he also lectured to rival researchers on the product secrets.[44]

The article notes that "such instances of corporate spying are on the rise, spurred by
increasingly tough global competition, a more mobile work force and the new premium placed on corporations' intellectual property." The American Society for
Industrial Security[45] estimates that intellectual property theft costs U.S. companies
as much as $24 billion per year.

The boundary between competitive intelligence and industrial espionage may
seem subtle to some. However, one activity can bring a hefty fine and even a jail
sentence, while the other does not. In the ever-changing world of cyberspace, the
legality of specific activities may be confusing. However, ignorance is often not a
valid legal defense.

Consider the following scenarios for your Web farming system:

1. The Web site of your biggest competitor is archived and indexed on a
   daily basis. The analysis focuses on changes and recent additions to its
   content. Is this activity espionage?

2. The competitor's Web site is scanned, and the Robot Exclusion statement for the site is ignored. Is this activity espionage?

3. Part of the Web site is reserved for "Press Only" and contains an archive
   of press releases that are up to date. This area is scanned on a daily basis
   to detect patterns in partnerships and recent large sales contracts. Is this
   activity espionage?

---

43. Lane, 1997, 44.
44. *Wall Street Journal,* Secrets and Lies: The Dual Career of a Corporate Spy, B1, October 23, 1997.
45. See http://www.asisonline.org/.

4. Part of the Web site has a special area for a customer forum devoted to a specific product of your competitor. A simple user ID and password protect this special area. It is common knowledge that the ID and password are *customer* and *password,* respectively. Looking for weakness in this product, your system scans this special area using the commonly known ID and password. Is this activity espionage?

5. The competitor's sales organization has implemented a special URL and secured protocol to coordinate its sales activities worldwide via the Internet. A friend working for the competitor gives you the weekly password in exchange for some vacation enhancements. Your system systematically monitors your competitor's sales activities in your region and issues confidential email to appropriate salespeople on your staff. Is this activity espionage?

The question is whether the operation of your Web farming system is legal. Will your activities hold up in a court of law when your competitor sues or the FBI prosecutes?

11.6 Information Warfare

The final social issue related to Web farming is information warfare—using information as a weapon to injure or harm another party. For the U.S. government, information warfare is a very serious issue. With many critical systems controlling large segments of society, the threat of another party to impair the operation of those systems is quite serious. The newspaper headlines usually note attempts by hackers to access classified information in military databases. However, hacking can also involve the sabotage of global financial systems (e.g., the New York Stock Exchange), national air travel control, train routings, electrical power distribution, oil pipelines, 911 emergency services, international telecommunications, and so forth. As a society, we have become highly dependent on complex systems to safely guide our daily life, down to the traffic control signs at our local intersections.

The U.S. government has taken this threat seriously. As stated in the *Wall Street Journal* article,[46] a task force of the Science Board for the U.S. Department of Defense issued an "Information Warfare—Defense" report warning of a possible "electronic Pearl Harbor." With over two million computers and 10,000 networks, the U.S. military can be quite vulnerable to attack unless strong measures are taken. In a closing comment, Duane Andrews, the task force chairman, said,

> Most of the stuff in there [the report] is a message to industry, too.... A large international bank has exactly the same problems and challenges as the Defense Department.[47]

46. *WSJ*, January 6, 1997, B6.
47. Ibid.

How does information warfare relate to Web farming?

The possibility is real that a competitor could intentionally cause damage to a company through disinformation. Unlike industrial espionage, which seeks to acquire confidential data by illegal means, industrial information warfare seeks to cause intentional damage. By feeding misleading information into a warehouse via a Web resource, a company could cause erroneous decisions leading to increased costs or loss of revenue. On a smaller scale, false information on comparative purchasing costs of components from suppliers can increase the cost of manufacturing. And on a larger scale, false information about potential acquisitions can cause a major loss of time, focus, and profitability for the acquiring company.

Consider the following: For several months, your Web farming system has been scanning a competitor's Web site. The competitor becomes aware of this activity. Its Web server is reprogrammed to reroute any HTTP requests from your Web crawler to a special dummy Web site. The competitor starts to systematically feed that site erroneous information about press releases, product specifications, pricing schemes, partnerships, and the like. All this deception is purely legal, and your company suffers. This situation is reminiscent of the British deception of the Germans just before D-Day.

The proper response to your knowledge of information warfare is to seriously assess the threat to your enterprise and to adequately verify external information sources involved with critical business processes. The Web farming function should be especially diligent in implementing that verification process.

For further information on information warfare, consult the following Web resources:

- Yahoo!'s directory on Government:Intelligence:Information Warfare,[48] which contains a good list of current Web resources
- The Information Warfare Research Center[49] of the Terrorism Research Center
- InfoWar.Com[50]
- The Journal on Information Warfare[51]
- JYA Cryptome,[52] which compiles various tidbits about the U.S. government, such as the Report of the Defense Science Board Task Force on Information Warfare and the House Report on Information Warfare Defense

---

48. See http://www.yahoo.com/Government/Intelligence/Information_Warfare/.
49. See http://www.terrorism.com/infowar/wwwlinks.html.
50. See http://www.infowar.com/.
51. See http://www.iwar.org/.
52. See http://jya.com/crypto.htm.

Getting Tough with Links to the Data Warehouse

After two years, the team finally proposed four areas in which they could provide enhancements to existing data within the data warehouse. So far, the team had provided information separate from the data warehouse to clearly distinguish the "valid" internal data from the "flaky" external data. Experience had shown that the "valid/flaky" distinction was often the opposite of what would have been expected. The data quality of internal systems in some areas was terrible, while the data quality of specific external Web sites was excellent. "Only experience with both enabled us to make that judgment," Alice concluded.

Careful planning preceded the team's proposal, to ensure that the Web content was reliable and the acquisition processes were stable. Debbie, who had extensive experience with DB2 and VSAM extractions, was transferred to the team as a data administrator to manage the validation and transformation effort. The initial attempts were very frustrating, since the primary key values never seemed to match; hence, joins between internal and external data often resulted in no rows retrieved. The team devoted considerable effort to the key-matching problem by refining the transformation algorithms and adding extra join tables to "fix-up" the values.

11.7 Code of Ethics for Web Farming

For Web farming to evolve into a responsible profession, we must struggle with the issues embodied within a code of ethics. In particular, any enterprise implementing a Web farming system should create its own code of ethics to direct its efforts in an appropriate manner.

Consider the following code of ethics for Web farming, which is indebted to the AIIP Code of Ethical Business Practice:[53]

- Honesty: Exhibit the highest standards for honesty and competence.
- Accuracy: Strive for the highest standards of accuracy and reliability within the information gathered and processed. Verify the accuracy and reliability of external sources on a periodic basis.
- Openness: Create written policies on the use of the Web farming system through widespread discussion of the issues.
- Enforcement: Stress the importance of enforcing these policies for all persons involved.

---

53. See http://www.aiip.org/ethics.html.

- Legality: Comply with all applicable laws and educate persons in the interpretation of those laws.

- Disclosure: Disclose the identity of your system to all data sources and respond honestly to any request about the purpose for which data is acquired.

- Restrictions: Abide by any standards that restrict or limit access to Web resources, such as robot exclusion policies.

- Copyright: Track the use of any content that may be protected by copyright, request permission of the author to use this content, and make any royalty payments requested.

- Confidentiality: Respect the confidential nature of any data with personal identifiers by limiting its disclosure. Especially respect the confidentiality of any financial information about specific persons.

- Security: Maintain appropriate security safeguards to ensure the integrity and privacy of information, especially for personal data.

- Notification: Inform any persons for whom personal data has been collected.

- Choice: To the person affected, offer a choice about whether and how personal data is gathered, analyzed, and disseminated.

- Review: Review and revise this code of ethics on a periodic basis, through discussions with the people involved with Web farming.

As you consider and adopt your code of ethics, please share your experience via the Web Farming Resource Center.[54]

This chapter has explored the various societal issues related to Web farming. From privacy to information warfare, the persons managing any Web farming system must be aware of the seriousness of these issues. It is strongly recommended that a code of ethics for Web farming be thoroughly debated, clearly posted, adequately enforced, and annually reviewed.

---

54. See http://webfarming.com/.

Your code of ethics for Web farming should be thoroughly debated, clearly posted, adequately enforced, and annually reviewed.

The issues discussed in this chapter are ones that we should ponder deeply over the coming years. Persons involved with Web farming will be at the cutting edge of these issues. They will have the responsibility of understanding and educating others. They will be viewed as role models for the next generation in their proper use of business intelligence technology.

The rapid evolution of information creation and sharing on the Web is creating wide gaps that our current laws cannot cover. An insightful article by Norderhaug and Oberding argues that more litigation and more legislation are not answers:

> Litigation will do nothing but slow the pace of any technological developments.... Unfortunately, lawsuits will be filed, and judges with limited knowledge or understanding of technology will make rulings that impact the future. Technologists must take action now to prevent improper precedent....
>
> It is not appropriate to adapt or contain technology to fit current laws and regulations, even if it were possible. Rather the law must change to fit the growth of technology.... Technology should be designed to minimize the need for legislation...[55]

The challenge for Web farming is to mold this technology so that it balances the rights of individuals against the benefits of information sharing. As Web farmers, we need to be on the leading edge of these societal developments to minimize their negative impacts. Are you up to the challenge?

---

55. T. Norderhaug and J. Oberding, Designing a Web of Intellectual Property, *Computer Networks and ISDN Systems,* 27 (6), 1995, 1037–46. Also see http://www.stud.ifi.uio.no/~terjen/pub/webip /950220.html.

## Chapter Twelve

Challenges

The farmer's life is filled with challenges—some good, some bad, but all eventful. For the farmer, it is not what the challenges are, but how you respond to the challenges that matters.

B y wading through the previous chapters, you have taken a journey through data warehousing, Web technology, and hundreds of other topics. It is a journey filled with challenges.

12.1 The Challenges—Chapter by Chapter

The first chapter, Motivation, describes the challenge of comprehending the Web and its use for business intelligence. The second chapter, Perspectives, poses the challenge of leveraging data into information and then into knowledge. The third chapter, Foundations, presents the challenge of remembering and utilizing the disciplines that are fundamental to Web farming.

The fourth chapter, Methodology, outlines the challenge of implementing Web farming through a prescribed sequence of stages. The fifth chapter, Architecture, continues the challenge by presenting the components and relationships required. The sixth chapter, Management, expands the challenge by noting the critical issues that will make Web farming successful.

The seventh chapter, Standards, describes the challenge of understanding current standards and evolving the proper future ones. The eighth chapter, Tools, proposes the challenge of finding and using the proper tools for Web farming. The ninth chapter, Resources, surveys the challenges of finding and using the diversity of Web resources. The tenth chapter, Techniques, explores the challenges of adequately using the specific methods of discovering, acquiring, structuring, and disseminating Web content. The eleventh chapter, Society, extends our challenges into the areas of privacy, confidentiality, intellectual property, and a code of ethics.

12.2 The Big Picture

As you have moved through these chapters, you should not have lost sight of the big picture. To help you, here are a few suggestions:

First, Web farming is not about technology or even about the Web. It is about basic business practices of thriving in today's turbulent markets. It is about being smarter in managing the intellectual capital that we so often take for granted. It is about changing the mindset of a wide cross section of your enterprise. It about landing your airliner at a crowded urban airport—safely.

Second, Web farming is exciting. It is exciting because of the potential the technology offers for the enterprises that can "get it together." It is particularly exciting in the potential to integrate your value-added chain, both downstream to the end consumer and upstream to suppliers.

Third, the development of Web farming is certain. It will become a standard function within data warehousing systems as companies strive in desperation for their next competitive advantage. And we will probably reach Stage Five faster than anyone expects. Web farming will soon blend into the enterprise system, vanishing with little mention or consideration in future years.

Finally, Web farming is frightening—at least it should be. It is frightening because of the potential for misuse of this emerging technology. There are moments in which this book seems like a recipe for a pipe bomb—common materials combined with simple skills that can result in much harm. It is like the thoughts of the early physicists who discovered the nuclear chain reaction: the delight at solving a deep mystery of nature combined with the hope of solving the energy needs of the entire world, while the fear of a nuclear explosion cast a dark pall over humanity. Quite a mixture of emotions!

Every time mankind is given more power, mankind is also given proportionally more responsibility. At times, we may wish to give back the power, just because the burden of responsibility is too great. Unfortunately, that choice is not an option. Progress marches on, and we are forced to mature and shoulder its burdens.

12.3 Your Response

By reading this book, you are now sharing the excitement and the burdens of Web farming. You must decide whether to assume leadership in Web farming within your enterprise and your industry. This is not an easy decision.

You must seriously reinvent yourself and then your enterprise. You can no longer be comfortable living along the road of past successes. You need to fix things before they break. You need to move beyond the rut of incremental improvements. The marketplace in which you are successful no longer exists; it quietly disappeared last night. Create innovative products that cannibalize your current products, before your competitors do it for you.

Understand the essentials of your enterprise from a business perspective. Know thy customer, and then know thy products or services. For the IT professional trained in systematic thinking, look for the big breakthrough opportunities that will cause radical changes in business processes.

Defend the virtues of sharing information across the enterprise. No one else will! Others will be focused solely on their small pieces of cyberspace. In business terms, define the common business objects that are critical to your business. Facilitate and guide the politics and emotions stemming from information sharing. Moreover, foster efforts toward effective data warehousing that will ensure the delivery of real business value to your enterprise.

12.4 Web Farmers, Unite!

An excellent way to shoulder the responsibilities for developing Web farming is to unite—to band together into a solid professional association. It does not matter whether this association is an extension of an existing one or a new creation. The real issue is whether the association takes responsibility for the proper education of its members, for effective direction within the vendor community, and for thoughtful advocacy of legal and political action. The Web Farming Resource Site[1] can be one focal point for this community building.

---

1. See http://webfarming.com/.

Glossary

This is the collection of key terms related to Web farming.

applet A small piece of executed code that is downloaded by the Web server to a Web browser for execution, usually in Java or a similar interpretive language.

application A program that performs a specific function.

attention economics Allocation of the scarce resource of the attention that a person queries to a subject.

automate To formalize a process to minimize human intervention.

bandwidth The number of bits (or bytes) per second that can be reliably communicated between nodes in a communications network.

browser A program executing on a client to interpret a Web page (usually in HTML) and render a proper image of that page.

business intelligence (BI) The next stage in decision support, in which there is direct impact on business processes.

channel A flow of messages (or goods) of a similar nature from producer to consumer via a broker.

client The node in a client-server architecture that initiates a request to a server and processes the results.

common gateway interface (CGI) A mechanism to execute a procedure within a Web server in response to a request by a Web browser.

confidentiality The right of a person or other legal entity to withhold and preserve information.

Critical External Factors (CEFs) Factors that significantly affect the business and that are external to the organization.

data mart A small version of a data warehouse that focuses upon a specific business function, rather than on the entire enterprise.

data warehouse A collection of data organized and packaged to enhance the business processes of an enterprise.

data warehousing A system that enables and supports the data warehouse.

data A collection of observations.

domain name server (DNS) A database that maps a domain name to a static IP address.

dynamic Web page A Web page whose content is dynamically created whenever the page is requested.

enable To formalize a process to enhance human intervention.

enterprise An organization of people who have a common purpose and a common set of resources to accomplish that purpose.

Extranet A TCP/IP network in which two or more physically separated nets are logically connected via the global Internet.

HyperText Markup Language (HTML) The language that encodes the content and presentation of a Web page.

HyperText Transfer Protocol (HTTP) The protocol that coordinates a Web browser with a Web server.

in-flow The flow of data into a data warehouse from operational systems and other sources.

informate To enable through information enrichment of the work environment.

information broker the third-party in the P&S architecture that decouples producers from consumers.

information ecology Understanding the enterprise-wide impacts of information design on maximizing information sharing and minimizing resource consumption.

information Data that changes individual decisions.

informational system A system that enhances decision making by management and by clerical personnel.

Internet The global network of computers that are directly addressable by each other.

intranet A TCP/IP network that is physically separated from the global Internet.

Knowledge Management System (KMS) A system that manages knowledge (which is much more complex than it sounds).

knowledge Information that changes organizational processes.

legacy Any information system that has become critical to the operation of your business, regardless of its age or complexity.

market The interaction of buyers and sellers with shared information and a mechanism to exchange objects of economic value.

network computer A client platform in which minimal code supports basic functions.

operational system A system that enhances the processing of business transactions.

out-flow The flow of data from a data warehouse to the consumers of that data.

platform. The layering of hardware, operating system, and communication protocols to support the execution of applications.

precision. The ratio of items retrieved to the total number of relevant items.

privacy The right of a person to withhold and preserve personal information.

Publish-and-Subscribe (P&S) A three-tier architecture in which producers and consumers are matched through a broker.

push versus pull Initiation of delivery of a message when it is created, rather than waiting for messages to be requested.

recall The ratio of relevant items to the total number of items retrieved.

request and reply (R&R) The traditional client-server architecture where the client requests and the server replies. As contrasted with publish-and-subscribe.

server The node in a client-server architecture that services a request from a client and responds with results.

stages of growth Necessary stages in the adoption of technology by an organization.

static Web page A Web page whose content is statically stored in a directory and retrieved whenever the page is requested.

Uniform Resource Locator (URL) Primary mechanism for linking documents on the Web.

up-flow The flow of data with the data warehouse that transforms and packages the data, thus adding business value.

Web or World Wide Web The information available on the Internet using the HTTP protocol.

Web farming The systematic refining of information resources on the Web for business intelligence.

Web-enabled databases The use of Web technology for accessing databases.

Acronyms

Every professional endeavor has its own language and culture, and the area of Web farming is certainly no exception. Because Web farming is the convergence of several I/T areas, these acronyms are complex and unobvious, each with its own folklore. Some acronyms have double or triple meanings. Conquer these acronyms, and you will be able to go toe-to-toe with the best. Don't be FUD'ed by YAA!

ACID Atomicity, Consistency, Isolation, Durability

ACM Association for Computing Machinery

AIIM Association for Information and Image Management International

AIIP Association of Independent Information Professionals

ANSI American National Standards Institute

API Application Programming Interface

ARL Association of Research Libraries

ASIS American Society of Information Science

BPR Business Process Reengineering

CCC Copyright Clearance Center

CDF Channel Definition Format

CD-ROM Compact Disk, Read-Only Memory

CEF Critical External Factor

CGI common gateway interface

CIA Central Intelligence Agency

CIO Chief Information Officer

CKO Chief Knowledge Officer

CLI Call-Level Interface

CNI Coalition of Networked Information

CORBA Common Object Request Broker Architecture

CRA Consumer Reporting Agency

CSA Client-Server Architecture

DBA Database Administration (or Administrator)

DBMS Database Management System

DCE OSF Distributed Computing Environment

DDB Distributed Database

DLL Dynamic Link Library

DNS domain name server

DP Data Processing

DSS decision support systems

DTD Document Type Definition

DW Data warehousing or data warehouse

EDGAR SEC Electronic Data Gathering, Analysis, and Retrieval system

EDI Electronic Data Interchange

EIRENE European Information Researchers Network

EIS executive information system

FCRA U.S. Fair Credit Reporting Act

FTP File Transfer Protocol

FUD Fear, Uncertainty, and Doubt

GUI Graphical User Interface

HTML HyperText Markup Language

HTTP HyperText Transfer Protocol

IAB Internet Architecture Board

IANA Internet Assigned Numbers Authority

IDL Interface Definition Language

IEEE Institute of Electrical and Electronics Engineers

IEFT Internet Engineering Task Force

IIOP Internet Inter-ORB Protocol

IP Internet Protocol

IS or I/S Information Systems

ISDN Integrated Services Digital Network

ISO International Standards Organization

ISOC Internet Society

ISP Internet service provider

ISV Independent Software Vendor

IT or I/T Information Technology

ITL NIST Information Technology Laboratory

KM Knowledge Management

KMS Knowledge Management System

LAN Local Area Network

LITA Library and Information Technology Association

MDIS Metadata Interchange Specifications

MIME Multipurpose Internet Mail Extensions

MIS Management Information System

NC Network Computer

NCITS National Committee for Information Technology Standards

NIST U.S. National Institute of Standards and Technology

NT Microsoft Windows New Technology operating system

OCLC Online Computer Library Center

OCR optical character recognition

ODBC Microsoft Open Database Connectivity

ODMA Open Document Management API

ODS Operational Data Store

OEM Original Equipment Manufacturer

OFE Open Financial Exchange

OLAP Online Analytical Processing

OLE Microsoft Object Linking and Embedding

OMG Object Management Group

OODM Object-Oriented Data Model

OSI ISO Open Systems Interconnection reference model

P&S Publish-and-Subscribe

PDF Page Definition Format by Adobe

POP Post Office Protocol

PTO U.S. Patents and Trademarks Office

R&R request and reply

RDBMS Relational Database Management System

RDF Resource Definition Framework

RDM Relational Data Model

RES Robot Exclusion Standard

RFC Request for Comment

RPC Remote Procedure Call

SCIP Society for Competitive Information Professionals

SDK. Software Development Kit

SEC. U.S. Securities and Exchange Commission

SGML Standard Generalized Markup Language

SIC Standard Industry Code

SIR Society for Insurance Research

SLA Special Libraries Association

SMTP Simple Mail Transport Protocol

SOIF Summary Object Interchange Format (from the Harvest Project)

SP Stored Procedure

SQL Structured Query Language (*also* SEQUEL)

TCP Transmission Control Program

TCP/IP Transmission Control Protocol/Internet Protocol

TP Transaction Program

UOW Unit of Work

URL Uniform Resource Locator

URN Uniform Resource Name

W3C World Wide Web Consortium

WAIS Wide Area Information Server

WAN Wide Area Network

WEBM Web Enterprise Management Initiative

WOSA Microsoft Windows Open Service Architecture

WYSIWYG What You See Is What You Get

XML Extensible Markup Language

YAA Yet Another Acronym

Bibliography

Abbott, E.A. *Flatland: A Romance of Many Dimensions.* New York: Dover Publications, 1992. Reprint of the classic 1884 publication.

Allee, V. *The Knowledge Evolution: Expanding Organizational Intelligence.* Boston: Butterworth-Heinemann, 1997.

Bachman, C.W. Data Structure Diagrams. *ACM Data Base,* 1(2), 4–10, Summer 1969.

Bair, J. It's About Time: Supporting Temporal Data in a Warehouse. *InfoDB,* 10(1), 1–7 (February 1996).

Bank, D. Know-It-Alls. *Wall Street Journal,* November 18, 1996, R28.

Basch, R. and H. Rheingold. *Secrets of the Super Net Searchers: The Reflections, Revelations and Hard-Won Wisdom of 35 of the World's Top Internet Researchers.* Wilton, CT: Pemberton Press, 1996.

Bates, M.E. *The Online Deskbook.* Wilton, CT: Pemberton Press, 1996.

Berinstein, P. *Finding Statistics Online: How to Locate the Elusive Numbers You Need.* Medford, NJ: Information Today, 1998.

Brackett, M.H. *Data Sharing: Using a Common Data Architecture.* New York: John Wiley & Sons, 1994.

Brodie, M.L. and M. Stonebraker. *Migrating Legacy Systems.* San Francisco: Morgan Kaufmann, 1995.

Christensen, C.M. *The Innovator's Dilemma: When New Technologies Cause Great Firms to Fail.* Boston: Harvard Business School Press, 1997.

Connolly, D. (ed.) XML: Principles, Tools, and Techniques, *World Wide Web Journal*, vol. 2, issue 4, Fall 1997.

Crossen, C. In This Tell-All Era, Secrets Just Aren't What They Used to Be, *WSJ,* March 31, 1998, A1.

Davenport, T.H. *Process Innovation: Reengineering Work through Information Technology.* Boston: Harvard Business School Press, 1993.

Davenport, T.H. *Information Ecology: Mastering the Information and Knowledge Environment.* New York: Oxford University Press, 1997.

Davenport, T.H. and L. Prusak. *Working Knowledge: How Organizations Manage What They Know.* Boston: Harvard Business School Press, 1997.

Davidow, W.H and M.S. Malone. *The Virtual Corporation: Structuring and Revitalizing the Corporation for the 21st Century.* New York: Harper Business, 1992.

Davis, G. *Management Information Systems: Conceptual Foundations, Structure, and Development.* New York: McGraw-Hill, 1974.

Davis, S. and B. Davidson. *2020 Vision: Transform Your Business to Succeed in Tomorrow's Economy.* New York: Simon & Schuster, 1991.

Devlin, B.A. and P.T. Murphy. An Architecture for a Business and Information System. *IBM Systems Journal*, 27(1), 60–80 (1988).

Devlin, B.A. *Data Warehouse from Architecture to Implementation.* Reading, MA: Addison-Wesley, 1997.

Diamond, D. Whose Internet is It, Anyway? *Wired*, April 1998, 172–195.

Donovan, J.J. *Crisis in Technology.* Cambridge, MA: Cambridge Technology Group, 1989.

Eskow, D. Harvest Profits from Web Farms, *Datamation*, March 1997, 44.

Friedman, G., M. Friedman, C. Chapman, and J.S. Baker. *The Intelligence Edge: How to Profit in the Information Age.* New York: Crown Publishers, 1997.

Gascoyne, R. Adapt to the Internet, *InformationWeek*, May 5, 1997, 89ff.

Gates, W.H. *Keynote Address to the 88th Annual Meeting of the Special Libraries Association,* Seattle, June 9, 1997.

Glossbrenner, A., and E. Glossbrenner. *Search Engines for the World Wide Web: Visual Quickstart Guide.* Berkeley, CA: Peachpit Press, 1998.

Glossbrenner, A., and J. Rosenberg. *Online Resources for Business.* New York: John Wiley & Sons, 1995.

Goldhaber, M.H. Attention Shoppers, *Wired*, December 1997.

Gray, J. Interview, *DataBase Programming and Design*, May 1996, 32.

Gray, J. and A. Reuter. *Transaction Processing: Concepts and Techniques.* San Francisco: Morgan Kaufmann, 1992.

Hackathorn, R.D. *Enterprise Database Connectivity: The Key to Deploying Enterprise Applications on the Desktop.* New York: John Wiley & Sons, 1993.

Hackathorn, R.D. Data Warehousing Energizes Your Enterprise, *Datamation*, February 1, 1995.

Hackathorn, R.D. Data Delivery When You Want It, *BYTE*, June 1997, 51.

Hackathorn, R.D. Publish or Perish, *BYTE*, September 1997, 65–72.

Halper, M. Everyone in the Knowledge Pool, *ComputerWorld Global Innovators*, December 8, 1997, 8.

Hammer, M. and J. Champy. *Reengineering the Corporation: A Manifesto for Business Revolution.* New York: Harper Business, 1993.

Hammer, M. and S.A. Stanton. *The Reengineering Revolution: A Handbook.* New York: Harper Business, 1995.

Hurwicz, M. Multicast to the Masses, *BYTE*, June 1997.

Inmon, W.H. *Building the Data Warehouse.* Somerset, NJ: Wiley-QED, 1992.

Inmon, W.H. and R.D. Hackathorn. *Using the Data Warehouse.* Somerset, NJ: Wiley-QED, 1994.

Inmon, W.H., C. Imhoff, and G. Battas. *Building the Operational Data Store.* New York: John Wiley & Sons, 1996.

Kahaner, L. *Competitive Intelligence: How to Gather, Analyze, and Use Information to Move Your Business to the Top.* New York: Simon & Schuster, 1996.

Kaplan, R.S. and D.P. Norton. The Balanced Scorecard: Measures That Drive Performance. *Harvard Business Review*, Jan.–Feb. 1992.

Kaplan, R.S. and D.P. Norton. *The Balanced Scorecard: Translating Strategy into Action.* Boston: Harvard Business School Press, 1996.

Keen, P.G.W. *The Process Edge: Creating Value Where It Counts.* Boston: Harvard Business School Press, 1997.

Keen, P.G.W. and Michael Scott Morton, M.S. *Decision Support Systems: An Organizational Perspective.* Reading, MA: Addison-Wesley, 1978.

Kelly, Sean. *Data Warehousing: The Route to Mass Customization.* New York: John Wiley & Sons, 1994.

Kimball, R. *The Data Warehouse Toolkit.* New York: John Wiley & Sons, 1996.

Kohonen, T. *Self-Organizing Maps,* second edition. Berlin: Springer, 1997.

Lanchaster, H. Web Sites That Help You Do Intelligence the Intelligent Way, *Wall Street Journal*, March 31, 1998, B1.

Lane, C.A. *Naked in Cyberspace: How to Find Personal Information Online,* Wilton, CT: Pemberton Press, 1997.

Lesk, M. *Practical Digital Libraries. San Franisco:* Morgan Kaufmann, 1997.

Lynch, C.A. The Z39.50 Information Retrieval Standard – Part I: A Strategic View of Its Past, Present and Future, *D-Lib Magazine*, April 1997.

Malone, T.W., J. Yates, and R.I. Benjamin, Electronic Markets and Electronic Hierarchies, *Communications of ACM*, vol. 30, no. 6, June 1987, 484–497.

Martin, J. *The Great Transition.* New York: AMACOM, 1995.

McLuhan, M., Q. Fiore, and J. Agel. *The Medium is the Massage: An Inventory of Effects,* Touchstone, 1967. Reprinted in 1996 by Hardwired.

Mealling, M. Where in the World is That Resource? *InterNIC News*, December 1997.

Mintzberg, H. *The Structuring of Organizations.* Englewood Cliffs, NJ: Prentice Hall, 1979.

Mintzberg, H. *The Rise and Fall of Strategic Planning: Reconceiving Roles for Planning, Plans, Planners.* New York: The Free Press, 1994.

Mowbray, T.J. and R. Zahavi, T*he Essential CORBA.* New York: John Wiley & Sons, 1995.

Mowshowitz, A. Virtual Organization, *Communications of ACM*, vol. 40 no. 9, Sept. 1997, 30–37.

Nolan, R.L. Managing Crises in Data Processing, *Harvard Business Review,* March/April 1979.

Norderhaug, T. and J. Oberding. Designing a Web of Intellectual Property, *Computer Networks and ISDN Systems,* 27(6), 1995, 1037–46.

Özsu, M.T. and P. Valduriez. *Principles of Distributed Database Systems.* Englewood Cliffs, NJ: Prentice Hall, 1991.

Peters, T. *Thriving on Chaos: Handbook for A Management Revolution.* New York: Alfred A. Knopf, 1987.

Peters, T. *Liberation Management: Necessary Disorganization for the Nanosecond Nineties.* New York: Alfred A. Knopf, 1992.

Peters, T. *The Tom Peters Seminar: Crazy Times Call for Crazy Organizations.* New York: Random House, 1994a.

Peters, T. *The Pursuit of WOW! Every Person's Guide to Topsy-Turvy Times.* New York: Random House, 1994b.

Peters, T.J. and R.H. Waterman. *In Search of Excellence.* New York: Harper & Row, 1982.

Pfaffenberger, B. *Web Search Strategies,* New York: MIS Press, 1996.

Porter, M.E. *Competitive Advantage: Creating and Sustaining Superior Performance.* New York: The Free Press, 1985.

Prusak, L. *Knowledge in Organizations.* Boston: Butterworth-Heinemann, 1997.

Rugge, S., and A. Glossbrenner. *The Information Broker's Handbook.* McGraw-Hill, 1997.

Schechter, B. Information on the Fast Track, *IBM Research,* no. 3, 1997, 18–21.

Schur, S.G. *The Database Factory: Active Database for Enterprise Computing.* New York: John Wiley & Sons, 1994.

Sengle, P. The Fifth Discipline: The Art & Practice of the Learning Organization. New York: Currency Doubleday, 1994.

Shaffer, S.L. *Strategic Database Technology: Management for the Year 2000.* San Francisco: Morgan Kaufmann, 1995.

Shaffer, S.L. and A.R. Simon, *Transitioning to Open Systems: Concepts, Methods and Architecture.* San Francisco: Morgan Kaufmann, 1996.

Smith, A. *The Wealth of Nations.* London: Dent, 1910.

Sonnenreich, W. and T. Macinta. *Web Developer.Com Guide to Search Engines.* New York: John Wiley & Sons, 1998.

Spewak, S.H. *Enterprise Architecture Plannning: Developing a Blueprint for Data, Applications, and Technology.* Somerset, NJ: Wiley-QED, 1992.

Steward, T.A. *Intellectual Capital: The New Wealth of Organizations.* New York: Doubleday Currency, 1997.

Sveiby, K.E. *The New Organizational Wealth: Managing and Measuring Knowledge-Based Assets.* San Francisco: Berrett-Koehler Publishers, Inc., 1997.

Tansel, A.Z. et al. *Temporal Databases: Theory, Design, and Implementation.* Redwood City, CA: Benjamin Cummings, 1993.

Tapscott, D. and A. Caston. *Paradigm Shift: The New Promise of Information Technology.* New York: McGraw-Hill, 1993.

Toffler, A. Future Shock. New York: Random House, 1970.

Tufte, E.R. *The Visual Display of Quantitative Information.* Cheshire, CT: Graphics Press, 1983.

Tufte, E.R. *Envisioning Information.* Cheshire, CT: Graphics Press, 1990.

Tufte, E.R. *Visual Explanations.* Cheshire, CT: Graphics Press, 1997.

Vaskevitch, D. *Client/Server Strategies: A Survival Guide for Corporate Reengineers.* San Mateo, CA: IDG Books, 1993.

Weick, K.E. *The Social Psychology of Organizing.* Reading, MA: Addison-Wesley, 1969.

White, C.J. and R.D. Hackathorn. Client/Server Computing on the World-Wide Web, *InfoDB*, 10(1), 12–19 (February 1996).

Wilder, C. Drucker: Look Outside, *InformationWeek*, February 16, 1998.

Yeager, N.J and R.E. McGrath. *Web Server Technology: The Advanced Guide for World Wide Web Information Providers.* San Francisco: Morgan Kaufmann, 1996.

Zachman, J.A. A Framework for Information Systems Architecture, *IBM Systems Journal*, vol. 26, no. 3, 1987.

Index

A

ABC Manufacturing (fictional story line)
  business intelligence, 105
  corporate library research, 124
  formal plan, 135
  implementation frustrations, 151
  information visualization, 251
  initial success, 71
  integrating the data, 195
  keeping goals in sight, 299
  overview, 23
  validating content reliability, 325
  Web farming experiment, 34
ABI (American Business Information),
    248–249
ACM (Association for Computing Machin-
    ery), 268
acquisition
  accessing dynamic Web pages,
    295–297
  acquisition server, 145
  organizing dynamic references,
    297–298
  overview, 18
  recall vs. precision, 88–89
  techniques, 293–298
  tools, 233
  Web crawling, 293–294
ActiveX controls, 70
Acxiom, 248
advanced searching, 290–291
agent programmer, 129
Agents Technologies (MEB) Corp., 186
AgentSoft Ltd., 186–187
Agentware i3, 216–217
AgeSearch, 253
AIIM (Association for Information and
    Image Management), 268
AIIP (Association of Independent Informa-
    tion Professionals), 269

Alexa Internet, 185–186
Alexandria Digital Library, 263
Allee, Verna, 36
AltaVista
  overview, 192, 238
  refining searches, 286, 288–290
Amazon.Com, 22
American Business Information (ABI),
    248–249
American National Standards Institute
    (ANSI), 174
American Society of Information Science
    (ASIS), 268
Amulet, Inc., 250
analyzing Web content, 112–113
anchor tags (HTML), 161
ANSI (American National Standards Insti-
    tute), 174
ANSI/NISO Z39.50 Information Retrieval
    standard, 166
applets, 69–70
architectures, 119–132
  components of Web farming, 120
  for data warehousing, 74–77
  Stage 1: Getting Started, 120–121
  Stage 2: Getting Serious, 121–126
  Stage 3: Getting Smart, 126–129
  Stage 4: Getting Tough, 130–131
  of Web connections, 67–68
  of Web warehousing, 83
Argus Clearinghouse, 238
ARL (Association of Research Libraries),
    269
ASIS (American Society of Information
    Science), 268
Association for Computing Machinery
    (ACM), 268
Association for Information and Image
    Management (AIIM), 268

Association of Independent Information
    Professionals (AIIP), 269
Association of Research Libraries (ARL),
    269
attention economics, 307–308
automation, 48–50
Autonomy, Inc., 216
Avert, Inc., 272

B

Babbage, Charles, 15
Bank, David, 36
bargaining power of buyers and suppliers,
    44
Basch, R., 283
Bates, M.E., 283
Behind the Peephole content, 281, 295
Berinstein, P., 283
Berkeley Digital Library SunSITE, 263
best-effort level of service, 61
Blue Squirrel, 189
body of messages, 59, 60–61
book distributors, 272
Booz-Allen & Hamilton, 32
brokers
    defined, 57
    information brokers, 144–145
    publish-and-subscribe mechanism,
        58–60
    responsibilities, 129
browsers. *See* Web browsers
buffers. *See* channels
building infrastructure, 107
building knowledge, 33, 34
bureaucracy, rise and decline of, 39
business analyst. *See* information analyst
business case, 105
business environment changes
    enterprise system crisis, 30–31
    rethinking the way we work, 38–50
    urgency of, 28–29
business intelligence, Web farming as, 105
business opportunities. *See* opportunities

business processes
    automating and enabling, 48–50
    defined, 42
    reengineering, 41–42
    sharing information among, 50–55
Business Researcher's Interests, A,
    246–247
business transaction quality, 48
buyers, bargaining power of, 44

C

Calvin Designer Label court case, 320
Cambio, 192–193
CARL Corp., 262
categorization. *See* structuring information
CCC (Copyright Clearance Center), 319,
    320
CD-ROM content, 282
CEF. *See* Critical External Factors (CEF)
Central Intelligence Agency (CIA) World
    Fact Book, 277
challenges, 330–331
change monitoring of Web content,
    108–110
channels
    defined, 57
    defining, 60
    namespace, 60–61
    publish-and-subscribe mechanism,
        59–60
chaotic systems, 29
Chevron, 32
Chief Information Officer (CIO), 138–139
Chief Knowledge Officer (CKO), 139–140
CIA World Fact Book, 277
CIO-centric organizational design,
    138–139
CKO-centric organizational design,
    139–140
classification. *See* structuring information
Coalition for Networked Information
    (CNI), 269
code of ethics for Web farming, 325–327

About the Author

Dr. Richard D. Hackathorn is a well-known innovator and educator with over 30 years of experience in the information systems field. In 1991 he founded Bolder Technology, Inc., to focus on professional education and technology innovation in enterprise systems and connectivity.

Dr. Hackathorn has recently founded WebFarming.Com as a client company in the Boulder Technology Incubator in Boulder, Colorado. He previously cofounded Micro Decisionware, Inc., in 1980, which pioneered SQL connectivity products for enterprise systems and was eventually acquired by Sybase.

Dr. Hackathorn was a professor at the Wharton School of the University of Pennsylvania and at the University of Colorado. He received a B.S. from the California Institute of Technology and a M.S. and Ph.D. from the University of California, Irvine. He has published two professional textbooks, *Enterprise Database Connectivity* and *Using the Data Warehouse* (coauthored with W.H. Inmon), both published by John Wiley.

He can be contacted through the Web site WebFarming.Com at http://webfarming .com/.